ONGOING CRISIS COMMUNICATION

To all those who have managed or will manage crises

ONGOING CRISIS
COMMUNICATION
PLANNING, MANAGING, AND RESPONDING
SECOND EDITION

W. TIMOTHY COOMBS
EASTERN ILLINOIS UNIVERSITY

SAGE Publications
Los Angeles · London · New Delhi · Singapore

For information:

Sage Publications, Inc.
2455 Teller Road
Thousand Oaks, California 91320
E-mail: order@sagepub.com

Sage Publications Ltd.
1 Oliver's Yard
55 City Road
London EC1Y 1SP
United Kingdom

Sage Publications India Pvt. Ltd.
B-42, Panchsheel Enclave
Post Box 4109
New Delhi 110 017 India

Printed in the United States of America

Library of Congress Cataloging-in-Publication Data

Coombs, W. Timothy.
Ongoing crisis communication : planning, managing, and
responding/W. Timothy Coombs. — 2nd ed.
    p. cm.
Includes bibliographical references and index.
ISBN-13: 978-1-4129-4991-0 (cloth)
ISBN-13: 978-1-4129-4992-7 (pbk.)
    1. Crisis management. 2. Communication in management. I. Title.

HD49.C664 2007
658.4'056—dc22   2006028040

This book is printed on acid-free paper.

07   08   09   10   10   9   8   7   6   5   4   3   2   1

Acquisitions Editor:	Todd Armstrong
Editorial Assistant:	Sarah Quesenberry
Production Editor:	Libby Larson
Copy Editor:	Marilyn Power Scott
Typesetter:	C&M Digitals (P) Ltd.
Proofreader:	Word Wise Webb
Indexer:	Michael Ferreira
Cover Designer:	Edgar Abarca

Contents

Preface

The prospect of writing a second edition of this book was very exciting. The field of crisis communication and management is very dynamic, and many things have changed since the first edition. Researchers have begun to yield additional insights into the crisis management process, and the Internet has added to the complexity of crises. Researchers in the evolving area of knowledge management have begun to recognize its connections to crisis communication, a link I outlined the foundation for in the first edition. Researchers are systematically examining the effects of crisis response strategies on stakeholders, and we are moving away from speculation to real knowledge about these strategies. Situational Crisis Communication Theory (SCCT) is one example of the systematic and social scientific study of crisis communication. The Internet is becoming a valuable tool for collecting information about warning signs and crisis as well as an option for communicating with stakeholders during a crisis. Oddly the Internet has also increased the crisis risks organizations face through computer hacking, denial of service, and amplifying challenges from stakeholders that management might be operating an organization in an inappropriate manner.

What has not changed is the need for crisis management: Mistakes still plague organizations facing crises, the emphasis remains on what is said and done after a crisis, there is increased pressure to perform in a crisis, and the field still provides scattered insights. Enron, the catastrophic events of 9/11, and hurricane Katrina are reminders that crises are a fact of organizational life. There is no truer statement in crisis management than "No organization is immune to a crisis." Managers may try to ignore the elephant in the room but that does not mean it is not there. All organizations must become prepared for crises. Merck, Cadbury, and Bausch & Lomb mishandled very public product harm crises that affected millions of consumers. This seems odd given the volumes written about crisis management. Clearly there is still a need to learn and know more about crisis management. Current crisis communication research features crisis response strategies. We still know little about the crisis communication aids that may prevent and prepare for crises.

Organizations face more pressure to manage crisis effectively than ever before. The 24-hour news cycle and Internet access create pressure to respond quickly to any crisis. Corporate social responsibility has resulted in greater stakeholder expectations of how an organization should behave and greater likelihood a crisis can be triggered by stakeholders believing an organization is acting inappropriately. This concern is compounded by the value organizations have placed on rep-utations as a strategic resource. The events of 9/11 have highlighted how crises can impact organizations not directly involved in a crisis, such as disrupting the supply chain.

Adding up all these concerns, we find a distinct need to know about crisis communication and crisis management. Surveys find that organizations are slow to see this reality. Crisis preparation is not as widespread as we would expect nor is it as thorough as it could be. Too many organizations are complacent with just having a crisis manage-ment plan without testing it and updating their crisis management efforts. Too little is done to systematically prepare or even to discover crisis warning signs. Part of this problem is the nature of writings on crisis management. The field has focused on plans and response, not preparation and prevention.

The vast writings about crisis communication and management are a blessing and a curse. It is great to have so much information. However, it is hard to find and organize it all. The writings about cri-sis communication and management are fragmented, as people write about crises from very different perspectives. This situation can leave managers struggling to organize bits of information or missing critical resources entirely. The multidisciplinary nature of crisis management can obscure the big picture. Shrivastava (1993) referred to the fragmen-tation as the "Tower of Babel Effect" (p. 33). Writers often focus on their specialties and fail to make connections to ideas and concepts devel-oped in other specialties. In turn, this fragmentation precludes a fuller understanding of crisis management that is gained by integrating the various perspectives. Add to this that a number of related communica-tion concepts have applications to crisis management but have yet to be integrated into the literature, and the situation becomes even more complicated. Practitioners, researchers, and educators are limited by this fractured approach.

A consideration of crisis response strategies illustrates the fragmen-tation. Crisis response strategies are a subset of crisis communication that focuses on what an organization says and does after a crisis hits. A crisis manager would have to review the business communication, consumer research, rhetoric, organizational communication, and public relations literatures to collect and integrate all the ideas needed to develop guidelines about what to say during a crisis. Such a comprehensive review requires a lot of research for a crisis manager. Researchers and educators are not accomplishing integration to any large degree. Research and reading materials in one discipline often either ignore or duplicate research in another discipline. Ironically, a 1998 article addressing the fragmented nature of crisis management research referenced no communication-based studies (Pearson & Clair, 1998). Virtually all aspects of the crisis management process are plagued by this same fractured approach.

The various ideas can be integrated into one, comprehensive crisis management process. A system that integrates the crisis management writings would benefit practitioners, researchers, and educators. Practitioners will have the lessons and recommendations of crisis management experts synthesized into a usable form. Helpful ideas from a variety of perspectives would be condensed into one, consistent framework. Researchers would benefit from exposure to fields they may not have known were involved in crisis management. Moreover, the framework can indicate where more research is needed to improve the crisis management process. Educators would have a tool that provides detailed lessons for teaching the crisis management process and recommends areas in need of further study. The purpose of this book is to provide a comprehensive analysis of the crisis management process as seen through the lens of crisis communication.

As with the original book, I hope to provide a resource that integrates and organizes a wide array of practitioner and research writings about crisis management. The book emphasizes the role of communication throughout the crisis management process and is designed to be a body of knowledge that aids managers, researchers, and educators. *Process* is an important word here. Too many people think that crisis management means having a crisis management plan or responding when a crisis hits. This is a very reactive and rather limited approach to crisis management. A richer, more proactive approach to crisis management explores the entire process.

Acknowledgments

I find that books are a collaborative effort even when there is one sole author. So I would like to acknowledge those who have helped with this revision. I appreciate the faith the people at SAGE have shown in updating this book and increasing its value as a reference for crisis communication and crisis management, especially Todd Armstrong and Sarah Quesenberry. I appreciate the feedback from the reviewers of the revision proposal: Phillip G. Clampitt, Hendrickson Professor of Business, University of Wisconsin—Green Bay; Keith M. Hearit, Western Michigan University; Kimberly A. Schwartz, APR, MA, University of Dubuque; Steven Venette, University of Southern Mississippi; and Debra A. Worley, Indiana State University. I would also like to thank Marilyn Power Scott for her work in the copyediting process.

I would also like to thank Bartel Van de Walle and the participants of the ISCRAM-TIEMS 2006 Summer School at Tilburg University for exposing me to new applications of technology in crisis management. Last, many thanks to Sherry for reading and commenting on various drafts of this book.

1

A Need for More Crisis Management Knowledge

Merck, BP, Enron, Bausch & Lomb, Hurricane Katrina, and the 9/11 attacks are all reminders that no organization is immune to crises. If no organization is immune, then all organizations should be prepared for a crisis. Pick any day of the week and you will find stories about train derailments, plane crashes, funds used inappropriately at nonprofit organizations, explosions in manufacturing facilities, workers shot or injured on the job, or E. coli-tainted beef, turkey, chicken, or even bean sprouts. The bottom line is that all organizations should learn as much as they can about crisis management.

Developing a comprehensive crisis management program (CMP) that captures the ongoing nature of crisis management is not an easy task. The crisis management process is varied and requires the integration of knowledge from such diverse areas as small-group decision making, media relations, environmental scanning, risk assessment, crisis communication, crisis plan development, evaluation methods, and reputation management. A diverse set of crisis management writings must be navigated in order to develop a complete CCMP that covers every stage and substage of the crisis management process. It is a daunting but necessary task to sort through the plethora of crisis management information. How else can a comprehensive crisis management program be developed?

The primary goal of this book is to offer an integrative framework that simplifies the task of organizing crisis management knowledge. An ongoing approach based upon a three-stage model of crisis management provides the foundation. The three stages are precrisis, crisis event, and postcrisis, with each stage being composed of three substages. The stages are used to summarize and to organize various insights into the crisis management process. Myriad ideas from different areas are synthesized into one continuous crisis management process. The end product is a guide for developing each stage in the ongoing crisis management process. The book is a living guide because future developments in crisis management can be easily assimilated into the comprehensive framework of the three-stage approach.

The three-stage model articulated in this book provides a variety of suggestions about "how to do" crisis management. This book is designed to aid those interested in practicing, researching, or teaching crisis management. To those interested in practicing crisis management, the book offers a comprehensive approach for structuring a crisis management program. For those interested in research, the book provides an analytic framework for the study of crisis management efforts. Those involved in teaching are offered an additional resource for educating future crisis managers. The book ends with a summary of key ideas and highlights some of the insights this book can offer to practitioners, researchers, and educators. In addition, an Appendix suggests a number of crises that can be used for study and research.

❖ CRISIS MANAGEMENT DEFINED

There are a lot of books written about crisis management but there is no one accepted definition of a crisis. Having a specific definition is important because how a subject is defined indicates how it is approached. I choose to start this book with a definition so readers will understand how this book approaches the subject.

Crisis Defined

A crisis is the perception of an unpredictable event that threatens important expectancies of stakeholders and can seriously impact an organization's performance and generate negative outcomes. This definition is a synthesis of various perspectives on crisis. It tries to capture the common traits other writers have used when describing crises.

A crisis is perceptual. What we typically think of as crises are events that are easy to perceive as such. That is why few people would dispute industrial accidents or hurricanes being crises. However, it is the perceptions of stakeholders that help to define an event as a crisis. A stakeholder is a person or group that is affected by or can affect an organization (Bryson, 2004). If stakeholders believe an organization is in crisis, a crisis does exist, and stakeholders will react to the organization as if it is in crisis. For nearly a decade, Audi told its customers there was nothing wrong with its transmissions. However, customers did perceive a crisis. Cars were jumping into gear from neutral—with sudden acceleration—resulting in injuries and deaths. Management must be able to "see" the event from the stakeholders' perspective to properly assess if a crisis has occurred.

A crisis is unpredictable but not unexpected. Wise organizations know that crises will befall them; they just do not know when. Crises strike suddenly, giving them an element of surprise or unpredictability (Barton, 2001; National Research Council, 1996). There are always exceptions to the rule; some crises offer a great deal of warning (Irvine & Millar, 1996). For instance, if a major television news magazine is planning to run a negative story about an organization, management will know the event months in advance. Metabolife, a diet supplement company, faced just such a crisis in 1999. They used the lead time to create an aggressive multimedia campaign to defend themselves from charges linking their product to harmful side effects. Radio and newspaper advertisements were used to drive people to a specially created Web site where people could watch an unedited video of the interview and learn how news shows can distort the truth.

Crises can violate expectations that stakeholders hold about how organizations should act. Planes should land safely, products should not harm us, management should not steal money, and organizations should reflect societal values. Crises disturb some stakeholder expectations resulting in people becoming upset and angry, which threatens the relationship between the organization and its stakeholders. That is why crises are considered dangerous to organizations' reputations (Barton, 2001; Dilenschneider, 2000). A reputation is how stakeholders perceive the organization. When expectations are breached, stakeholders perceive the organization less positively: the reputation is harmed.

The difference between incidents and crises illustrates the meaning of "serious impact." An *incident* is a minor, localized disruption. Say a water valve breaks and sprays water in the vending and meeting areas of a plant. The valve is repaired, some meetings are rescheduled, and vending machines are down for a day. The valve is replaced without harming the larger organizational routine, making it an incident not a crisis. If the broken water valve leads to the plant being shutdown, then it becomes a crisis as it disrupts the entire organization (Coombs, 2006b; Pauchant & Mitroff, 1992). A crisis disrupts or affects the entire organization or has the potential to do so.

Last, crises have the potential to create negative or undesirable outcomes. If business is disrupted, an organization will usually suffer financial losses (e.g., lost productivity or a drop in earnings). Crisis damage extends beyond financial loss, however, to include injuries or deaths to stakeholders, structural or property damage (on and off site), tarnishing of a reputation, and environmental harm (Loewendick, 1993). The damage can affect a variety of stakeholders. An entire industry can be affected by a crisis in one of its member organizations. An industry can suffer financial loss (e.g., new, costly regulations) or reputational damage as people project a localized crisis on to an entire industry. In 2006, the cruise ship industry became involved in the Carnival Cruise line fire because the crisis was an industrywide threat, not just a company-specific one. Fires were a risk on every cruise ship, and people needed to feel safe. Employees, customers, or community members can be injured or killed by industrial or transportation accidents. A plane crash can kill crew members, passengers, and people on the ground.

Environmental damage is another outcome of accidents. Community members can suffer structural or property damage from accidents as well. Explosions can shatter windows, and evacuations can cost members of the community in money, time, and disruption. Careless handling of an accident can add to the damage. Investors can lose money from the costs of the crisis. For example, an organization can incur repair expenses from an accident while a faulty product can result in product liability lawsuits and recall costs. A crisis presents real or potential negative outcomes for organizations, their stakeholders, and their industries. Crisis management is designed to ward off or to reduce the threats by providing recommendations for properly handling crises.

What Would You Do?

BP and Texas City: Act 1

It's 1:20 p.m. on March 23, 2005, in Texas City, Texas. You work at the BP refinery in the town. Suddenly an explosion rocks the ground. You go outside and see large flames and smoke coming from direction of the isomerization unit. You know that workers were performing a startup at the isomerization unit today, and startups are one of the most dangerous procedures at refineries. Alarms are going off, people are running and shouting, and some personnel are heading over to help. You are the public relations person on the BP Texas City crisis team. What do you do now? What does the organization need to do to respond to this event?

Crisis Management

Crisis management represents a set of factors designed to combat crises and to lessen the actual damage inflicted. Put another way, crisis management seeks to prevent or lessen the negative outcomes of a crisis and thereby protect the organization, stakeholders, and industry from harm. Crisis management has evolved from emergency preparedness. Drawing from that base, crisis management is a set of four interrelated factors: (1) prevention, (2) preparation, (3) response, and (4) revision.

Prevention, also known as mitigation, represents the steps taken to avoid crises. Crisis managers often detect warning signs and then take actions designed to prevent the crisis. For instance, a faulty toaster is recalled before its overheating problem causes any fires or injuries to customers. Prevention is largely unseen by the public. News stories about crises that did not happen are rare.

Preparation is the best known factor in crisis management because it includes the crisis management plan (CMP). If people know nothing else about crisis management, they know an organization should have a CMP. The CMP is the tip of the crisis management iceberg. Although people think the CMP is the crisis management process, in actuality most of the process is unseen. Preparation also involves diagnosing crisis vulnerabilities, selecting and training a crisis management team and spokespersons, creating a crisis portfolio, and refining a crisis communication system.

Response is the application of the preparation components to a crisis. A crisis can be simulated (as in an exercise) or real. The preparation components must be tested regularly. The testing involves running simulated crises and drills that determine the fitness of the CMP, crisis team members, spokespersons, and communication system. A real crisis involves the execution of the same crisis management resources, only the outcomes are real rather than hypothetical. Response is very public during an actual crisis. An organization's crisis management response is frequently reported and critiqued in the news media (Pearson & Clair, 1998). Many publications critiqued Bausch & Lomb's failure to recall ReNu with MoistureLoc when it was linked to a 2006 outbreak of Fusarium keratitis, a form of fungal eye infection that can produce blindness (e.g., Bausch & Lomb, 2006; Dobbin, 2006). Bausch & Lomb did stop shipping the product and eventually asked retailers to remove the product from the shelf. It was not until May 15, a month after the crisis began, that an official recall was issued (Bausch & Lomb, 2006; Important message, 2006). Remember, crises make for good news stories and news of the ReNu with MoistureLoc was everywhere.

Part of the response is recovery. *Recovery* denotes that the organization attempts to return to normal operations as soon as possible following a crisis. *Business continuity* is the name used to cover the efforts to restore operations to normal. As noted earlier, downtime from a crisis is a financial drain. The quicker an organization can return to normal operations, the fewer financial losses it will incur.

Revision is the fourth crisis factor. It involves the evaluation of the organization's response in simulated and real crises, determining what it did right and what it did wrong during its crisis management performance. The organization uses this insight to revise its prevention, preparation, and response efforts. Ideally, in the future, the right moves are replayed while the mistakes are avoided and replaced by more appropriate actions. Revision is the development of an institutional or organizational memory, which can improve the effectiveness of crisis management by expanding the organization's perception of crises and its response capacity (Li, YeZhuang, & Ying, 2004; Weick, 1988). The more and varied the crises an organization experiences through practice sessions, the better it can handle those same situations in reality. The factors are linked in a spiral. If prevention fails, preparation is required for optimal performance. Revision is derived from performance and informs both the prevention of and preparation for future crises. In turn, improving preparation should improve response. To recap, crisis management is a process of preventing, preparing for, responding, and revising from crises.

What Would You Do?

Bausch & Lomb and ReNu with MoistureLoc: Act 1

It is early April of 2006, and you work for Bausch & Lomb, an eye health company. You have just received a call from the Food and Drug Administration (FDA) and the Centers for Disease Control and Prevention (CDC). These two agencies are tracking an unusually large outbreak of an eye fungus known as Fusarium keratitis, which can cause blindness. There have been over 100 reported cases. So far, the only link the government has found is that a high percentage of those infected had used Bausch & Lomb's ReNu with MoistureLoc contact lens solution. The FDA and CDC are not saying your product is the cause, but it is the only product that stands out in their investigation. This is your newest product line, and the company is hoping it will help to increase profits. The FDA and CDC tell you that they will be issuing a warning about Fusarium keratitis to the media and on their Web sites. These warning will mention ReNu with MoistureLoc but not state it as the source of the problem. Who are the key stakeholders in this situation? What actions should your organization take? How should they communicate those actions to key stakeholders?

❖ IMPORTANCE OF CRISIS MANAGEMENT

The first paragraph of this chapter offers a reminder that crises are ubiquitous. In fact, today's environment seems to be placing higher premiums on crisis management; unprepared organizations have more to lose today than they ever have before. A variety of developments has made all types of organizations more susceptible to crises. In turn, a higher premium is placed on crisis management as mismanagement costs seem to escalate. To recap, the developments increasing the need for effective crisis management are increased value of reputation, stakeholder activism through communication technologies, broader views of crises, and negligent failure to plan.

Value of Reputations

As late as the 1990s, writers were still debating the value of reputation. A reputation is evaluative, with organizations being seen as having favorable or unfavorable reputations (Coombs & Holladay, 2005). There is a strong consensus in the practitioner and academic writings that a reputation is an extremely valuable intangible organizational resource. Favorable reputations have been linked to attracting customers, generating investment interest, attracting top employee talent, motivating workers, increasing job satisfaction, generating more positive media coverage, and garnering positive comments from financial analysts (Alsop, 2004; Davies, Chun, da Silva, & Roper, 2003; Dowling, 2002; Fombrun & van Riel, 2004). An impressive list of key stakeholders that control resources vital to an organization's success is represented here (Agle, Mitchell, & Sonnenfeld, 1999). A reputation is built through the direct and indirect experiences stakeholders have with the organization (Fombrun & van Riel, 2004). Positive interactions and information about the organization build favorable reputations while unpleasant interactions and negative information lead to unfavorable reputations. A crisis poses a threat to reputational assets (Barton, 2001; Davies et al., 2003; Dilenschneider, 2000). As greater emphasis is placed on reputation, a corresponding emphasis must be placed on crisis management as a means of protecting reputational assets (Coombs & Holladay, 2002).

Stakeholder Activism

Today, angry stakeholders are more likely to generate crises (Changing landscape, 2002). Consumers, shareholders, employees, community groups, and activists are becoming increasingly vocal when dealing with organizations and are using the Internet to voice those concerns (Coombs, 2002; Heath, 1998). The Internet provides various means of stakeholder expression, including Web pages, discussion boards, and blogs (Weblogs). Collectively, these Internet expressions are known as *consumer-generated media* (CGM). Actually, CGM is a bit of a misnomer because stakeholders other than customers can and do create what is termed CGM. The vast majority of CGM never finds an audience. However, when disgruntled stakeholders strike a responsive chord and connect with opinion leaders online, a crisis can occur. These crises evolve from the value of the organizational reputation. Legitimate criticism that spreads among stakeholders poses a direct threat to the organization's reputation. Here's an example: Kryptonite manufactures one of the most popular and expense bicycle locks available. When the company did not respond quickly to consumer concerns about a certain type of lock being easy to pick, the complaints appeared in CGM and created a crisis for Kryptonite. The company appeared to be forced to recall the product by consumer pressure rather than concern for the consumers. Kryptonite looked unresponsive and uncaring. CGM has the potential, even if remote, to create a crisis.

Activist groups are using the Internet to organize and to pressure organizations to change their behaviors. CGM is part of a mix of pressure tactics, along with negative publicity campaigns and boycotts. The Internet has the potential to increase the power of activist groups, thereby making them audible to managers and on an organization's agenda for consideration (Coombs, 1998, 2002; Heath, 1998; Putnam 1993). Consider how People for the Ethical Treatment of Animals was able to pressure Burger King and Wendy's to change their purchasing practices for beef and poultry through integrated pressure campaigns orchestrated on the Internet. The campaigns had the not-so-subtle titles, "Murder King" and "Wicked Wendy's." Stakeholder activism is now global. Concerns over environmental issues in Europe encouraged Chiquita to change how it grows bananas in Central and South America. Partnering with the Rainforest Alliance, Chiquita has had 100% of its banana farms certified as Better Banana Grower (Corporate Conscience, 2003).

Communication Technology

The discussion of stakeholder activism demonstrates one of the ways advances in communication technologies has begun to shape crisis management. These advances make the transmission of communication easier and faster. Another way to think about communication technologies is that they make the world more visible. Events that would have gone unnoticed a decade ago are now highly visible. There are no remote areas of the world any more. The 24-hour news networks, or even just concerned individuals, have the opportunity to reveal crises, complete with video clips. Moreover, crises are now global, thanks to communication technologies. Because news is global, news of an event in an isolated area of Africa appears rapidly around the world. Organizations no longer have isolated crises because the once remote or far flung areas of the world are accessible to the media and to other stakeholders. A crisis may appear on CNN or some other international news service or be the subject of a Web site on the Internet. Coca-Cola's issues with worker abuses in South America became known globally in 2005 and 2006, due in large part to the Killer Coke Web site. PepsiCo was forced to sell operations in Myanmar due to a consumer pressure campaign emanating from CGM (Coombs, 1998). Crises are now more likely to be seen and to be seen by the world thanks to advances in communication technologies.

Broader View of Crises

Prior to the horrific events of 9/11, most organizations were focused on their own little world. Crisis management was driven by what might happen to them on their sites.

However, 9/11 showed that attacks or events at other locations can affect your organization. An event does not have to be a major terrorist event to create collateral damage. An explosion at a nearby chemical facility can create a need to evacuate and close your facility. An airplane crash may prevent vehicles from reaching your offices or plant.

Consequently, organizations are now broadening their view of crises to include nearby facilities that could create crises for them. A second way that the 9/11 attacks have broadened the view of crisis management is the increased emphasis on security and emergency preparedness. Security is one element of prevention and mitigation. Spending and managerial focus on security spiked dramatically after 9/11 and continues to stay high on the list of managerial priorities. While driven by terrorism concerns, security can help with other crises, such as workplace violence. In addition, the security focus has been coupled with the recognition of the need for emergency preparedness. Organizations should be prepared for an evacuation or to provide shelter in place, the two basic emergency responses. Emergency preparedness will help organizations with any crisis they face, not just with terrorism (Coombs, 2006b). The tragic events of 9/11 have been a wakeup call to crisis managers to expand their view of crisis management. The expectation is that this broader view will serve organizations well by saving lives in future crises.

Negligent Failure to Plan

Organizations have long been considered negligent if they did not take reasonable action to reduce or eliminate known or reasonably foreseeable risks that could result in harm. This liability is based on the 1970 Occupational Safety and Health Act (Headley, 2005). The scope of foreseeable risks is expanding to include workplace violence, industrial accidents, product tampering, and terrorist attacks (Abrams, n.d.). This new area of liability is known as negligent failure to plan and is closely tied to crisis management. Organizations can be found legally liable if they did not take precautions to prevent potential crises and were not prepared to respond. Both crisis prevention and crisis preparation serve as defenses against negligent failure to plan. Juries are already punishing organizations that are not engaging in proper crisis management (Blythe & Stivariou, n.d.; Headley, 2005). Crisis management is becoming firmly established as a form of due diligence (efforts to avoid harm to others or the organization) that will protect an organization not only from the immediate harm of a crisis but from secondary harm resulting from lawsuits.

❖ CONCLUSION

As the potential for crises increases, so does the potential for negative outcomes. Organizations are playing for high stakes when confronting crises. The developments just reviewed demonstrate that the need for crisis management is increasing, not decreasing. The value of crisis management is greater now than when experts first began preaching about the need for crisis preparedness in the late 1970s. The end result is a higher premium on effective crisis management. Organizations must continue to improve their crisis management processes. Crisis management acts as a hedge against the negative outcomes of crises. Effective crisis management can protects lives, health, and the environment; reduce the time it takes to complete the crisis life cycle; prevent loss of sales; limit reputation damage; preclude the development of public policy issues (i.e., laws and regulations); and save money. Today's operating environment demands that organization be prepared to manage crises.

❖ DISCUSSION QUESTIONS

1. What would be some arguments managers would use against implementing a crisis management system?

2. Do you agree or disagree with the idea that a crisis is perceptual?

3. What do you think makes an event a crisis?

2

Outline for an Ongoing Approach to Crisis Management

This chapter discusses the different models for the crisis management process and the approach that guides the remainder of this book.

❖ THE INITIAL CRISIS MANAGEMENT FRAMEWORK

The idea that crises have an identifiable life cycle is a consistent theme that permeates the crisis management literature. The crisis manager needs to understand this life cycle because different phases in the life cycle require different actions (Gonzalez-Herrero & Pratt, 1995; Sturges, 1994). The crisis life cycle has been translated into what I term *staged approaches* to crisis management. A staged approach means that the crisis management function is divided into discrete segments that are executed in a specific order. Moreover, the life cycle perspective reveals that effective crisis management must be integrated into the normal operations of an organization. Crisis management is not merely developing a plan and executing the plan during a crisis. Instead, it is appropriately viewed as an ongoing process. Every day, organization members can be scanning for potential crises, taking actions to prevent them, or considering any number of the aspects of the crisis management process detailed in this book. Crisis management should be a part of many people's full-time jobs in an organization, not a part-time fancy. Each working day, crisis managers can be doing something to improve crisis prevention and response (Coombs, 2006a).

The life cycle perspective has yielded a variety of staged approaches to crisis management. These provide a mechanism for constructing a framework for organizing the vast and varied crisis management writings and for creating a unified set of crisis management guidelines. Regardless of discipline, the various topics addressed in crisis management can be placed within a comprehensive, incremental approach to crisis management. An overarching framework organizes the scattered crisis management insights and permits crisis mangers to easily envision their best options during any stage of the crisis management process. Crisis managers can find it easier to access and to apply available resources, thereby improving the crisis management process. The framework I use in this book is influenced by existing models of the crisis management process. Reviewing these models will reinforce the importance of process in crisis management.

Past Staged Approaches to Crisis Management

Three influential approaches emerge from a study of the various crisis management models. Influence was gauged by the number of people citing the approach in the development of their crisis models. These three are Fink's (1986) four-stage model, Mitroff's (1994) five-stage model, and a basic three-stage model. Fink's (1986) is the earliest and can be found in his seminal book, *Crisis Management: Planning for the Inevitable*. His cycle is well represented in writings appearing in the 1990s and even today. He uses a medical illness metaphor to identify four stages in the crisis life cycle: (1) prodromal, clues or hints of a potential crisis begin to emerge, (2) crisis breakout or acute, a triggering event occurs along with the attendant damage, (3) chronic, the effects of the crisis linger as efforts to clean up the crisis progress, and (4) resolution, there is some clear signal that the crisis is no longer a concern to stakeholders—it is over.

Fink's (1986) approach is one of the first to treat a crisis as an extended event. Of particular note is his belief that warning signs precede the trigger event. The job of crisis managers expands and becomes more proactive when they know and read the warning signs.

Well-prepared crisis managers do not just enact the crisis management plan when a crisis hits (being reactive); they are also involved in identifying and resolving situations that could become or lead to a crisis (being proactive). In addition, Fink divides the crisis event into three stages. A crisis does not just happen, it evolves. It begins with a trigger event (acute phase), moves to extended efforts to deal with the crisis (chronic phase), and concludes with a clear ending (resolution). The different stages of the crisis life cycle require different actions from the crisis manager. As a result, crisis management is enacted in stages and is not one simple action.

Sturges's (1994) elaborations on Fink's (1986) model illustrate how different actions are required during various crisis phases. Sturges (1994) proposed that different types of communication are emphasized during the various phases of the crisis life cycle. The acute phase is dominated by the eruption of the crisis. Stakeholders do not know what is happening; therefore, they require information about how the crisis affects them and what they should do to protect themselves. For example, information such as to whether community members should evacuate an area or whether employees should report for the next shift is highly relevant. In contrast, the resolution stage sees the end of the crisis. At that point, stakeholders would be receptive to messages designed to bolster the organization's reputation. Stakeholders need to know how a crisis affects them when it breaks but are open to reputation-building messages once the crisis ends (Sturges, 1994). The demands of the crisis stage dictate what crisis managers can and should be doing at any particular time. The later chapters of this book detail the different actions required during the various stages.

The second influential approach is from prolific crisis writer and expert Ian Mitroff (1994). He divided crisis management into five phases: (1) signal detection: new crisis warning signs should be identified and acted upon to prevent a crisis, (2) probing and prevention: organization members search known crisis risk factors and work to reduce their potential for harm, (3) damage containment: a crisis hits and organization members try to prevent the crisis damage from spreading into uncontaminated parts of the organization or its environment, (4) recovery: organization members work to return to normal business operations as soon as possible, and (5) learning: organization members review and critique their crisis management efforts, thereby adding to the organization's memory.

While subtle differences are apparent, the similarities between the Fink (1986) and Mitroff (1994) approaches are strong. Mitroff's stages reflect Fink's crisis life cycle to a large degree. Signal detection and probing can be seen as part of the prodromal phase. The difference is the degree to which Mitroff's model emphasizes detection and prevention. While Fink's model implies that crises can be prevented, the Mitroff model actively identifies them, seeking to prevent them.

There is a strong correspondence between the damage containment and crisis breakout stages and the recovery and abatement stages. Both damage containment and crisis breakout focus on the trigger event—when the crisis hits. However, Mitroff's (1994) model places greater emphasis on limiting the effects of the crisis. Augustine (1995) and Ammerman (1995) both highlight the need to limit the spread of a crisis to healthy parts of the organization. The recovery and chronic stages reflect the natural need to restore normal operations. In fact, one measure of success for crisis management is the speed with which normal operations are restored (Mitroff, 1994). Mitroff's model emphasizes how the crisis management team can facilitate the recovery while Fink's (1986) model simply documents that organizations can recover at varying speeds.

Both the learning and resolution stages signal the end of the crisis. The additional review and critique of the learning stage is a function of Mitroff's (1994) focus on crisis management rather than just crisis description. Fink's (1986) model simply notes that the resolution stage occurs when a crisis is no longer a concern. For Fink, termination marks the end of the crisis management function. In contrast, Mitroff's model is cyclical because the end also represents a new beginning. The crisis management effort is reviewed and critiqued in order to find ways to improve the system. The last stage signals the start of implementing improvements in the crisis management system. Hence, the learning phase can feed back to either the signal detection phase or the probing and prevention phase. Gonzalez-Herrero and Pratt (1995, 1996) extend Mitroff's (1994) thinking by treating the final stage as a continuation of the recovery phase. In addition to evaluation and retooling, the final stage involves maintaining contact with key stakeholders, monitoring the issues tied to the crisis, and providing updates to the media (Gonzalez-Herrero & Pratt, 1995, 1996). Communication and follow-up with stakeholders from the recovery phase are carried over to the learning phase.

The essential difference between the Fink (1986) and Mitroff (1994) models is revealed by comparing the last phases. Mitroff's is active and stresses what crisis managers should do at each phase. Fink's is more descriptive and stresses the characteristics of each phase. This is not to say that Fink is not offering recommendations to crisis managers.

Rather, the Mitroff model is more prescriptive than Fink's. Fink is concerned with mapping how crises progress while Mitroff is concerned with how crisis management efforts progress. Early models tended to be descriptive so this essential difference is not unexpected.

The three-stage model has no clearly identifiable creator but has been recommended by a variety of crisis management experts (e.g., Birch, 1994; Guth, 1995; Mitchell, 1986; Seeger, Sellnow, & Ulmer, 2003). However, Richardson (1994) provided the first detailed discussion of one. His model was composed of (1) precrisis or predisaster phase, where warning signs appear and people try to eliminate the risk; (2) crisis impact or rescue phase, where the crisis hits and support is provided for those involved in it; and (3) recovery or demise phase, where stakeholder confidence is restored.

Following from this three-stage approach, I divided the crisis management process into three macro stages: precrisis, crisis, and postcrisis. The term *macro* means that the stages are general and that each stage contains a number of more specific substages: the micro level. This is similar to economics where macroeconomics deals with all the forces at work on the economy while microeconomics deals with specific factors. Both the Fink (1986) and Mitroff (1994) models fit naturally within this general three-stage approach. The precrisis stage encompasses all of the aspects of crisis preparation. Prodromal signs, signal detection, and probing would be included in the precrisis stage. The crisis stage includes the actions taken to cope with the trigger event—the time span when the crisis is being actively dealt with. Damage containment, crisis breakout, and recovery or chronic phase all fall within the crisis stage. The postcrisis stage reflects the period after the crisis is considered to be over or resolved. Learning and resolution are each a part of the postcrisis stage.

❖ OUTLINE OF THE THREE-STAGE APPROACH

The three-stage approach to crisis management was selected as the organizing framework for this book because of its ability to subsume the other staged approaches used in crisis management. The ideal crisis management model would accommodate all of the various models plus additional insights provided by other crisis management experts. Not all crisis managers have placed their ideas within a phased model. Therefore, a comprehensive model must be able to place random insights into the crisis management process.

The three-stage approach that provides the organizing framework for this book has the appropriate macro-level generality for constructing the comprehensive framework necessary for analyzing the crisis management literature. The three stages are general enough to accommodate the other two dominant crisis management models and to allow for the integration of ideas from other crisis management experts.

Within each stage there are separate substages or set of actions that should be covered during that stage. Each substage integrates a cluster of writings about that particular crisis management topic. Each cluster of writings has been carefully examined in order to distill the essential recommendations the clusters could offer to crisis managers. For each substage, the crisis wisdom and any tests of that wisdom are reported along with a discussion of its utility to crisis managers. Moreover, this three-stage approach provides a unified system for organizing and utilizing the varied insights crisis managers offer.

Precrisis

The precrisis stage involves three substages: (1) signal detection, (2) prevention, and (3) crisis preparation. Chapters 3, 4, 5, and 6 are devoted to the development of this stage. Organization members should be proactive and take all possible actions to prevent crises. The precrisis stage entails actions to be performed before a crisis is encountered. However, not all crises can be prevented, so organization members must prepare for crises as well.

Chapter 3 deals with signal detection. Most crises do emit early warning signs. If early action is taken, these crises can be avoided (Gonzalez-Herrero & Pratt, 1995). Crisis managers must identify sources for warning signs, collect information related to them, and analyze the information. For example, a pattern in customer complaints could identity a product defect. Reporting the complaints to the appropriate manufacturing sector of the organization could result in corrective action being taken. In turn, the corrective action could prevent further complaints and the potential of a highly visible recall or battle with customers or both. Crisis managers must develop a system for detecting potential crises and responding to them.

Chapter 4 is devoted to crisis prevention. Once the potential is detected, actions must be taken to prevent the crisis. Preventative measures fall into three categories: issues management, risk aversion, and reputation management. Issues management means to take steps to prevent a problem from maturing into a crisis. Risk aversion eliminates or lowers risk levels. Reputation management seeks to resolve problems in the stakeholder–organization relationship that could escalate and damage the company's reputation. Chapters 5 and 6 develop the idea of crisis preparation. Crisis managers must be prepared for a crisis happening. Preparation typically involves identifying crisis vulnerabilities, creating crisis teams, selecting spokespersons, drafting crisis management plans (CMPs), developing crisis portfolios (a list of the most likely crises to befall an organization), and structuring the crisis communication system.

Crisis Event

The crisis event stage begins with a trigger event that marks the beginning of the crisis. The crisis stage ends when the crisis is considered to be resolved. During the crisis event, crisis managers must realize that the organization is in crisis and take appropriate actions. The crisis phase has two substages: (1) crisis recognition and (2) crisis containment. Communication with stakeholders is a critical facet of this phase. An organization communicates to stakeholders through its words and actions.

Chapter 7 is devoted to crisis recognition. People in an organization must realize that a crisis exists and respond to the event as a crisis. Crisis recognition includes an understanding of how events get labeled and accepted as crises—how to sell a crisis to management—and the means for collecting crisis-related information. Chapter 8 covers the crisis response and includes topics related to crisis containment and recovery. Crisis containment focuses on the organization's crisis response, including the importance and content of the initial response, communication's relationship to reputational management, contingency plans, and follow-up concerns.

Postcrisis

Crises are resolved and organizations must consider what to do when a crisis is deemed to be over. Postcrisis actions help to (a) make the organization better prepared for the next crisis, (b) make sure stakeholders are left with a positive impression of the organization's crisis management efforts, and (c) check to make sure that the crisis is truly over. Chapter 9 addresses evaluating crisis management, learning from the crisis, and other postcrisis actions, such as follow-up communication with stakeholders and continued monitoring of issues related to the crisis.

❖ CONCLUSION

Generally we experience crises through the news media and the Internet. As a result, it is easy to view crisis management as a short-term process and crisis managers as having few demands on their time. However, what the public sees of the response to a crisis is a small part of crisis management. Effective crisis management is ongoing. Crisis managers continually work to reduce the likelihood of a crisis occurring and to prepare the organization for the day when a crisis does occur. Moreover, crisis managers carefully dissect each crisis in order to improve prevention, preparation, and response. An appreciation of the phases of crisis management helps people to better appreciate the complexity and ongoing nature of crisis management and communication.

❖ DISCUSSION QUESTIONS

1. What alternatives are there to a staged approach to crisis management?

2. Some people question the value of precrisis activities. What reasons do you see that argue for and against precrisis activities?

3

Prevention:
Finding Warning Signs

In 1986, crisis management pioneer Steve Fink (1986) proclaimed that all crises had warning signs or prodromes, indicating that a situation has the potential to develop into a crisis. The search for warning signs is known as *signal detection*. A crisis can be prevented if appropriate action is taken on the warning signs. Prevention is the ideal form of crisis management because the best-managed crisis is the crisis that is prevented. Unfortunately it is unrealistic to expect that all crises can be prevented (Pauchant & Mitroff, 1992). Some warning signs are difficult to see. The old adage of hindsight being 20/20 fits well with crisis warning signs: they are easy to see after a crisis. We know what happened, so it is simple to identify the connections between events. A led to B and that led to a crisis. Before a crisis, people must anticipate how A will affect B and if a crisis will occur. Signal detection is like putting together a jigsaw puzzle when you do not know how the finished puzzle should look. Crisis managers can and will miss some warning signs and misinterpret others. But that does not mean that signal detection should be ignored. In fact, crisis management must develop a system designed to scan and monitor for crisis warning signals—what I term the *crisis-sensing mechanism*.

The basic element of signal detection is *scanning*, an active search for information. Crisis managers must scan for information that might contain warning signs. A variety of information sources, both internal and external, must be scanned due to the diversity of crises that could befall an organization. As part of this process, crisis managers must evaluate the information they have collected for warning signs. Those warning signs with the greatest potential for signaling danger are then monitored for further developments. Scanning is a form of radar: it identifies as many warning signs as possible. Monitoring is a form of focused tracking; it keeps a close watch on the warning signs that have the greatest potential to become crises. Therefore, the signal detection stage must include collecting and analyzing information that may contain warning signs.

Signal detection is a three-part process. First, the sources of information to be scanned must be identified. The crisis managers want to search sources that are related to crises in some way. For instance, customer complaints can signal a potential crisis in product quality or customer relations. Second, the information must be collected. The crisis managers must decide how the information will be collected from the source. And third, the information must be evaluated for its crisis potential: how strong the warning sign is, how likely the situation is to develop into a crisis. Scanning is a systematic search and analysis of events. Crisis managers scan both outside of the organization (the environment) and inside of the organization for warning signs. Neglecting either area could result overlooking important warning signs of an impeding crisis.

What Would You Do?

Verizon and Swedish Research

You work for Verizon wireless, and you love to see people talking on their cell phones. Researchers at the Swedish National Institute for Working Life have released a story linking cell phone use to cancer. They studied 2,200 cancer patients and an equal number of healthy people. Of the cancer patients with malignant brain tumors, about 10% were heavy cell phone users. Heavy use was defined as at least one hour per day. Heavy users were 240% more likely to run the risk of a malignant tumor on the side of the head where the phone was used. The story makes the news in this country. Is this a warning sign? What action would you recommend be taken by Verizon?

❖ CONTRIBUTING ORGANIZATIONAL FUNCTIONS

So how does a crisis manager go about building a scanning system? The first step is to examine existing scanning resources. Issues management, risk assessment, and reputation management can all serve to scan information that could be relevant to crisis management. Examining the three areas provides the foundation necessary to construct a crisis-sensing mechanism.

Issues Management

An issue is "a trend or condition…that, if continued, would have a significant effect on how a company is operated" (Moore, 1979, p. 43). An issue is a type of problem whose resolution can impact the organization. Issues management includes the identification of and actions taken to affect issues (Heath, 1990). It tries to lessen the negative impact of an issue. It is a systematic approach intended to shape how an issue develops and is resolved. It is a proactive attempt to have an issue decided in a way favorable to an organization. While issues management can address internal concerns (Dutton & Jackson, 1987; Dutton & Ottensmeyer, 1987), the emphasis is on societal and political issues that populate the organization's environment—external issues (Coombs, 1992). Societal issues relate to standards of corporate social performance (Heath & Cousino, 1990), while potential political issues involve regulatory and legislative decisions (Buchholz, 1990; Hainsworth, 1990). Because some issues can develop into crises, issues management contributes to crisis scanning (Gonzalez-Herrero & Pratt, 1996).

Risk Assessment

Risk assessment attempts to identify risk factors or weaknesses and to assess the probability that a weakness will be exploited or developed into crises (Levitt, 1997; Pauchant & Mitroff, 1992). Every organization faces a variety of risk factors. Typically, they include personnel, products, the production process, facilities, competition, regulations, and customers (Barton, 2001). Risk factors exist as a normal part of an organization's operation. The following incidents illustrate their crisis potential. In January 2006, an ex-postal worker entered a mail-processing facility in Santa Barbara, California, killing five employees—personnel risk. In April 2006, a blast at the AK Steel plant near Middletown, Ohio, caused several small fires and injured three workers—production process risk. In April 2006, Disney recalled personal DVD players because the batteries could heat up and burst when recharged—product and customer risk. While not daily events, the existence of employee, production process, and other risk factors can lead to serious crises from which no organization is immune. Risk can never be eliminated completely.

Risk assessment has more of an internal rather than an external focus. The internal weaknesses identified through risk assessment provide vital information for crisis management scanning. For instance, Occupational Safety and Health Administration (OSHA) records might reveal a pattern of mishandling acids. The crisis team concerned would look for ways to break the pattern, thereby preventing injuries and reducing a crisis-inducing risk factor.

Reputation Management

A reputation is an evaluation stakeholders make about an organization. Hence, we can talk about favorable and unfavorable reputations. Stakeholders can be any group that can affect or be affected by the behavior of an organization (Bryson, 2004), a point developed in more detail shortly. As noted in Chapter 1, reputations are widely recognized as a valuable if intangible asset.

Reputations are formed as stakeholders evaluate organizations based upon direct and indirect interactions. Direct interactions form the basics of the organization–stakeholder relationship (Fombrun & van Riel, 2004). Positive interactions build favorable reputations while unpleasant interactions lead to unfavorable ones. Favorable stakeholder relationships can be taken as a marker of a positive reputation. The relationship history—how the organization has treated stakeholders in the past—is a function of an organization meeting or failing to meet stakeholder expectations (Finet, 1994). Organizations build favorable relationship histories and reputations by meeting and exceeding stakeholder expectations (Coombs, 2004b).

Indirect interactions are mediated reports of how the organization treats its stakeholders. News reports, comments from friends or family, and messages sent by an organization are important sources of information for evaluating organizations. Do you dislike Enron? Did you meet anyone from Enron, buy Enron stock, or purchase products from Enron? The odds are that you build your opinion of Enron based upon media reports. In fact, stakeholders are more likely to draw upon indirect than direct experiences when crafting their personal views of an organization's reputation (Carroll & McCombs, 2003; Power Shift, 2006). Being evaluative, reputations are based in large part on how stakeholders assess an organization's ability to meet their expectations for how they are treated. How well an organization meets stakeholder expectations is a rough guide for determining if a reputation will be positive or negative.

In some respects, a reputation is a reflection of the organization–stakeholder relationship. A threat to the relationship is a threat to the reputation. It is important to dig deeper into the relationship to appreciate its connection to reputations. Crisis experts agree that favorable organization–stakeholder relationships are a benefit during crisis management (e.g., Ulmer, 2001). As Alsop (2004) stated, "They [organizations] build up 'reputation capital' to tide them over in turbulent times. It's like opening a savings account for a rainy day. If a crisis strikes . . . reputation suffers less and rebounds more quickly" (p. 17). A crisis will inflict some reputation damage. "A crisis or other negative development will certainly tax any reputation and rob a company of some of its stored-up reputation capital" (Alsop, 2004, 17).

But what does the term *relationship* mean? Talking about organizational relationships with stakeholders assumes that we all understand and agree on what is meant by relationship and stakeholder. For crisis management, a useful definition of relationship is the interdependence of two or more people or groups. This definition is a modification of one developed by O'Hair, Friedrich, Wiemann, and Wiemann (1995). The definition centers on interdependence, some factor that binds the two people or groups together. The interdependence definition of relationship is useful because it is consistent with the stakeholder theory that guides most business thinking (Rowley, 1997).

Stakeholder theory posits that an organization's environment is populated with various stakeholders. An organization survives or thrives by effectively managing these stakeholders (Bryson, 2004; Clarkson, 1991; Wood, 1991). Stakeholders are generally defined as any persons or groups that have an interest, right, claim, or ownership in an organization. Stakeholders have been separated into two distinct groups: primary and secondary. Primary stakeholders are those people or groups whose actions can be harmful or beneficial to an organization. Failure to maintain a continuing interaction with a primary stakeholder could result in the failure of the organization. Typical primary stakeholders include employees, investors, customers, suppliers, and the government. For instance, organizations cannot operate without employees, while government officials may close a facility for a variety of legal or regulatory reasons. Secondary stakeholders or influencers are those people or groups who can affect or be affected by the actions of an organization. Typical influencers include the media, activist groups, and competitors. Influencers cannot stop an organization from functioning, but they can damage it (Clarkson, 1995; Donaldson & Preston, 1995).

Primary and secondary stakeholders are interdependent with an organization, thus the relevance of the earlier definition of relationship. Each of the stakeholders has a connection with the organization that links them in some way. The links include economic, social, and political concerns. Reputation management is the management of the relationships between the organization and its various stakeholders, and organizational success is predicated on maintaining an effective balance in these relationships (Donaldson & Preston, 1995; Rowley, 1997; Savage, Nix, Whitehead, & Blair, 1991). It follows that stakeholders can play an important role in crisis management.

Primary stakeholders can stop organizational operations and trigger a crisis. Conflict with an organization can lead primary stakeholders to withhold their contributions. As a result, an organization may stop operating if those contributions cannot be replaced. For instance, unhappy workers can strike, and discontented customers can boycott. In 1997, the Teamsters 15-day strike against UPS cost the company $600 million in revenues. A total of 185,000 Teamsters, nearly two-thirds of the UPS American workforce, joined the strike. At best, UPS was able to operate at only 10% capacity, using management personnel and drivers who did not strike. UPS found it could not function without the drivers, so it conceded to their demands (Sewell, 1997).

In 2004, Kryptonite announced it would recall some of its popular and high-priced bicycle locks. The problem was that many locks could be picked using just the outside casing of a Bic pen. The impetus for the recall was a complaint from a group of angry bikers taking their case to the Internet via discussion group postings and blogs. Some people even posted videos showing how to pick the lock, to prove the claim was true. The bikers were angry that their very expensive bikes were being stolen or were at risk from the faulty locks. It took Kryptonite a week to respond to customer concerns, a long time in the Internet world (Wagstaff, 2006). Primary stakeholders are powerful because it is difficult and often impossible to replace the contributions they provide the organization (Mitchell, Agle, & Wood, 1997).

For crisis management, it would be a mistake to focus solely on primary stakeholders. Problems in relationships with secondary stakeholders can also harm reputations and trigger crises. The media can expose organizational misdeeds or generate other negative publicity, competitors can instigate lawsuits that bind an organization's operations, and activists can launch boycotts or protests against an organization.

A few examples illustrate the role of secondary stakeholders in creating crises.

On February of 2006, Airbourne was brought down to earth by a "Good Morning America (GMA)" special report. On its packaging, Airbourne claimed to fight colds. In fact, it claimed to be a miracle cold buster that could cure colds in an hour. The GMA investigation reported that the product was no more effective than hand washing during cold and flu season—it was not a cure. The key finding was that the clinical study Airbourne used to support its claim was highly questionable. GMA found that the research firm was created just to study Airbourne and that the main researcher had false credentials. Airbourne promised to remove any mention of the study from its Web site and promotional materials (Does Airborne, 2006). The company had to publicly address the concerns about its claims and documentation. A media story had precipitated a crisis.

In February of 2006, Procter and Gamble Company (P&G) filed a lawsuit against Vi-Jon Laboratories, Inc., a manufacturer of health and beauty products. P&G alleged that Vi-Jon had infringed and diluted the unique trade dress of its Crest Pro-Health Rinse: The Vi-Jon packing looked too much like Crest's, and consumers could be confused and buy the wrong product. P&G also alleged Vi-Jon's advertising for its Vi-Jon Rinse was false and misleading (Procter & Gamble files, 2006). In April 2006, a settlement was reached between P&G and Vi-Jon. Vi-Jon agreed to remove its product from the market, to stop using a bottle design similar to Crest Pro-Health Rinse, and to stop making gingivitis efficacy claims in its advertising (Procter & Gamble reaches, 2006)

In both cases, a secondary stakeholder had influenced organizational actions. Secondary, as well as primary, stakeholders can create a crisis for an organization. Mismanaging the organization–stakeholder relations can damage an organization's reputation. Moreover, a damaged organization–stakeholder relationship can evolve into a crisis (Grunig, 1992; Heath, 1988). Therefore, watching organization–stakeholder relationships contributes to crisis scanning as a part of reputation management. Early problems related to reputations are signs that a crisis could erupt.

Summary

Issues management, risk assessment, and reputation management all can contribute to crisis scanning. Combined, the three functions provide a broad radar system for detecting warning signs. The challenge for crisis managers is to integrate the three organizational functions into an effective crisis-sensing mechanism. To meet the challenge, crisis managers should know what sources to scan, how to collect information, and how to evaluate information for its crisis potential. The next three sections discuss the basic elements needed to construct a crisis-sensing mechanism.

❖ SOURCES TO BE SCANNED

Crisis managers cannot begin looking for warning signs until they

Table 3.1   Potential Crisis Sources to Monitor

Issues Management Sources

TRADITIONAL

News media: Newspapers, television news, news and business magazines

Trade journals	Medical and science journals
Newsletters	Government publications
Public opinion polls	Public opinion experts
Stakeholder actions	

ONLINE

News and business wires
Online newspapers, magazines, and trade publications
Archives for professional associations, special interest groups, and
    government agencies
Consumer-generated media: Web sites, blogs, and discussion groups
Newsgroups

Risk Assessment Sources

Total quality management	Liability exposure	Natural disaster exposure
Environmental crisis exposure	Criminal exposure	Product tampering exposure
Legal compliance audits	Financial audits	Ethical climate surveys
Workers compensation exposure	Safety, accident records	Behavioral profiling
Internet use monitoring		

Reputation Sources

Consumer-generated media: Web sites, blogs, and discussion groups
Stakeholder comments sent to the organization

know what sources they will be scanning. Table 3.1 provides a list of potential crisis threat information sources derived from issues management, risk assessment, and reputation management sources.

Issues Management Sources

Environmental scanning is a tool that is popular in issues management (Gonzalez-Herrero & Pratt, 1996; Heath, 1997; Heath & Nelson, 1986; Pauchant & Mitroff, 1992). Roughly, environmental scanning is watching the environment for changes, trends, events, and emerging social, political, or health issues. The information is used to guide organizational decision making to plot future actions (Lauzen, 1995). Unfortunately, environmental scanning strategies used by organizations are not well developed. Still, crisis managers must consider the sources involved in external scanning that would be helpful in locating warning signs.

External scanning uses both traditional print and online sources. In fact, most traditional sources can now be found online as well. A common traditional source used to monitor the environment is to watch, listen to, or read the news media (Heath, 1988). The news media include leading or elite newspapers (e.g., *New York Times, Wall Street Journal, Washington Post*), news and business magazines (e.g., *Time, Newsweek, Fortune*), and television news programs, such as the evening news and TV news magazines (e.g., "60 Minutes," "20/20"). Futurists such as John Naisbitt locate trends and issues by examining the media (Heath, 1997). Of special interest are stories about crises in similar organizations. Case studies of similar organizations in crisis are a valuable resource for crisis managers, allowing crisis teams to learn from someone else's crisis rather than their own (Pauchant & Mitroff, 1992).

Other useful publications include trade journals, relevant medical or scientific journals, newsletters, and public opinion surveys. The trade outlets are likely to carry stories about crises suffered by similar organizations. The trade journals and other publications provide information about issues the industry is facing as well as industry-specific complaints. Both may help to identify possible crises for individual organizations within that industry. Medical or scientific journals may contain studies that might affect how people view an industry. The dangers of cholesterol and concerns over the link between using cell phones and automobile accidents are two such examples. The public's first exposure to these two health concerns was through medical and scientific publications, not the news media.

Newsletters include reports published by special interest groups, foundations, and government agencies. Each can indicate potential threats to an organization. Special interest publications inform organizations about the concerns of the activist stakeholders and indicate if anger is being focused on their industry or their specific organization. Foundations can identify emerging issues. Government publications offer insights into possible regulatory or legal changes as well as identifying emerging issues. For example, the *Federal Register* has information about potential regulatory changes, the *Congressional Record* and *Congressional Quarterly Weekly Report* provide information about new legislation, and the *Congressional Quarterly Researcher* provides information about salient issues in U.S. society. Public opinion surveys can indicate changes in attitudes, lifestyles, and values (Heath, 1997).

Individuals are another source of environmental information. Crisis managers should focus on two broad categories: the public opinion experts and their own stakeholders. Public opinion experts, like the published data, provide insights into public attitudes, lifestyles, and values. Stakeholders can tell the organization how they feel about issues and organizational actions (Heath & Nelson, 1986). It is easy to become overly dependent on the mass media and forget about people as resources for environmental information. (There is more about people as a source of information in the reputation management section.)

Online resources are becoming more popular in environmental scanning (Coombs, 2002). Online, there are news and business wire services, newspapers, magazines, trade journals, archives from professional associations, special interest group newsletters, and records from government bodies. The array is similar to the published sources but is stored and accessed electronically. A particular source may have a searchable archive or offer live, continuous feeds of information. Another option is to hire a service, such as Cyberalerts, that will search for stories on specific topics or provide industry-specific news and information. The online options simply provide information more quickly and make it easier to track events over time.

Information spreads through the Internet by ways other than the conventional media or publication sources. Discussion groups, message boards and forums, Web pages, dedicated complaint sites, and Weblogs (blogs) are information sources that should not be overlooked. As noted earlier, these online communication vehicles are known as consumer-generated media or CGM but are used by a variety of stakeholders, not just consumers.

CGM is easy to use, and I would bet you have already created some CGM yourself. CGM is simply the ability to post messages to the

Internet that other people can read. All a person needs is Internet access and the ability to use a keyboard. Admittedly, most CGM is of little interest to anyone. However, CGM is a potentially powerful form of word-of-mouth (WOM) information distribution (Laczniak, DeCarlo, & Ramaswami (2001). WOM is recognized as serious force that can shape consumer decisions; hence, it should not be ignored (Blackshaw & Nazzaro, 2004). Consider how concerned organizational leadership can be with attack sites—Web sites designed to criticize an organization (Holtz, 1999). Tuning in to CGM can be a very effective way to listen to stakeholders. Again, most CGM is irrelevant to an organization. Crisis managers must carefully identify the CGM most relevant to their concerns or hire firms such as BuzzMetric to collect CGM data for them. Table 3.1 identifies some basic categories of CGM to consider.

As of this writing, if you typed www.killercoke.org into your Web browser, you would arrive at the Killer Coke Web site. As the name implies, the site is hostile toward the Coca-Cola Company and supports the Campaign to Stop Killer Coke. So how is Coke a killer? The site maintains that security forces in Colombia have kidnapped, murdered, and tortured members of SINALTRAINAL (National Union of Food Industrial Workers) who work at Coca-Cola bottling plants. The claim is that the Coca-Cola bottlers hire violent, paramilitary security guards who commit these atrocities. The Coca-Cola Company disputes this claim. However, the Web site is composed of testimonials, photographs, and resources attacking the company. A key element of the campaign in the United States is to target college campuses. Students pressure their schools' administration to terminate vending contracts with Coca-Cola. Michigan State University, Rutgers University, and Hofstra University are but a handful of the schools that have ended contracts with Coca-Cola. Killer Coke moved from the Internet to the business press when *BusinessWeek* did a feature on the campaign in January 2006 (Killer Coke, 2006). The Killer Coke campaign continues to pressure Coca-Cola through lost contracts, and the Internet is the epicenter of this effort.

The Internet is more than a source of fear for an organization. It is a resource that can be used to anticipate and to respond to potential problems. An organization concerned with human rights, for example, can peruse a variety of human-rights-oriented Web sites to get a feel for stakeholder sentiments and the development of human rights issues. These insights can guide actions designed to prevent possible crises, a point further developed in Chapter 4.

The Internet is a source that organizations should not overlook. The Internet user population continues to grow, making it an increasingly important environmental information resource. The Internet serves as a dual information source. It can be used to access information also found in print or broadcast form and it can be used to collect information unique to CGM.

Risk Assessment Sources

Risk assessment sources provide information about an organization's weaknesses that could become crises. This section briefly explains each source and notes its connection to certain crises. Total quality management systematically assesses the manufacturing process in order to improve quality. Part of that process is to locate sources of defects (Milas, 1996). Product defects can trigger the need for recalls (Mitroff, 1994). Environmental crisis exposure includes pollution abatement actions and threats to the environment posed by an organization. Polluting can lead to accidents, lawsuits, protests, or regulatory fines. Legal compliance audits make sure an organization is complying with all federal, state, and local laws and regulations. Failure to comply can result in lawsuits or fines. Financial audits review the financial health of the organization, which can indicate financially oriented crises such as shareholder rebellion.

Traditional insurance coverage indicates risks worth insuring against. Insurance risks include liability exposure, criminal exposure, and worker compensation exposure. All three areas can produce lawsuits and extremely negative publicity. Natural disaster exposure identifies what Mother Nature might do to the organization. Administration must know if facilities are at risk of crises caused by floods, earthquakes, or volcanoes—natural actions typically not covered by insurance.

Safety, maintenance, and accident records reveal minor problems which could become crises. These records should be examined for patterns. Organizations have what are called near misses—something bad that almost happened. A series of near misses runs the risk of escalating into a major crisis. If there are a number of near misses or small hand injuries with a piece of equipment, it is possible that a major injury, such as amputation or death, could also occur. Action should be taken in the prevention phase to break the pattern of minor accidents. Similarly, a history of the same safety violation indicates that a major accident and injury could occur. Obviously, safety precautions are designed to prevent accidents and injuries. Unheeded, the workplace becomes unsafe and ripe for these troubling and preventable events (Komaki, Heinzmann & Lawson, 1980).

Employee use of the Internet and e-mail are sources of risk. Misuse of these online communication tools can result in information leaks, computer viruses or worms, discrimination and harassment lawsuits, or reduced bandwidth capacity. Concerns over online risks have led most companies to create Internet and e-mail use policies and to utilize software design to monitor employee online behavior. A 2006 study found that 38% of large companies in the United Kingdom and the United States hired people to read worker e-mails (Study finds, 2006). Online use policies lack any real meaning if the organization cannot effectively determine whether or not their policies are being violated. The monitoring software can block access to inappropriate Web sites, review all e-mails for inappropriate language, or record and evaluate all employee Web activity in terms of business-related and non-business-related site visits. Organizations assume unnecessary risk if they do not have and enforce employee Internet and e-mail use policies.

Product-tampering monitoring examines the manufacturing process and packaging for susceptibility to product tampering. Product tampering leads to recalls and lawsuits. Behavior profiling identifies the characteristics of potentially dangerous employees, typically those who may become violent. Violent employees can trigger workplace violence crises. Ethical climate surveys assess the organization for temptations and cultural blinders to problems. Such blinders are located by examining management attitudes and values about important concerns, such as sexual harassment. A weak ethical climate can encourage organizational misdeeds, such as check fraud, sexual harassment, or racial discrimination (Mitroff & McWinney, 1987; Soper, 1995).

Very few people have not heard of Enron and its fall from the list of "Most Admired" to "Most Reviled" corporations. At heart, the Enron tale is story of an organization's culture precipitating a crisis. As Enron was winning honor after honor from the business press, its culture was characterized as "aggressive." Enron was among the Most Admired, the Best Companies to Work For, and the Most Innovative. However, an aggressive culture also made for a risk-taking culture. The company rapidly expanded into areas it knew little about (Normand, McKittrick, Roberts, & Kline, n.d.). The expansion was required because Enron needed to keep its earnings high in order to maintain a strong stock price. Members of Congress referred to this as a "culture of greed" (Lawmakers, 2002).

Enron's risk taking had its downfall. Top management, led by Ken Lay, Jeffrey Skilling, and Andrew Fastow, had become arrogant and overly optimistic. They believed Enron could not fail, and its risk taking intensified. But Enron did fail, and this meant revenues would drop. Being aggressive, top management engaged in very creative and illegal bookkeeping methods to hide losses and to feature gains. Enron crafted a fake financial front that cost investors billions of dollars when it went bankrupt (Schuler, 2002). Enron's aggressive actions led it to ignore ethics in the pursuit of stock prices and profits (Brewer, Chandler, & Ferrell, 2006). It is safe to say that Enron was an ethically challenged organization; it had a morally bankrupt ethical climate. A similar fate can befall any company that fails to monitor and to correct its own ethical climate and aspects of its culture that can promote rather then retard crises.

Reputation Sources

Unlike issues management and risk assessment, the sources for reputation monitoring are not well developed, but Table 3.1 identifies some logical choices, and they reflect the importance of stakeholders to reputation management, particularly the investor, customer, activist, and community stakeholders. Shareholder resolutions reflect the values and attitudes of those owning stocks. For instance, Wal-Mart investors rejected six different social responsibility shareholder resolutions in 2006. Resolutions can reflect social concerns, such as support for the UN Global Compact (a set of 10 environmental and social principles), or financial concerns, such as resolutions preventing the "poison pill" as a takeover defense. Most resolutions are designed to address social concerns. Shareholder resolutions provide insight into how the stockholders feel about important issues or the organization itself. Stakeholder complaints and inquires help to detect discontent among customers and to discover rumors. Early identification of discontent means that the organization can act to resolve the problem and make a customer happy, maintaining a positive relationship with this stakeholder (Dozier, 1992).

Profit-making organizations cannot survive without customers, which makes them a critical source for reputation signs. Organizations must identify when their actions place customers at risk and when customers are unhappy with organizational operations or policies. In October 1996, an E. coli outbreak linked to Odwalla juices killed 16-month-old Anna Gimmestad and sickened over 70 other people. Odwalla juice was not pasteurized at that time. Pasteurization kills bacteria, but natural juice makers felt it harmed the product. Odwalla began flash pasteurization after the incident. The company launched a quick recall and covered medical expenses for those who were stricken.

In addition, Odwalla was one of the first companies to use the Internet as part of its crisis management. It has been praised for its quick and caring response (Baker, n.d).

From a warning signs detection stand point, Odwalla was a dismal failure. There were a number of warning signs prior to the October 1996 E. coli tragedy. Dave Stevenson, the head of Odwalla's quality assurance, had recommended using a chlorine rinse to increase the killing of bacteria. Senior executives rejected the idea and kept the far less effective acid-wash method. Even the supplier of the acid wash told Odwalla it was only 8% effective at killing E. coli. In the lawsuits that followed the outbreak, Odwalla admitted to more than 300 reports of bacterial poisoning prior to the 1996 event. Moreover, the U.S. Army had denied Odwalla access to military commissaries. Just four months before the outbreak, Army inspectors found an unacceptably high bacteria count in its sample and decided the risk was too high to sell in commissaries (Entine, 1998, 1999). Had Odwalla taken the warning signs seriously and either changed to the chlorine wash or switched to flash pasteurization, the 1996 outbreak would probably not have occurred.

One important source of concern is public criticism of the organization. Heath (1988) recommends that "All public criticism should prompt corporate leaders and operations managers to conduct studies to determine whether the charges are true and whether key publics are believing the allegations" (p. 105). Complaints can be found in inquires customers make to an organization or protests from activists. Inquiries may reveal an actual problem or a rumor, as people call to confirm the information they heard. Consider the toy maker Hasbro's online run-in with fathers. In May of 2006, Hasbro announced it had cancelled plans to manufacture and market a line of dolls based on the popular singing group, the Pussycat Dolls. The toys were targeting girls as young as four. The Pussycat Dolls are infamous for sexy clothes and sexy lyrics, such as "Don'tcha wish your girlfriend was hot like me; Don'tcha wish your girlfriend was a freak like me?" Dads & Daughters, a nonprofit group that promotes fathers spending time with daughters, and the Campaign for a Commercial Free Childhood both launched Internet-based attacks on Hasbro's plans. They felt the sexily charged group and dolls were not suitable for young girls. As Dads & Daughters President Joe Kelly said, "We asked Hasbro executives to imagine encouraging their own six-year-old daughters and granddaughters to engage in developmentally unhealthy behavior. It appears they did that, and then made the right decision for their families, our families, and the company" (Pussycat dolls, 2006). Both organizations stated their concerns about the dolls at their Web sites and provided a form visitors could complete and e-mail to Hasbro management. By scanning the two Web sites and watching e-mail traffic, Hasbro was able to detect a potential problem and take action before it escalated.

Here's another example. Febreze is a fabric refresher manufactured by Procter & Gamble. One of its main selling points is its ability to eliminate pet odors. So when a rumor began circulating on the Internet that Febreze kills pets, there was reason for concern. Here is a sample message:

> There have been multiple instances of dogs and birds that have died or became very ill after being exposed to Febreze, a deodorizer/ air freshener. Febreze contains zinc chloride, which is very dangerous for animals. Please do not use Febreze anywhere near your pets! If you have used it near your pets or on their bedding, clean the bedding area thoroughly to remove the Febreze, and move the animals away from the area. Please pass this information on to other pet owners/caretakers, before more animals are injured or killed, and find a safer method of odor control. (Febreze warning, 1999)

P&G soon began receiving phone calls and e-mails asking if Febreze was safe around pets. The P&G response was "Yes!" The product had been tested and proven safe around dogs and cats. P&G created a special section of its Febreze Web site to debunk the myth. People were told of Febreze's safety along with testimonials from National Animal Poison Control Center and the American Society for the Prevention of Cruelty to Animals (Hanging, 1999). P&G used the consumer concerns to fight the rumor and protect the sale of Febreze.

❖ REPUTATION AND SOCIAL PERFORMANCE

Corporate social responsibility (CSR) is an important consideration in how stakeholders feel about organizations. It is based on how organizations handle nonfinancial concerns and has significant implications for reputation (Fombrun, 2005). Broadly, CSR is the realization that organizations have responsibilities beyond investors (Husted & Salazar, 2006) and focuses on how the operations of an organization impact society (Werther & Chandler, 2006). Thus, a working definition of CSR is the management of actions designed to affect an organization's impacts on society. CSR can be measured by examining community relations, treatment of women and minorities, employee relations, treatment of the environment, and quality of services and products. Weaknesses in any one of these areas could develop into a conflict with certain stakeholders. For instance, neglect of community relations can lead to protests from community groups or new local regulations that can hurt the organization in some fashion. Unhappy stakeholders can create a crisis by taking their problem public by using protests, boycotts, lawsuits, or other forms of confrontation.

❖ INFORMATION COLLECTION

Once potential environmental information sources are located, crisis managers face the challenge of gathering the information. Content analysis, interviews, surveys, focus groups, and informal contacts are among the most frequently used collection tools. A familiarity with these tools is an important crisis management asset.

When utilizing any published, online, or broadcast source, content analysis can be useful. It involves the systematic coding and classification of written materials, be they news stories, articles in other publications, or transcripts of focus groups or interviews. Effective content analysis requires the development of coding categories and expertise in using the categories. Coding categories are the boxes in which discrete pieces of information are placed. Each category needs a thorough written definition that indicates what is appropriate for it, and these categories must be mutually exclusive—no message should fit into more than one category (Stacks, 2002; Stewart, 2002). People who use the categories, the coders, must be trained in their use. Coders must be able to place similar messages in the same categories. This consistency is called *reliability*. Reliability allows different people to code messages consistently. Such consistency allows for comparisons of the coded data. Content analysis converts the written information into quantifiable data—the words become numbers that can be analyzed using statistics. Some examples may help to clarify the content analysis process.

Most organizations have established categories for accidents and safety violations. People are trained to understand the differences in the accident and safety categories so that they can accurately record these events. An organization can examine the data to see if certain accidents or safety violations have increased or decreased over time. For example, an organization might be interested in the number of falls in a particular area of the organization. Systematic coding of accidents permits an accurate analysis of the fall data. Similarly, organizations should develop categories for coding customer complaints. It is not enough to know the sheer number of complaints received; an airline, for example, needs to know the type and frequency of different varieties of complaints. By categorizing customer complaints, organizations can identify problem areas by the increase of complaints in those areas. If an airline receives increasing complaints about how canceled flights are handled, it needs to improve its customer service relative to canceled flights. Systematic coding allows for comparisons that could not be made if the written information had not been quantified. It is the recording and quantifying of the material that qualifies content analysis as a form of information collecting.

The first step in soliciting information from stakeholders is for the crisis team to construct a stakeholder map that lists all possible stakeholders (Grunig & Repper, 1992). Then the crisis team would identify the stakeholders relevant to the most highly ranked crises. Interviews, surveys, focus groups, or key contacts can be used to collect information from stakeholders. Interviewers ask people questions about a particular subject in an organized fashion. The interviewer develops and follows an interview schedule. Preparation is essential. The person collecting the information must have an organized approach to the interview if it is to yield useful information (Stewart & Cash, 1997). Surveys collect information about people's perceptions, attitudes, and opinions. Surveys can be conducted by having people complete questionnaires or by having researchers ask stakeholders the questions. Focus groups are collections of specific stakeholders who are brought together to listen and to respond to questions as a group. Open-ended questions are used to encourage interaction and to probe the nature of people's beliefs. Key contacts are community, industry, or organization leaders who are selected because of their expertise on a subject. Using public opinion or issue experts is a form of key contact (Baskin & Aronoff, 1988).

❖ INFORMATION ANALYSIS EQUALS KNOWLEDGE CREATION

Collecting information about issues, risks, and stakeholder relationships is of no value unless it is analyzed to determine if the information contains crisis risks. Analyzing information creates knowledge (Geraghty & Desouza, 2005). Crisis managers determine if the information really does suggest a possible crisis. The premise behind finding warning signs early is to locate those that can significantly impact the organization and to take action to manage them (Dutton & Duncan, 1987; Gonzalez-Herrero & Pratt, 1996; Heath & Nelson, 1986). Analysis is the process of understanding if and how a warning sign might impact the organization (Heath & Nelson, 1986). Crisis managers need criteria for evaluating issues, risks, and reputation threats.

Issues Threat Assessment

Two criteria stand out for assessing issues: (1) likelihood and (2) impact (Heath, 1988, 1997). *Likelihood* is the probability of an issue gaining momentum. An issue with momentum is developing and more likely to affect the organization. Some indicators of momentum are sophisticated promotion of the issue, heavy mass media coverage, strong Internet presence, and a strong self-interest link between an issue and stakeholders. The anti-Alar campaign in 1989 illustrates an issue with momentum. Alar is a chemical that was used to treat apples. Within a year of launching its campaign, the anti-Alar coalition headed by the Natural Resources Defense Council (NRDC) had removed Alar from use. The Alar issue had professionals crafting the publicity effort: sophisticated promotion. Celebrity appearances, including Meryl Streep, helped to garner massive publicity: heavy media coverage. And Alar was treated as a threat to innocent children, a strong self-interest link between Alar and consumers (Center & Jackson, 1995).

Impact refers to how strongly the issue can affect either profits or operations. It involves the use of forecasting, which projects the potential effect of an issue on the organization. There are at least 150 forecasting techniques used in business. A detailed discussion of fore-casting is beyond the scope of this book; Coates, Coates, Jarratt, and Heinz (1986), Ewing (1979), and Heath (1997) offer more details on forecasting techniques. Organizations should use those forecasting methods with which they are familiar. Only issues with high impact would be considered crises because a crisis must be disruptive to orga-nizational operations.

Issues can be given scores from 1 to 10 for the two dimensions of likelihood and impact. The highest scoring issues should be tracked carefully, and the organization should consider taking action to pre-vent or to lessen the threat of the issue.

Risk Threat Assessment

Not all risks have the potential to be crises. Crisis managers must be able to separate minor risks from crisis-producing risks. Again, the two criteria already mentioned can be used to assess risk: (1) likelihood and (2) impact. In this context, likelihood is the probability that the risk can or will become an event—the risk will cause something to happen. This estimates the possibility of the risk being exploited or maturing into an event. Impact is, again, how much the event might impact the organization. In this context, it includes disruption to organizational routines and potential damage to people, facilities, processes, or reputation (Levitt, 1997). Again, the anticipated impact must be strong enough to warrant labeling the event as a crisis. Each risk should be rated on a 1 to 10 scale for both likelihood and impact. The scores high enough to be deemed crises should be identified for preventative action. While an organization might want to manage all risks (Smallwood, 1995), time and resource constraints allow organizations to address only the top priority risks (Heath, 1997).

Reputation Threat Assessment

Assessing reputational threats is a two-step process. The first step is to determine if there is a gap between how the organization wants to be perceived and how it is perceived by stakeholders. If there is a difference between the two, the second step is to determine the salience of the stakeholder holding the expectation gap.

As noted earlier, reputations are built around stakeholder expectations. Different stakeholder groups will have different expectations for organizational behaviors. For instance, investors want the organization to make money, employees want adequate pay and medical benefits, and community groups want it to be engaged in the life of the community. The point is that crisis managers must identify the expectations held by each major stakeholder group. Through research, crisis managers can isolate stakeholder expectations. Expectations reflect values. Stakeholders perceive that they share values with an organization when that organization meets their expectations.

Once the expectations are known, crisis managers must determine whether or not the stakeholders perceive the organization as meeting those expectations: they search for gaps. There are two types of gaps illustrated in Figure 3.1. The first gap is based on performance; the organization is not doing what it needs to do to meet expectations. The second gap occurs when stakeholders fail to perceive that the organization is meeting expectations. Perceptions are the key. Even if an organization has made significant efforts to reduce pollution, if the stakeholders do not know about it, there is a gap.

Figure 3.1   Expectation Gaps

Performance Gap: Organizational actions do not match stakeholder expectations.

Organizational Actions   Stakeholder Expectations

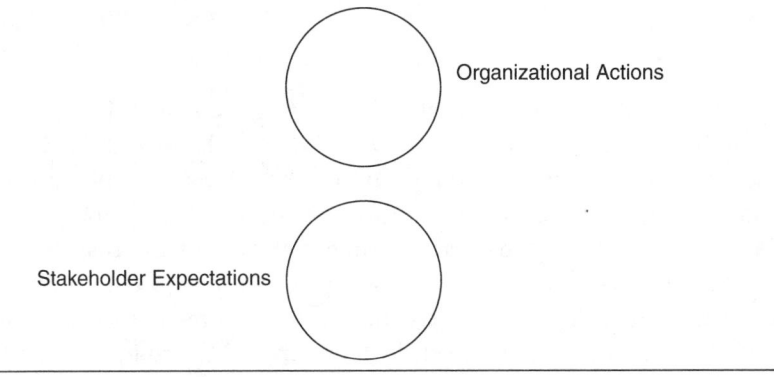

Perception Gap: Organizational actions do match stakeholder expectations, but stake-holders do not see the match.

Organizational Actions

Stakeholder Expectations

What Would You Do?

FedEx and Environmental Defense

The best way to avoid an expectation gap is to anticipate it and make changes before stakeholders become angry. This requires an organization to anticipate where stakeholder expectations and values are going. FedEx is one of the top package delivery companies in the world. Delivering packages requires the use of a lot of trucks. Trucks burn fuel and create pollution. The Environmental Defense (formerly Environmental Defense Fund) is a proenvironmental group with a track record of successfully working with corporations. They approach FedEx with a plan to work together to fight pollution. The plan requires the development, building, and using of fuel-efficient, low-pollution trucks. What are the advantages and disadvantages of this partnership? What possible expectation gaps could be closed? What would you recommend to FedEx management about the proposal and why did you make that recommendation?

If stakeholders have concerns based on expectation gaps, they can become a reputation threat by taking action against the organization and generating negative publicity. No organization has the time, money, or personnel to address every expectation gap. So what is an organization to do? The answer is to prioritize stakeholders and focus your resources on those that have the greatest potential to initiate crises. Not all expectation gaps lead to crises. Crisis managers must be able to differentiate between mild threats and serious reputation threats. The strength of the reputation threat is a function of the salience (importance) of the stakeholder holding the expectation gap. Three criteria can be used to evaluate the salience of stakeholders to an organization: (1) power, (2) legitimacy, and (3) willingness to confront (Mitchell et al., 1997).

Power

Power is the ability of the stakeholder to get the organization to do something it would not do otherwise. Power relates to the ability of the stakeholder to disrupt organizational operations. Stakeholders who control essential resources or can form coalitions have strong power. Control over essential resources permits a stakeholder to disrupt organizational processes. For instance, employees can stop the production process or the delivery of goods and services. As mentioned earlier, in 1997, UPS drivers launched a strike that crippled the company's ability to deliver its primary service.

Coalition formation supplies power through numbers. As stakeholders join forces with one another, their power increases (Mitchell et al., 1997; Rowley, 1997). An example would be an activist group that persuades shareholders and customers to join its efforts to pressure an organization for change. The combination of activists, customers, and shareholders was instrumental in convincing Levi Strauss to close its production facilities in Myanmar. Activists persuaded customers and shareholders that facilities in Myanmar contributed to human rights violations there. In turn, customers and shareholders questioned Levi Strauss's operations there. Levi Strauss felt the stigma of human rights abuse was reason enough to leave Myanmar (Cooper, 1997). The Killer Coke campaign has followed a similar strategy. Alone, the activists would have little impact but combined with shareholders and customers, they can exercise great power.

Stakeholder power is enhanced by the ability to take action against the organization. Stakeholders need resources (e.g., money) and skill in using communication channels if they are to put pressure on an organization (Ryan, 1991). Let us return to the NRDC's effort to ban

Alar, a plant growth regulator that was used on apples. The NRDC had money to hire professional communicators to develop a major publicity campaign promoting the danger of Alar. The campaign raised awareness of Alar danger from 0% to 95% in less than a month (Center & Jackson, 1995). Money and publicity skills created the perception of Alar as a cancer threat to children.

Legitimacy

Legitimacy refers to actions that are considered desirable, proper, or appropriate according to some system. A stakeholder concern is more serious when it is deemed legitimate by other stakeholders. Ignoring a legitimate concern makes the organization appear callous to the other stakeholders. They ask, Why doesn't the organization address this reasonable concern? Offending other stakeholders increases the risk of the threat spreading to additional organization–stakeholder relationships. Crisis managers should determine if other stakeholders will view the concern as legitimate. This requires knowing the values and social responsibility expectations of various stakeholder groups in order to assess a concern's legitimacy potential (Mitchell et al., 1997).

Willingness

Willingness refers to the stakeholder's desire to confront the organization about the problem. A problem must be important for the stakeholders, and their relationship to the organization must be relatively weak. Importance prompts the stakeholder to take action. Why push a problem if it is unimportant? And stakeholders are less likely to pursue a problem when they have a favorable relationship with the organization. Once more, the Alar case illustrates the point. The NRDC considered Alar to be salient; it was the major concern of the NRDC at the time. The NRDC seemed to have no real relationship with the apple growers, the group affected most by the anti-Alar campaign. Documentation of the case makes no mention of the two sides ever meeting to discuss the concern prior to the launch of the NRDC's anti-Alar publicity campaign (Center & Jackson, 1995). A favorable relationship encourages both sides to seek a nonconfrontational approach to problem solving (Grunig & Repper, 1992).

Power, legitimacy, and willingness are related to the criteria of impact and likelihood associated with issues management and risk assessment. High power and legitimacy indicate a strong impact. Such stakeholder can disrupt the organization and are likely to be perceived by others as having a valid (legitimate) reason for doing so. Legitimacy and willingness suggest a strong likelihood of occurrence. Willingness increases the chance of a stakeholder taking action while legitimacy increases the possibility of other stakeholders supporting the action. Each stakeholder expectation gap can be rated on a 1 to 10 scale for power, legitimacy, and willingness. The highest scoring threats should be tagged for immediate consideration.

From Scanning to Monitoring

The information analysis ends the scanning process and begins the monitoring process. Monitoring involves following the development of the warning sign. The crisis team continuously collects and analyzes information about the warning sign. The team looks for changes that indicate whether the risk is becoming more or less likely to evolve into a crisis. The information sources, collection tools, and analytic criteria used in scanning are employed in monitoring. The key differences are a search for more detailed information and the continuous application of the search process in monitoring.

❖ CRISIS-SENSING MECHANISM

The discussion of scanning and monitoring presupposes that issue, risk, and stakeholder information is received by crisis managers. As noted in the introduction of this chapter, crisis sensing is a critical crisis management function. The first edition of this book talked about a concept I developed known as the *crisis-sensing mechanism*. A crisis-sensing mechanism is a systematic means of collecting crisis risk information and is built on three points: (1) locating the source of crisis risk information, (2) funneling the information to a central location, and (3) making sure the information is analyzed—converted into knowledge. Sources, collection tools, and evaluation criteria are the raw materials used to construct the crisis-sensing mechanism—the crisis radar and tracking system. No one crisis-sensing mechanism is right for all organizations. Each organization has quirks which must be accommodated, but some basic ideas can be offered.

Since the first edition, knowledge management (KM) has emerged as an important influence on organizations. KM is a mechanism for finding and sharing what is known by an organization or its external stakeholders. KM differentiates between *information* and *knowledge*. Information simply places facts in context, while knowledge analyzes the information so that it is usable by people in the organization

(Halonen-Rollins & Halinen-Kaila, 2005; McKeen, Zack, & Singh, 2006). There is a close connection between knowledge management and some aspects of crisis management. Knowledge is essential to all phases of crisis management. "Managing knowledge well is key to enhancing an organization's ability to deal with business crises" (Wang & Belardo, 2005, p. 7).

In this edition of the book, I draw out these connections. The first connection is the crisis-sensing mechanism, a knowledge-management strategy, a means of finding the knowledge an organization needs (Wang & Belardo, 2005). The crisis-sensing mechanism attempts to create a repository of warning sign knowledge by locating, collating, and analyzing the crisis risk information or existing crisis knowledge.

Crisis sensing begins by determining what information-sensing mechanisms already exist in your organization. Avoid recreating the wheel. Review the issue management sources, risk sources, and reputation sources to see if they are comprehensive. Find out where your organization currently collects warning-sign-related information or already processes it into knowledge. New procedures should be developed only if key sources are being overlooked. For instance, if no efforts are being made to scan relevant activist groups, add that as a source. A similar review should be undertaken for information-gathering techniques. Keep in mind that if you have the financial resources, you can hire vendors to help you scan, especially for issue and reputation information. Pay particular attention to how information and knowledge, such as publicity, are coded. A common weakness in information collection is a coding system that is too general and misses important details contained in the information (Denbow & Culbertson, 1985).

An example illustrates the importance of details. Let's say a retail store tracks its media coverage by collecting and analyzing news stories which mention the organization. A general coding system might simply count the total number of positive and negative comments about the retail store. The analysis provides a global evaluation of the reputation: is it favorable or unfavorable? No insight is provided into why the media image is favorable or unfavorable. A more specific coding system might include the following categories: sales staff, customer service, selection, merchandise quality, value and pricing, store appearance, and parking. The retail store would have separate evaluations for the seven categories. Store managers would know the exact areas where the store's image was strong and where it needed improvement.

Second, the organization must establish mechanisms and procedures for funneling relevant information and knowledge to the crisis manager or the crisis department. An organization should have at least one person who is dedicated full-time to crisis management (Coombs, 2006a). Crisis sensing is easier if there is an entire department, but many organizations are lucky to have one crisis manager. Crisis managers cannot process information they have not received nor attend to warning signs (knowledge) never encountered. The crisis managers must receive the scanning information and knowledge in a timely fashion and must carefully analyze the information for the warning signs. Various areas of the organization and possibly some vendors are likely to be responsible for different pieces of internal information and knowledge. Some organization units involved in scanning include operations and manufacturing, marketing and sales, finance, human resources, legal, customer communications and satisfaction, environmental and safety engineering, public relations and public affairs, engineering, shipping and distribution, security, and quality assurance.

The many organization units and vendors hired to scan must send this information and knowledge to the crisis team as soon as possible after they first receive and evaluate the information. A crisis manager becomes the center of a larger crisis-sensing mechanism. The crisis manager must act as a functioning unit that is integrated within the flow of organizational activities, information, and knowledge exchange. Channeling information and knowledge sounds easier than it is. Consider that most organizations have difficulty collecting and analyzing information from customers (Rollins & Halinen, 2005). Now add information from a number of additional stakeholders, and your crisis-sensing mechanism becomes a real challenge.

Third, the crisis manager's assessment criteria for warning-sign-related information must be carefully developed. This discussion provides general criteria for assessing issues, risks, and reputation threats. Crisis managers may wish to add their own, organization-specific assessment criteria. The crisis team must determine which criteria they would like to use, develop additional criteria if need be, and determine precise definitions for the assessment criteria. Without precise definitions, the crisis manager is not able to apply the assessment criteria consistently. Last, the crisis-sensing mechanism must be tested to determine if the various parts are integrated effectively. Running carefully selected and controlled information through the system is one way to assess the integration's effectiveness.

Wal-Mart, for instance, has a crisis-sensing mechanism for staying ahead of crises. Jason Jackson, Wal-Mart's director of emergency management, uses what he terms *watchdog positions*. The watchdogs monitor a variety of sources, including the Internet, news reports, and information from local stores, to identify possible disruptions to business. One source they monitor is weather, and hurricane Katrina stands as testimony to the value of weather scanning. When watchdogs find a threat, they relay that information to the emergency management team. The emergency management team evaluates the information and decides what action, if any, should be taken. Johnson conducts regular training and testing of Wal-Mart's system (Rojas, 2006). The Wal-Mart watchdogs concentrate on risk management and operational concerns, such as weather and security.

Wal-Mart's crisis-sensing mechanism has not been tuned to issues management and reputation management. In 2005 and 2006, Wal-Mart moved to improve both of these aspects through the hiring of external agencies and internal personnel. One example of the changes is the Web site http://Wal-Martfacts.com, which responds to issues involving Wal-Mart, such as health care for workers, gender discrimination, and hiring of illegal immigrants. Wal-Mart also launched its first ever reputation advertising campaign during this time period. This effort was designed to shore up Wal-Mart's reputation with customers and employees (Hays, 2003; Kaiser, 2004). However, these issues management and reputation management efforts are not connected with the risk management efforts to build a comprehensive crisis-sensing mechanism. Wal-Mart still has room to expand and to improve its crisis-sensing mechanism.

What Would You Do?

Bic and the Exploding Lighters

You work for Bic, and one of the products you make is a disposable butane lighter. Your lighters have always conformed to accepted safety standards. However, over the past three years there have been a number of complaints about exploding lighters. Your competitors experience similar complaints. The lighters could fail to extinguish completely after use, then explode moments later. People could be and were badly burned from lighters exploding in their pockets. The lighter was redesigned last year, but the redesign had nothing to do with the exploding lighters. A total of 147 exploding-lighter lawsuits have been filed against your company; one involved a death. You have learned that the New York Times and a major television network news show are collecting information about the exploding lighters. There is also a Web site called "Fire in Pants" that has people relate their stories of exploding lighters. Is this a warning sign? Is this a crisis? What would you recommend Bic do, and why do you recommend this course of action?

❖ CONCLUSION

The first step in an ongoing approach to crisis management is to find potential crises before they find your organization. The crisis team must scan for crisis warning signs. Crisis scanning requires the crisis team to collect and to analyze a wide array of environmental and internal data. But remember, the crisis team is not alone. Invariably other organization units (such as issues management, customer relations, or investor relations) can supply much of this data to the crisis team. The organization should formalize this information gathering into a crisis-sensing mechanism. *Formalizing* means setting procedures for funneling scanning information to the crisis team. Once information is received and analyzed, crisis teams can move into the prevention phase, the subject of Chapter 4.

❖ DISCUSSION QUESTIONS

1. What are some organizational barriers to creating a crisis-sensing mechanism? How might you overcome those barriers?

2. While this chapter separates issues, risk, and reputation management, the three areas are interrelated. How can a risk become an issue, an issue become a risk, a risk threaten reputation, or an issue threaten reputation? How do you see these three functions being interrelated?

3. How do you think perception gaps form? Does this inform how you would correct a perception gap?

4

Taking Preventative Measures

C risis experts Chris Skinner and Gary Mersham (n.d.) note, "Prevention, then, versus reaction, is the ultimate key to successful crisis communication" (n.p.). The problem is that people outside of an organization rarely see crisis prevention when organization members act on the warning signs and try to curtail the onset of a crisis. Just because it is not visible does not mean it is unimportant. While communication plays a lesser role than in crisis response, it is still vital to crisis prevention.

Slightly different preventative measures are needed to stop issue, risk, and reputation-affecting warning signs from becoming crises. Then, specific consideration is given to prevention measures regarding issues, risks, and reputation as well as the role of communication in preventative measures. Issues management and risk abatement already have established programs, but work on reputation management is still evolving.

❖ BASIC CRISIS PREVENTION PROCESS

An organization avoids crises by taking action on crisis warning signs and reducing its risk factors. Crisis managers must determine the exact nature of a crisis prevention program that can work in their organization. This section explains the basic process that undergirds any crisis prevention program.

The goal of a crisis prevention program is to defuse a crisis by attending to the warning signs and risks. The organization is taking actions it hopes will eliminate the potential crisis identified during the signal detection stage (Pauchant & Mitroff, 1992). The crisis prevention program has two basic components: (1) change and (2) monitoring. The first component involves making changes that eliminate or reduce the likelihood of a warning sign becoming a crisis. Actions are taken to manage issues, to reduce risks, and to build or maintain reputations. A few examples will illustrate this point. Say that the issues management unit of a company learns of a proposal to tighten air quality standards. Action is taken to prevent or postpone the new regulation, thereby averting a possible plant closing while the plant implements ways to reduce emissions. Or a safety review finds that workers are not following the unloading directions for hazardous chemicals. A refresher training course is offered along with new, stricter safety procedures regulating the unloading of chemicals. The risk of a hazardous materials accident is reduced. And another: a number of complaints appear about chain guards falling off of a chain saw. Customers are offered replacements and design changes made to prevent the guards from falling off. Accidents and a major conflict with customers are averted, and the reputation is maintained.

Without monitoring, the organization does not know if the change has been effective—has it reduced or eliminated the chance of a crisis. For example, an organization would want to know if the new safety procedures and policies made the workplace less hazardous. The only way to know if safety has improved is to monitor workplace behaviors. If workers are now engaging in safer behavior—fewer violations of safety procedures—then the safety changes are working. Never assume any change is for the better. Some changes produce no results while others may intensify the warning signs or risks, thereby moving an organization closer to a crisis. Monitoring involves a regular review of any changes designed to reduce warning signs. The review determines the effectiveness of the changes and if any additional modifications are warranted (Pauchant & Mitroff, 1992).

Communication is an essential part of the crisis prevention process. It is communication that helps to locate warning signs and relay that knowledge to the relevant units. A redesigned product, for example, will not be made if designers do not know there is a specific problem with the original product. Issues management requires communication with stakeholders; risk reduction, such as training, is a communication process; and reputation management is heavily dependent on communication to relay action and policies to stakeholders.

❖ ISSUES MANAGEMENT

After issues have been identified and analyzed, issue managers apply systematic procedures designed to influence the issue's resolution in a manner favorable to the organization. The approach is systematic. The Jones and Chase model is the dominant issues management model (Coombs, 1992). The model provides crisis managers with directions on actions to take to prevent an issue from becoming a crisis and ways to evaluate the issues management effort.

Issues Management Process

Managing an issue involves attempts to shape how the issue is resolved. The idea is to have the issue resolved in a manner that avoids a crisis. For instance, say that legislation is proposed that would threaten the financial viability of the railroad by making trucking companies more competitive with rail transportation. The issues management effort prevents a crisis by persuading the Congress to reject the legislative proposal. Communication is used to influence an issue's resolution.

The Jones and Chase (1979) model is the classic issue identification, analysis, change strategy option, action program, and evaluation model familiar to most people involved in issues management. The action step centers on communicating the organization's position on the issue to stakeholders involved with the issue. Goals and objectives for the communication program are developed, followed by the selection of the means and resources needed to achieve them. Decisions are made about the specific messages to be communicated, when to communicate them, and the channels of communication to be used (Jones & Chase, 1979). Developing the transportation example can clarify the issue action program. The railroad company decides the goal is to prevent passage of the protrucking legislative proposal. Legislators, the media, and voters are the stakeholders to be targeted. The message centers on the danger to automobile drivers created by the protrucking legislation, and the message must be sent immediately because a vote will be held in a few months. Advertisements, publicity, and lobbying are the communication channels utilized.

The laxative market offers an example of how issues management can both avert and create a crisis. Until the 1990s, the main ingredient in the two leading laxatives, Correctol and Ex-Lax, was phenolphthalein. In the early 1990s, the Food and Drug Administration (FDA) began investigating a link between phenolphthalein and cancer. In 1995, the preliminary study with rats indicated phenolphthalein could be a carcinogen. The FDA now thought about banning phenolphthalein. Novartis, the manufacturers of Ex-Lax, did not see a problem and defended the use of phenolphthalein. Schering-Plough, the makers of Correctol, decided to switch from phenolphthalein to bisacodyl and supported the FDA move to ban phenolphthalein.

Additional evidence was collected by the FDA that supported the phenolphthalein–cancer link. In April of 1997, the FDA went public with its cancer concern over phenolphthalein. Schering-Plough supported the decision and informed customers that they had removed phenolphthalein from Correctol over a year earlier, while Ex-Lax still used it. Novartis kept fighting the phenolphthalein ban issue. They advocated a public education campaign to curb laxative abuse. The idea was that proper, limited use would not place people at risk, that only those who abuse laxatives were at risk for cancer. In August of 1997, the FDA proposed a ban on phenolphthalein. At that time, Novartis recalled Ex-Lax and introduced a new formula shortly thereafter. However, Correctol had already established its competitive advantage by demonstrating greater concern for customers because Schering-Plough had acted much faster to protect customers from the phenolphthalein threat (McGinley, 1997).

Issues management can also involve changing the organization. Issue managers may decide that the best way to resolve an issue would be to correct or improve operating standards and plans. McDonald's illustrated this point when it abandoned the polystyrene "clamshell" burger boxes. Environmentalists had been complaining about the environmentally unfriendly clamshell packaging for years. McDonald's original plan was to win acceptance of the clamshell by emphasizing recycling. By recycling, McDonald's would eliminate the complaint that its packaging would clog landfills for hundreds of years. McDonald's was trying to change stakeholder attitudes. Consumers did not respond well to the early recycling tests. So McDonald's abandoned the clamshell recycling campaign and simply ended their use (Snyder, 1991).

McDonald's changed its procedures rather than trying to change its stakeholders' opinions.

Issues management can be a form of crisis prevention when the issues management effort prevents an issue from developing its crisis potential (Grunig & Repper, 1992). An example of issues management prevention is the pharmaceutical companies' use of direct-to-consumer (DTC) advertising. You have no doubt seen many DTC messages but may not have realized it. Have you seen television advertisements for drugs to address cholesterol, high blood pressure, social anxiety, acid reflux, or sexual dysfunction? Then you have been exposed to DTC. The United States and New Zealand are the only major countries to allow DTC efforts.

In 2005, the U.S. Senate and the FDA began deliberating on the need to regulate DTC. To prevent government regulation, the pharmaceutical industry decided to self-regulate. In August of 2005, PhRMA, the industry association for major pharmaceutical manufacturers, announced a new 15-point Guiding Principles document for DTC. Most of the principles repeated existing FDA regulations, such as that DTC information should be accurate and not misleading. New measures included educating physicians prior to a DTC campaign and allowing no DTC messages in media targeted to age-inappropriate audiences (PhRMA, 2005). Most of the major pharmaceutical companies publicly endorsed the plan. Talk about regulating DTC all but disappeared. PhRMA used the complete spectrum of issues management communication tools: advocacy advertising, direct lobbying, grassroots lobbying, letter writing, e-mail, Web pages, and publicity.

As you can understand, the exact mix of communication strategies depends upon the stakeholders involved in the issues management effort and the current stage of the issue's progression (Crable & Vibbert, 1985).

Issues Management Evaluation

To evaluate the results of issues management, the final resolution of the issue is examined. Evaluation consists of comparing the actual resolution of the issue to the intended or desired one. Success is measured by how closely the actual resolution matches the desired one (Jones & Chase, 1979). In the earlier examples, the railroad and pharmaceutical issue managers were successful. The trucking legislation was defeated, and the government stopped pressing for DTC regulation—the actual and intended resolutions were a match. Evaluation does not end with the issue's resolution. Issues are cyclical, and they have the potential to reappear. For example, the health care debate of the 1990s is much like the debate that took place in the 1940s and 1950s. During his first term, President Clinton introduced the idea of health insurance for all Americans. The government would help to insure Americans who were currently uninsured for various reasons. In the 1940s and 1950s, President Truman advocated national health insurance. His idea was to make health insurance a reality for all Americans through government assistance. The national health insurance issue may disappear for a while but never dies. The cyclical nature of issues means an issue should be reexamined at least annually to see if it is gaining new momentum and might once again threaten the organization (Crable & Vibbert, 1985).

❖ RISK MANAGEMENT

Risk management represents attempts to reduce the vulnerabilities faced by an organization (Smallwood, 1995). Vulnerabilities are weaknesses that could develop into crises. Basically vulnerabilities are risks. Like crises, not all risks can be avoided or completely eliminated. Hence, risk management involves a number of strategies that vary in their crisis prevention potential.

Two factors drive the use of risk management strategies. The first factor is cost. Risk managers use procedures such as risk balancing to compare the costs of the risk (e.g., costs of deaths, injuries, litigation, and property damage) to the costs of risks reduction (e.g., equipment and actual work needed to prevent or reduce the risk). Organizations may take no action when the costs of risk reduction outweigh the costs estimated from the risk. However, ignoring risk can be a more costly move than anticipated. If stakeholders discover their safety was sacrificed for profit, a different and much worse type of crisis erupts. The Pinto case taught Ford Motor Company the cost of privileging profit over people. Internal documents proved that Ford knew that the Pintos produced between 1970 and 1976 could explode in rear-end collisions. The crashes caused a differential housing bolt to puncture the gasoline tank and spark an explosion. Ford engineers tested a rubber bladder for the gasoline tank in 1970. The tests showed that the bladder did correct the puncture problem. A cost-benefit analysis of the corrective action was performed. The corrections would cost $137 million, while the estimated injuries, deaths, and litigation would cost only $49.5 million (Birsch & Fielder, 1994).

Ford executives decided it was more profitable to sell the faulty Pintos and litigate than to correct the flaw and protect customers. Ford knowingly placed its Pinto customers at risk of serious injury or death. Ford's decision was based on financial not customer safety concerns (Lerbinger, 1997; Levitt, 1997). The second factor is technical: can the risk actually be eliminated or reduced? No action is taken if there is no means for reducing the risk.

Risk Aversion Process

Risk management becomes crisis management when risk aversion (the avoidance or reduction of risk) is possible. Actions are taken to completely eliminate the risk or to reduce the risk to as low a level as reasonably possible (Levitt, 1997). The use of dangerous chemicals in a manufacturing process illustrates this point. Using inherently safer practices is an approach to designing safer chemical plants, storage facilities, and chemical processes. Three common risk reduction strategies in inherently safer practices are to (1) reduce the amount of hazardous material on site, (2) substitute a less hazardous substance, and (3) use a less hazardous process or storage condition. If less hazardous materials are on site, the effect of a crisis is reduced: The Chevron Richmond Refinery reduced the amount of anhydrous ammonia it stored on site and moved the storage facilities farther from the residential area. If a nontoxic or less hazardous chemical can be substituted for a hazardous chemical, a risk can be eliminated or reduced: The Mt. View Sanitary District, a wastewater treatment facility, replaced three hazardous chemicals (chlorine, sulfur dioxide, and ammonia) with an ultraviolet light system to disinfect wastewater. Changes in the chemical process used or the state in which a chemical is stored can reduce a hazard: Acrylate producers have switched from manufacturing with the Reppe process to the safer propylene oxidation process, and Dow Chemical Company switched from using liquid chlorine to the less hazardous gaseous form.

Using inherently safer practices is one among a variety of approaches for eliminating or reducing risk. Another common effort is training, and topics for risk aversion can range from chemical safety to e-mail use. The exact action taken by an organization to reduce a risk varies according to the actual risk (Lerbinger, 1997). For instance, many companies face computer rather than chemical risks. Antivirus software, firewalls, and employee Internet use polices are ways to prevent risks. Consider the threat of viruses, such as Melissa, that could damage an organization's computer systems and databases. Cognos Corporation, a software developer, knew that the Melissa virus contained a file that was over 25K-bytes in size. The company set a 25-K limit on incoming messages to keep Melissa out. Managers acted quickly; within one hour of identifying the risk, a policy was created and relayed to employees along with a rationale for the new policy (Meserve, 1999). The basic process involves determining if the risk aversion is possible and then implementing the risk aversion program.

Risk Aversion Evaluation

The evaluation of risk aversion is an ongoing concern. Periodic reviews of the risk are conducted to determine the effectiveness of the risk aversion program (Pauchant & Mitroff, 1992). Evaluation compares the level of risk before and after the risk aversion program is implemented. The review is continued to determine if the program works over time. Was the risk reduction a statistical aberration or has the lower level of risk been maintained over the course of the risk aversion program? The risk must be monitored continually to ensure that the threat does not reemerge.

❖ REPUTATION MANAGEMENT

Reputation management attempts to build and maintain a favorable perception of an organization among its stakeholders. As mentioned earlier, common stakeholders for an organization include customers, investors, community members, employees, government agencies and actors, news media, suppliers, activists, and competitors. To review, there are two dominant sources of reputational threats: specific stakeholder concerns and expectation gaps. Specific stakeholder concerns are those that stakeholders tell the organization about, indicating that there is a problem that can threaten the relationship. Expectation gaps indicate that stakeholders do not perceive the organization as delivering on desired performance standards. For instance, an organization can view itself as an environmental champion while stakeholders perceive it as a polluter. Organizations that meet expectations avoid criticism, are viewed favorably, and receive support from stakeholders. Conversely, failure to meet expectations leads to criticism and conflict with stakeholders (Finet, 1994). As stakeholders become aware of an expectation gap, they are very likely to pressure the organization to change its behavior. This pressure can precipitate a reputation-based crisis.

What Would You Do?

McDonald's and CIW

The Coalition of Immokalee Workers (CIW) has worked for four years to get Yum! Brands to change its relationship with tomato growers in Florida, the main constituency of CIW. Yum! Brands own Taco Bell, among other fast food restaurants. Now the CIW has turned its attention to McDonald's. They want McDonald's to agree to a similar deal as Yum! Brands: one penny more per pound of tomatoes for workers and help in protecting the human rights of workers. McDonald's has resisted, using a study critics say has methodological flaws that make the results suspect. CIW has protested at the McDonald's shareholder meetings; connected with six college organization to boycott stores; and enlisted leading economic figures, such as former Secretary of Labor Robert Reich, to urge McDonald's to negotiate with CIW. Is this a reputational threat? What course of action would you recommend to McDonald's, and what led you to that conclusion?

Reputation Management Process

Specific problems are easy to identify because the stakeholders tell the organization what their concerns are and how the concerns should be addressed. Dads & Daughters e-mailed their feeling about the proposed PussyCat Doll action figures directly to Hasbro. Had you ever heard of the CIW before the previous paragraph? CIW represents mostly immigrant farm workers in Florida and tries to improve their working conditions. Yum! Brands, the parent company of Taco Bell, have heard of CIW. As mentioned, in 2005, Yum! Brands agreed to add one penny to each pound of tomatoes to be passed along to workers and to partner with CIW to improve working conditions in Florida tomato fields. The CIW placed pressure on Yum! Brands through boycotts of Taco Bells, public protests, and a Web site designed to educate people about the boycott and poor working conditions in the Florida tomato fields (Coalition, 2005). Organizations can agree with the stakeholders and make the recommended changes. Hasbro cancelled the proposed dolls, and Yum! Brands agreed to pay more for tomatoes.

An organization can disagree with the stakeholders and decide not to take action. Management can dialogue with the stakeholders to develop an agreeable alternative. Keep in mind that there are times when an organization and its stakeholders will simply have to agree to disagree. Ford Motor Company hit just such an impasse with the conservative group, American Family Association (AFA). AFA demanded that Ford end all support for gay and lesbian groups, such as donations of money and vehicles and advertising in gay and lesbian publications. The AFA called for a boycott of Ford, then suspended the boycott for six months while it talked with Ford. During that same time, leaders of gay and lesbian groups met with Ford as well. Although Ford at first wavered and appeared to sell out its own convictions, management eventually renewed its support of gay and lesbian groups. The AFA then restated its intent to pressure Ford to change and join its side in the "culture wars" (Ford, 2006). Ford is among a number of corporations that recognize and hope to connect with the lucrative gay and lesbian market. Hence, Ford has both economic and moral reasons to not change its policies. As of the middle of 2006, the AFA and Ford have agreed to disagree.

As noted in Chapter 3, an expectation gap between an organization and stakeholders can be a result of the organization's performance not meeting expectations (performance gap) or stakeholders not realizing the organization is meeting expectations (perception gap). The reputation management process can serve to identify and resolve expectation gaps. The Pussycat Dolls situation illustrates the performance gap. Hasbro was creating a product many parents felt was inappropriate for the target market (young girls). British retail chain Marks and Spencer is trying to close a perception gap: They have launched a public relations and marketing campaign to educate people about their positive social and environment efforts, such as using more recycling and providing healthier food (less salt and fat). The campaign is known as "Look behind the Label" (Look, n.d.).

An expectation gap demands that an organization know its stakeholders expectations. The only way to learn stakeholders' expectations is by listening to them. Listening can include initiating surveys, focus groups and interviews, and town hall meetings and reviewing comments from stakeholders (online postings, media statements, and direct message from stakeholders).

The first step is to determine what expectations a specific stakeholder group holds. Focus groups are an excellent way to discover expectations. Focus groups are designed to answer "why" questions and to explore how stakeholders feel about topics such as expectations for organizational behavior (Stacks, 2002; Stewart, 2002).

The next step is to determine if the organization is meeting expectations. Management first reviews the organization's performance against the expectations. Management must honestly determine if they are engaging in the desired behaviors. Then stakeholder perceptions are assessed. Surveys are designed to collect data about how well or poorly the organization is perceived to be meeting these expectations. Stakeholders could be asked to rate the organization on its dominant performance expectations and the overall quality of the organization–stakeholder relationship. The individual dominant performance expectations provide details about the relationship. The organization learns more precisely why a relationship is weak or strong. For instance, stakeholders might expect an organization to buy supplies locally, exceed clean air and water standards, offer day care to its workers, and be involved in the social fabric of the community. The organization would identify the dominant performance expectations through formative research with each stakeholder group. Surveys should also include measures of trust, a key component of virtually every existing reputation evaluation system (Beren & van Riel, 2004) and stakeholder relationship evaluation system (Hon & Grunig, 1999; Ledingham, 2005).

What Would You Do?

Adidas and the Collector Shoe

Did you know there was a market of sport shoe collectors? I don't mean shoes worn by athletes; I mean people who collect makes of sports shoes. Adidas, often in the shadow of market leader Nike, does create limited-edition shoes for the collector market. One such shoe appeared in 2006 designed by famed underground artist Barry McGee. A total of 1,000 of the Yellow Series shoes were created and retailed for $250 a pair. Part of McGee's design was an Asian face on the tongue of the shoe. McGee said the design was a caricature of himself—he is part Asian. However, many Asian Americans and groups representing them were offended by it. The face was viewed as a negative stereotype, with bowl-cut hair, slanted eyes, pig nose, and buckteeth. Bloggers were among the first to condemn Adidas for producing the shoe. Does the situation warrant a response from Adidas? If so, how should Adidas respond to the criticisms?

Listening facilitates two-way communication between the organization and its stakeholders. It is the use of regular, two-way communication that helps an organization to understand the expectations of its stakeholders. The communication must be regular because the organization and the stakeholders change. Understanding is lost if the parties drift out of contact and fail to appreciate even minor changes in each party. For example, protecting human rights is a social concern that is gaining acceptance among stakeholders as an expectation for corporations. Only by listening to stakeholders can organizations learn about societal trends that impact expectations. Communication must be two-way if both parties are to receive information about the other. One-way communication privileges the sending party and does not facilitate mutual understanding (Grunig, 1992). The goal is to determine when an expectation gap occurs and the nature of that gap. You cannot address an expectation gap until you understand it.

Expectation gaps are addressed through communication. A performance gap can be addressed in one of two ways. The first option is to change behaviors. As mentioned previously, Hasbro abandoned the Pussycat Doll action figure to meet the expectations of parents for appropriate dolls for young girls. The second option is for the organization to attempt to alter stakeholder expectations. Mutual understanding allows organizations not only to identify but perhaps to shape stakeholder expectations. When these expectations are unrealistic, the organization can engage in a dialogue with the stakeholders. They may try to convince stakeholders that the expectations are unrealistic and need to be modified.

A perception gap can be addressed by informing stakeholders about how the organization is meeting expectations. Public relations, advertising, and marketing need to effectively develop and deliver messages to stakeholders in order to increase awareness of the organization's actual performance. An example would be to increase knowledge of socially responsible acts by organizations, such as the Marks and Spencer "Look behind the Label" campaign. Stakeholders say they want to know this information but often do not know that an organization has acted in a socially responsible action. As a result, publicity, advertising, cause marketing, and parts of the organization's Web presence are often used to inform stakeholders about the organization's socially responsible actions.

Visit a Starbucks and you will see brochures detailing their socially responsible actions on topics such as access to water and fair trade coffee. (If you are unfamiliar with either of these issues, visit www.star bucks.com to learn what fair trade coffee is and why access to water is an important global issue.) You will find the same information on their Web site and references to social concerns in their marketing and advertising.

Reputation Management Evaluation

For specific problems, stakeholders have stated what the concern is and have probably offered advice on how to solve the problem. If the organization decides to take action, management should ask the disgruntled stakeholders if the resolution was satisfactory. The feedback from the stakeholders will serve as the measure of success.

Success in closing an expectation gap is determined by whether or not stakeholders perceive the organization as meeting expectations. The organization and stakeholders must co-create meaning—they must share a similar interpretation of the organization's performance on the desired expectations—for expectation gaps to be closed (Botan & Taylor, 2004). The most effective way to determine if an expectation gap has been closed is to use surveys to assess stakeholder perceptions of expectation performance before and after efforts are initiated to close the gap. The survey provides the evaluative data necessary to determine if stakeholder perceptions have changed. For example, one item can ask stakeholders to rate on a scale of 1 to 7 (7 being the highest), "Does the organization reflect your concern for the environment?" If the original evaluation was 2.5, a post-communication-effort score of 4 would be considered a success, as stakeholders see greater similarities between their concerns and the organization's behavior.

❖ CONCLUSION

Crisis management works best when it includes avoiding or preventing crises. Issues management, risk management or aversion, and reputation management all can be used to avoid crises or at least their most dire consequences. Some issues can evolve into crises; issues management can be used to prevent such crises. Risks have the potential of becoming crises; risk aversion is used to lessen the chance. A threat to a reputation can be identified and resolved; by understanding and working with one another, the organization and its stakeholders can resolve reputation-related problems early on, before they escalate into crises. For example, customer complaints can be corrected before the customers become outraged and publicly protest about a product or service.

A crisis prevention program is a valuable part of the crisis management process. The crisis team uses the warning signs from signal detection to target situations that could become crises. The team then takes actions designed to eliminate or reduce the likelihood of the warning signs developing into crises.

Prevention is not as easy as it sounds. Finding potential crises is a type of warning environment, and a warning environment involves ambiguous information and penalties for incorrect actions. Possible crises can be hard to detect, and failure to do so can result in a crisis. Unfortunately, organizational politics can complicate or even block efforts to reduce risks (Chapter 7 offers suggestions for combating resistance to preventative actions).

Ideally, crisis teams must remember to monitor their corrective actions on a regular basis to determine if preventative actions have produced the desired effects. However, an organization cannot count on avoiding all crises. Hence, the need remains for crisis preparation, the subject of Chapters 5 and 6.

❖ DISCUSSION QUESTIONS

1. Locate and read information about fair trade coffee. Do you think it is an idea that will gain additional support among coffee growers? Is Starbucks wise to increase its support for fair trade coffee?

2. What barriers do you see to organizations taking preventative measures? How might they be overcome?

5

Crisis Preparation: Part I

During crisis preparation, an organization readies itself for the inevitable crises that will befall it. Organizations should not fall victim to hubris and assume that their preventative measures will protect them from harm. All organizations should prepare to handle crises by addressing six concerns: (1) diagnosing vulnerabilities, (2) assessing crisis types, (3) selecting and training a crisis team, (4) selecting and training a spokesperson, (5) developing a crisis management plan (CMP), and (6) reviewing the communication system. This chapter covers the first four points, and Chapter 6 is devoted to the CMP and the communication system.

❖ DIAGNOSING CRISIS VULNERABILITIES

As noted at the beginning of this book, an array of potential crises can happen to an organization. However, every organization has specific crisis vulnerabilities (Fink, 1986). These are a function of the organization's industry, size, location, operations, personnel, and risk factors. For example, a hotel must ensure the safety of hundreds of people who are in an unfamiliar building, and food producers run the risk of contamination that can poison their customers. Put another way, different types of organizations are prone to different types of crises. Location should not be overlooked, either. Location dictates which natural disasters are likely to strike. In addition, if your organization is near a facility that could have a serious crisis, such as a chemical leak or be a strategic target for terrorists, their crisis can become your crisis. Crisis managers must identify the crises for which their organizations and some neighbors are most vulnerable. Vulnerabilities affect the development of the CMP (Pauchant & Mitroff, 1992).

Vulnerabilities typically are assessed using a combination of likelihood of occurrence and of severity of damage. Crisis managers start by listing all possible crises that could affect their organizations. The list of potential crises can result from brainstorming by the crisis management team or an assessment done by a consultant (Barton, 2001). Once a final list of potential crises is developed, each crisis should be assessed. A common approach is to rate each crisis from 1 to 10 for likelihood and impact (with 10 being the strongest score) (Fink, 1986). *Likelihood* represents the odds that the crisis might happen. *Impact* is the amount of damage a crisis can inflict on an organization. The crisis manager then multiplies the likelihood and impact ratings to establish a final crisis vulnerability score. The higher the score, the greater the potential damage (Barton, 2001; Fink, 1986). Crisis managers should focus their attentions on crises that have the highest crisis vulnerability scores. Summaries of the crisis assessments are often included in the CMP.

❖ CRISIS TYPES

The list of potential crises for organizations is extremely long. It includes accidents, activist actions, boycotts, earthquakes, explosions, chemical leaks, rumors, deaths, fire, lawsuits, sexual harassment, product harm, strikes, terrorism, and whistle-blowing, to name but a few. There is a point to the laundry list of crises—an organization faces different threats, not just one, when it comes to crises. Different crises can necessitate the use of different crisis team members, an emphasis on different stakeholders, and warrant different crisis response strategies. For instance, a product harm crisis is not the same as a rumor. A crisis involving product harm requires the organization to respond to those hurt, tell consumers how to return the product, and inform shareholders of the financial impact of the recall. A rumor requires a response designed to present the truth to consumers and to stop the source of the rumor.

While crises possess different characteristics, they tend to cluster into identifiable types (Coombs & Holladay, 2001). A variety of crisis typologies can be found in the crisis writings (e.g., Egelhoff & Sen, 1992; Lerbinger, 1997; Marcus & Goodman, 1991; Pearson & Mitroff, 1993). These typologies have been synthesized into one master list:

Natural disasters: When an organization is damaged as a result of the weather or "acts of God" such as earthquakes, tornados, floods, hurricanes, and bad storms

Workplace violence: When an employee or former employee commits violence against other employees on organizational grounds

Rumors: When false or misleading information is purposefully circulated about an organization or its products in order to harm the organization

Malevolence: When some outside actor or opponent employs extreme tactics to attack the organization, such as product tampering, kidnapping, terrorism, or computer hacking

Challenges: When the organization is confronted by discontented stakeholders with claims that it is operating in an inappropriate manner

Technical-error accidents: When the technology utilized or supplied by the organization fails and causes an industrial accident

Technical-error product harm: When the technology utilized or supplied by the organization fails and results in a defect or potentially harmful product

Human-error product harm: When human error results in a defect or potentially harmful product

Human-error accidents: When human error causes an accident

Organizational misdeeds: When management takes actions it knows may place stakeholders at risk or knowingly violates the law

It would be impossible for an organization to prepare a CMP for every single crisis, but it can prepare CMPs for the major types it may face. Organizations should have crisis portfolios composed of CMPs for the primary types of crises they might face. Because of the similarities of the crises within each type, one CMP can be used to address any crisis within a particular crisis type (Pauchant & Mitroff, 1992).

The crisis portfolio prepares an organization to cope with a wide array of crises.

The organizational vulnerabilities and crisis types can help crisis managers to construct their crisis portfolios, addressing the specific crises that could affect an organization. Here is the way to proceed: First, organize the list of potential crises by crisis type. Second, select at least one crisis from each type. Select the crises with the highest vulnerability rating. The highest rated crisis in each crisis type becomes part of the crisis portfolio. Third, develop variations of the CMP for each of the crises in the portfolio.

❖ CRISIS MANAGEMENT TEAMS

The crisis management team (CMT) is a cross-functional group of people in the organization who have been designated to handle any crises and is a core element of crisis preparation. Oddly, the American Management Association (AMA) found that only 56% of companies with CMPs had a dedicated crisis team (AMA, 2005). Typically the CMT is responsible for (a) creating the CMP, (b) enacting it, and (c) dealing with any problems not covered in it. The CMT crafts the CMP after thoroughly researching its organization's vulnerabilities. As just discussed, the CMP planning includes anticipating the most likely crises to befall an organization (Pauchant & Mitroff, 1992). To develop the crisis plan, the crisis team needs information about different crisis types and all information about potential crises (scanning) and actions being taken to prevent crises (prevention). Any background information relevant to crises is helpful when the crisis team is writing the CMP.

A second CMT responsibility is to enact the CMP during simulated or real crises. CMPs must be tested to see if they work by running the entire organization, certain departments, or just the crisis team through drills and simulations. The simulations help to discover any holes in the CMP or weaknesses in the CMT (Pauchant & Mitroff, 1992; Regester, 1989). The CMTs are responsible for implementing the CMP during real crises as well. We must remember that CMPs are contingency plans. This means that a CMT must be able to adapt to situational experiences and not just mindlessly follow a CMP (Fink, 1986; Littlejohn, 1983).

This brings us to the third major responsibility of the CMT: dealing with factors not covered in the CMP. It is impossible for a CMP to anticipate all possible contingencies in every crisis. During an actual crisis, the CMT must be able to provide counsel on and to resolve issues not dealt with in the CMP (Barton, 2001; Register, 1989). It falls to the CMT to make the necessary decisions when a crisis presents an unanticipated challenge. A CMP is an outline, not a road map, for how to manage a crisis. The CMT must fill in the details.

Development of an effective CMT is essential to the crisis management process. The best CMP is worthless if the CMT cannot fulfill its crisis duties (Wilson & Patterson, 1987). An effective CMT is developed through careful selection and training. Selection involves choosing the people best suited for the tasks whereas training helps people to improve skills and to become more proficient at performing tasks (Goldstein, 1993). Careful selection and training produces more effective workers; that is why organizations spend millions of dollars a year on each.

Functional Areas

Crisis team selection is not as simple as finding the people best qualified to work on the CMT. Selection is complicated by the need to have specific functional areas within the organization represented on the CMT. The dominant selection criterion in the crisis management writings is the functional approach. It posits that team members must represent specific functional divisions or positions within the organization, including legal, security, public relations or communications, operations or technical, safety, quality assurance, human resources, information technology, finance, government relations, marketing, and the CEO or representative (Barton, 2001; Creating the best, 2003). The logic behind the functional selection is that certain knowledge bases (e.g., operations and legal), skills (i.e., media relations and public relations), and organizational power sources (i.e., CEO) are required on a crisis team. For instance, a crisis team often needs to integrate technical information about the organization's operations, assessment of legal concerns, and information collected by security when enacting a crisis plan. Furthermore, media relations skills are needed when addressing the press, and the CEO or a representative legitimizes the crisis team within the organization and empowers the team to take action. Human resources can address compensation issues for employees during a crisis, and financial can project the costs of the crisis.

The composition of the crisis team should reflect the nature of the crisis (Weddle, 2001). One example would be that a product harm crisis is unlikely to involve information technology, but a computer-hacking crisis would. The core members of the crisis team are typically operations or manufacturing, legal, public relations or communication, security, and representative or CEO. Keep in mind that a CMT may not be the best place for a CEO during a crisis. That is why a representative with authority is recommended. In some cases, the full-time, dedicated crisis manager will have such decision-making power.

Task Analysis

The key to selection and training is the identification of the characteristics (knowledge, skills, and traits) people need to perform their jobs (Goldstein, 1993). *Task analysis* is the technical term for identifying the key characteristics needed for job performance. A task analysis of crisis management should isolate the characteristics required by crisis team members. Once tasks are identified, the knowledge, skills, and traits needed to perform each task should be determined. Through interviews with crisis managers and an analysis of crisis management writings, four specific tasks were isolated: (1) group decision making, (2) functioning as a team, (3) enacting the CMP, and (4) listening (Coombs & Chandler, 1996). Table 5.1 summarizes the task analysis.

Very little information exists about the characteristics of crisis team members. The discussions tend to be vague or limited. The personal characteristics mentioned in the literature include being a team player, having decision-making ability and listening skills, and being able to handle stress (Barton, 2001; Dilenschneider & Hyde, 1985; Littlejohn, 1983; Mitchell, 1986; Regester, 1989; Walsh, 1995). Unfortunately, little detail is provided about what actually constitutes these characteristics—the knowledge and skills needed to meet them. The following section is dedicated to providing specific information about the tasks, knowledge, skills, and traits that make for an effective crisis team member. The task serves as the organizing point for the explanations.

Decision Making

Crisis management is a group decision-making process (Fink, 1986; O'Connor, 1985; Olaniran & Williams, 2001; Williams & Olaniran, 1994). Decision making involves selecting an option to meet the needs of the situation or reaching a judgment. The three primary responsibilities of the crisis team all involve decision making. As previously mentioned, the CMT decides what goes into the CMP (Pauchant & Mitroff, 1992; Wilson & Patterson, 1987), when and how to enact it (Mitroff, Harrington, & Gai, 1996; Walsh, 1995), and how to extemporaneously handle those factors not covered in the crisis plan. If crisis management

Table 5.1   Crisis Team Task Analysis

Task Statement	Knowledge	Skills	Traits
Work as a team to facilitate the achievement of crisis team goals.	1. Understand various styles of conflict resolution. 2. Understand components of an ethical conflict resolution.	1. Ability to use cooperation-based conflict management style 2. Ability to apply components of ethical conflict resolution	1. Cooperative predisposition
Apply the CMP to crises in order to facilitate an effective organizational response to the crisis.	1. Understand how to use the CMP. 2. Understand specialized information of one's functional area. 3. Understand mechanisms for coping with stress. 4. Understand mechanisms for coping with ambiguity.	1. Ability to follow directions given in the CMP 2. Ability to supply area-relevant information 3. Ability to use the mechanisms for coping with stress 4. Ability to use the mechanisms for coping with ambiguity	1. Stress tolerance 2. Ambiguity tolerance
Make the group decisions necessary to effectively solve the problems encountered by the crisis team.	1. Understand the critical vigilant decision-making functions. 2. Understand the value of argumentation. 3. Understand how to structure arguments. 4. Understand the value of group participation	1. Ability to apply the elements of critical vigilant decision making 2. Ability to create arguments 3. Ability to speak in groups	1. Argumentativeness 2. Willingness to speak in groups
Listen to others as a means of collecting information.	1. Understand the steps to effective listening.	1. Ability to use the steps to effective listening	

is decision making, the knowledge, skills, and traits associated with group decision making should be essential to the effective performance of a crisis team.

Determining how to handle a crisis is an example of dynamic decision making and is characterized by time pressure, risk, and a changing situation. Researchers find that decision making in a crisis follows one of three styles: intuitive, rule based, or analytical.

The intuitive method is derived from naturalistic decision making, how people use experience to make real-world decisions. Recognition-primed decision making is a form of intuitive decision making that has been applied to crisis management. The decision makers use their experience to recognize cues in crisis situations and to react. This is more than so-called gut instinct. The decision makers use their experience to gauge the situation and evaluate whether or not their past experiences are appropriate. The advantage of intuitive decision making is its speed and the limited negative effects of stress (Flin, 2006). It's safe to say that intuitive decision making seeks a viable solution rather than the optimal one.

Rule-based decision making involves finding a rule that can be applied to events in the crisis. There is an assumption that a set of rules does exist. Government reporting requirements and actions are examples of existing rules that crisis managers can use. For instance, the government has a checklist for executing a product recall. However, most crisis situations cannot be managed with a list of rules. There simply are not enough to address all the possible factors a crisis team might encounter. Rules are useful for novices, but there is always the risk of applying the wrong rule. A rules approach would work well for deciding when to enact the CMP, however.

Analytic decision making is the type most commonly used in training. Decision makers are taught a process for making decisions. The focus is on identifying and evaluating options. Analytic decision making is thoughtful and requires time, and some feel it is ill suited to crisis decisions (Flin, 2006). However, the analytic approach is perfect for creating a CMP and has its place in crisis decisions, especially the decision whether or not or when to enact the CMP. A well-trained crisis team can use processes like vigilance in a short period of time. The following discussion of vigilance is an analytic approach to decision making. An extended discussion of vigilance is offered because it is such a valuable tool for the crisis team.

Group decision-making research has consistently found vigilance to be valuable in making effective decisions and avoiding ineffective decisions (Hirokawa, 1985, 1988; Hirokawa & Rost, 1992). Vigilance is a form of critical thinking, and that can be defined as "a structured process whereby people actively and carefully conceptualize, apply, analyze, synthesize, and/or evaluate the information they have collected from, or created by, observation, experience, reflection, reasoning, or communication, as a guide to their actions or their beliefs" (Scriven & Paul, 1996, p. 1). Critical thinking involves learning and applying skills used to evaluate information. Vigilance applies critical thinking to group decision making by emphasizing the need for careful and thorough analysis of all information related to a decision (Hirokawa & Rost, 1992; Olaniran & Williams, 2001; Williams & Olaniran,1994). *Analysis* is a process of dissecting a whole into its parts in order to examine something in more detail.

Hirokawa and Rost (1992) identified a specific set of four critical vigilant decision-making functions which aid the decision-making process: (1) problem analysis, (2) standards for evaluating alternative choices, (3) understanding the important positive aspects of an alternative choice, and (4) understanding the important negative aspects of an alternative choice. Each of these skills is a corrective for a factor that could contribute to faulty decision making. First, a decision is threatened when a group fails to a see a problematic situation or fails to identify its correct cause. The group must analyze and assess the problem thoroughly and systematically. The group must understand what it is supposed to accomplish.

Second, a decision is threatened if the group improperly evaluates the alternative choices for solving a problem. Three critical vigilant decision-making functions address the evaluation of alternative choices. One, the group identifies appropriate standards for evaluating alternative choices; the group discusses and specifies criteria for evaluating the alternative choices. Two, the group applies the criteria to consider the important positive aspects of each alternative choice; it identifies and seeks clarification of these positive aspects. And three, the group applies the criteria to understand the important negative aspects of each alternative choice; it identifies and seeks clarification of the negative aspects. Research in laboratories and in the field has found these four critical vigilance decision-making functions to be related to higher-quality decisions in groups (Hirokawa & Rost, 1992).

Vigilance is a composite of a variety of knowledge (K), skills (S), and traits (T). First, group members must know some process for evaluating situations (K) and be able to apply these processes (S) to their situations. Second, group members must know how to develop the criteria to evaluate decision alternatives (K) and be able apply these criteria (S). And third, group members must be able to argue for thoroughness of analysis and to present their views on the matters being discussed (S). *Arguing,* in this context, refers to giving reasons for and against a proposal, not fighting or having an emotional disagreement (Paul & Elder, 1995). Group members must be motivated to use their skills if analysis is to be thorough (Hirokawa & Rost, 1992). This requires groups to continually argue for thoroughness. Group members must be willing to argue their positions (T) since group decisions become less effective when members do not voice concerns and allow one perspective to dominate the group's discussion (Hirokawa, 1985, 1988; Rancer, Baukus, & Infante, 1985). Group members are required to have the skills for argumentation and the disposition to argue (the argumentativeness trait). Table 5.1 provides the knowledge, skills, and traits associated with decision making.

Communication apprehension is the fear or anxiety some people feel in a communication setting. A team member with a high level of communication anxiety in a group setting is unlikely to fully contribute (Richmond & McCroskey, 1997) and will likely be silent and let others do the talking. As a result, communication apprehension can cause the team to lose the valuable knowledge that that team member was to bring to the team.

Working as a Team

Members of the crisis team must be able to work together as a group. Team members must be able to function in a cooperative manner in order to maximize the gains for themselves and others (Daniels, Spiker, & Papa 1997; Paton & Flin, 1999). Some people are naturally cooperative, while others are competitive (Baron, 1983). Part of working together is resolving the conflicts which occur inevitably within groups (Kreps, 1990; O'Connor, 1985). Conflict happens when people are interdependent with one another but have differing goals, which may prevent either from reaching their goals (Putnam & Poole, 1987). People in groups often disagree and can blame one another for the disagreements. Conflict can be beneficial to a group. Vigilance is fostered through conflict, including arguing different perspectives. Cooperation is the key to conflict becoming productive rather than destructive (Kreps, 1990).

People seem to have preferred conflict styles, the typical modes they use to handle disputes (Putnam & Poole, 1987). There are systems for identifying conflict styles (Daniels et al., 1997; Kilmann & Thomas, 1975). The key is to emphasize the use of cooperation-based conflict styles in crisis team deliberations.

Enacting the Crisis Management Plan

The crisis team must be able to enact the CMP. For this reason, groups train by reviewing and practicing the CMP. Creating the CMP should give the team members greater understanding of the plan (Barton, 2001; Wilson & Patterson, 1987). This is where each team member's functional organizational area becomes important. One reason to appoint a team member is his or her particular knowledge of a functional area that is important during a crisis (e.g., legal, media relations, investor relations). The knowledge and skills of these functional areas are important to executing the crisis plan effectively. Stress enters the crisis management equation most fully during the execution of the plan (Dilenschneider & Hyde, 1985; Shrivastava & Mitroff, 1987). When the crisis team faces deadline pressures and needs to deal with ambiguous information, the stress it experiences increases (O'Connor, 1985). Table 5.1 includes the knowledge, skills, and traits associated with enacting the crisis plan. Part of enacting the CMP is managing the concomitant stress and ambiguous information. Stress can hinder job performance (Baron, 1983), and ambiguity can create stress (Tsui, 1993).

Listening

Crisis team members frequently use listening. Collecting information when creating or enacting the CMP often means that CMT members must listen to others. Working together to make decisions requires listening to the others in the group. Obviously, listening is an important part of many tasks. However, many crisis managers felt listening was important enough to be considered as a separate, distinct task.

Implications for Crisis Team Selection

As the Corporate Leadership Council (2003) noted, "Every crisis management program begins with a competent crisis management team" (p. 4). As mentioned earlier, team members must bring certain area-specific knowledge and skills to the crisis team, which will facilitate the execution of the crisis plan—the functional approach to selecting team members. However, as Shrivastava and Mitroff (1987) noted, crisis team members also should have a set of general crisis management skills. The knowledge, skills, and traits that were shown in Table 5.1 represent a set of general crisis management skills that are vital to the effective operation of a crisis team. The full range of knowledge, skills, and traits should be considered when identifying those people most likely to contribute positively to a crisis team. Assessment is vital in the screening of crisis team candidates. An organization may be in a position to choose among a number of people to represent a functional area. For instance, there might be a pool of five people from operations who possess the requisite skills and knowledge from their area. Only one person from operations is needed, and the organization wants the person best suited for work on a crisis team. The assessment instrument would indicate which of these potential candidates best matches the demands of being a crisis team member, particularly in terms of traits, because people can learn to cope with the limits of their traits but not to develop completely new ones.

It is possible to develop profiles of desirable and undesirable crisis team members from the traits shown in Table 5.1. A desirable crisis team member would be low in communication apprehension in groups, high in cooperation, high in ambiguity tolerance, moderate in argumentativeness, and well equipped to handle stress. The desirable profile produces a crisis team member who can work under stress, is not bothered by the ambiguity of a crisis, will work with the team to find the best solution, is willing to express opinions and ideas, and is willing to argue the merits and weaknesses of various solutions. An undesirable profile would be high in communication apprehension in groups, high in competitiveness, low in ambiguity tolerance, high in verbal aggressiveness, and poorly equipped to handle stress. The undesirable profile produces a team member who functions poorly under stress, feels increased stress in ambiguous situations, works poorly in problem solving by fighting, and may be unwilling to contribute ideas and opinions. Combining the functional and task-based approaches results in being able to select the most competent crisis management team.

Applications for Training

Crisis experts frequently mention the need to train crisis teams (e.g., Augustine, 1995; Mitroff et al., 1996; Pauchant & Mitroff, 1992; Walsh, 1995; Williams & Olaniran, 1994). In any job, a person must possess the necessary knowledge and skills to perform effectively. Current training practices include group review of the CMP and crisis drill (Wilsenbilt, 1989). Box 5.1 describes the basic forms of crisis exercises.

Box 5.1	Training Options for Crisis Management

Orientation Seminar: An overview of the crisis management process. The crisis team reviews roles, procedures, policies, and equipment.

Drill: A supervised exercise that tests one crisis management function, such as employee notification or evacuation.

Tabletop: A guided analysis of a crisis situation. A facilitator leads the team through a discussion of what they would do in a particular crisis situation. This exercise does not have the time pressures of a real crisis.

Functional Exercise: A simulated interactive exercise. It can be done in a large meeting room. It tests the complete crisis management system and unfolds in real time to create crisis pressures. The CMT will need to interact and coordinate with the groups it would encounter in a crisis, such as first responders. A CMT should conduct one functional exercise a year.

Full-Scale Exercise: The simulation of a real crisis as closely as possible. People are on site and in the field. The actual equipment and people that would be used in a situation are deployed. There will be simulated injuries as well. Full-scale exercises are time consuming and expensive, so they should only be done every few years.

As you may have noticed, the exercises are listed in order of increasing complexity. A crisis team needs to work its way up to functional and full-scale exercises through the orientation seminars, drills, and tabletops.

Discussions of crisis team training are dominated by proponents of practice based on running simulations of crises (Augustine, 1995; Birch, 1994; Mitchell, 1986; Pauchant & Mitroff, 1992; Regester, 1989; Walsh, 1995). There is sound logic to this application; simulations enable the CMT to determine how well it can enact the CMP and how the CMP might be improved. Part of group training is determining whether the team can accomplish group tasks (Goldstein, 1993). Crisis simulations emphasize group tasks with their focus on enacting the CMP. Decision making is a critical group-level task that demands training attention. While managers know how to make decisions, the decision-making dynamic changes in a team, especially one that must make time-pressured decisions based on limited information. Training can improve the decision making of teams and of crisis teams. One promising training tool is called *thinkLets*. It is a set of facilitation techniques that can aid decision making during a crisis. Some techniques are as basic as brainstorming options and using a straw poll to have group members evaluate options against a single criterion. Work on collaborative teams and crisis teams has shown that thinkLets can facilitate and improve team decisions (Kolfschoten & Appelman, 2006; Kolfschoten, Briggs, de Vreede, Jacobs, & Appelman, 2006).

While useful, the group-level approach to training overlooks the need to train the individuals in skills needed to complete crisis team tasks. People need individual knowledge and skills to function as effective team members (Paton & Flin, 1999; Stohl & Coombs, 1988). Williams and Olaniran (1994) noted that crisis team members must be trained in specific crisis duties, which include the individual-level knowledge and skills needed to be effective team members.

Individual-level assessment would be composed of the knowledge, skills, and traits listed in Table 5.1. The individual-level assessment of each team member indicates specific areas where that person is strong or weak and identify a person's specific training needs. Training should be specific; people should be trained only in those areas in which they are deficient. A crisis team assessment system not only determines a person's strengths and weaknesses but also evaluates a person's progress in acquiring knowledge and skills (Goldstein, 1993). The initial assessment is the benchmark or baseline against which subsequent assessments are compared. Specific training modules should be developed for each of the major knowledge and skills important to a crisis team. When needed, modules designed to help people cope with the limits of specific traits could be added, such as a module designed to develop listening skills.

A 2006 study found that 80% of crisis managers learned on the job. That means only 20% had any training in crisis management (New survey, 2006). A study of the Fortune 1,000 found that less than one-third of organizations with CMPs ever tested them (Levick, 2005). A 2005 study by the American Management Association (AMA) found that only 50% of U.S. companies with CMPs have engaged in any type of crisis training in the past year (AMA, 2005). This suggests that even many organizations that have CMPs and CMTs are not truly prepared to face a crisis. How can an organization know if its team members can perform or if the CMP will work if the team has not trained using some form of crisis exercise? A crisis exercise seeks to simulate a crisis for educational purposes. Team members should know the point is learning, not being critiqued, when they engage in exercises. It is important to create an atmosphere that is supportive rather than punitive in order to maximize the educational benefits of the crisis exercise.

It bears repeating: Crisis teams need training. Effective crisis team training requires the inclusion of both individual-level and group-level knowledge and skills. Crisis exercises are excellent ways to test group-level knowledge and skills. However, part of evaluating the crisis exercise should be dedicated to examining individual-level skills, a point that is missing in most current discussions of crisis team training. Remember, if a team does not exercise, an organization does not really have a dependable CMT or CMP.

❖ SPECIAL CONSIDERATIONS

CMTs have two special considerations they may need to address: coordination with external agencies and the need for a virtual team. An organization may find that its crisis is part of a larger disaster, a large-scale event that may require government intervention and involve multiple organizations and agencies. Crises are smaller in scope and may involve just one organization. Disasters include acts of God and acts by humans, such as terrorism and major hazardous material releases. Hurricane Katrina taught organizations not to count on government agencies coming in to help them. However, CMTs may need to coordinate their efforts with firefighters, police, emergency medical teams, or the Red Cross. In disasters, agencies are supposed to follow the incident command system, more specifically, the national incident command system (NIMS). Box 5.2 has a description of NIMS. CMTs should visit the Federal Emergency Management Agency (FEMA) Web site, which contains the complete NIMS training module. While FEMA may be unreliable during some disasters, it offers very good online training. By being familiar with NIMS, a CMT will understand the basic language and chain of command needed to function within the NIMS environment.

Box 5.2	National Incident Management System (NIMS)

NIMS was developed by the Department of Homeland Security to allow for easier integration of agencies (public and private) that respond to disasters. NIMS provides a common set of incident command procedures, multi-agency coordination, standardized command and management structures, mutual aid, and public information procedures. The idea is that responders from different jurisdictions and disciplines can work together better to respond to disasters, both natural and terrorist initiated. Government responders from the federal, state, local, and tribal jurisdictions are required to take NIMS training. The training for NIMS is standardized as well. Nongovernment responders, such as corporations, are encouraged to understand NIMS. This is part of a larger effort to maximize the use of private resources during a disaster. NIMS did not seem to perform well during hurricane Katrina, but it had not been in place for very long. Knowledge of the structure and terminology of NIMS would help crisis teams during disasters, as they would fall under the purview of NIMS at that point.

The second special consideration is the possibility of virtual teams. A virtual team does not meet in a designated crisis control center. Instead, members are assigned tasks, share information, and make decisions via the Internet and telephones with no face-to-face communication. The team uses mediated communication instead. Most virtual teams are really partially distributed teams (PDT). A PDT involves a mix of people, some in a shared location and some in remote locations. Some team members would be in the same room or area of the field and able to interact face-to-face while others would be in one or more different geographic locations and linked via mediated communication (Hiltz, 2006). Team members on the scene of a crisis have the ability to interact with team members in various geographic locations. A PDT may be needed if an organization has lost all possible crisis control center locations or needs to assemble a team that is geographically dispersed and travel time would be prohibitive for managing the crisis. Also PDT members can begin managing a crisis as soon as they have been contacted. Any team member can begin to execute individual tasks as soon as she or he is notified. However, if a team has to wait until members arrive at the crisis command center to begin discussions, the team is losing time. A PDT can be having team discussions as the members are traveling to their respective locations. A PDT increases the risk of problems for the team because any communication technology failure could doom the team. Still, it is worth considering and training for virtual teams or PDTs as an option (Well-provisioned, 2005).

❖ THE SPOKESPERSON

The spokesperson is the voice of the organization during the crisis. As such, the spokesperson is a very important and specialized function within the crisis management team. A poorly trained or unskilled spokesperson merely exacerbates the crisis situation (Donath, 1984; Mitchell, 1986). Again, selection and training require the identification of tasks and the knowledge, skills, and traits associated with those tasks. The discussion of the spokesperson begins with an analysis of the spokesperson's role and responsibilities during a crisis. The spokesperson's role provides a foundation for locating the requisite knowledge, skills, and traits.

The Spokesperson's Role

The primary responsibility of the spokesperson is to manage the accuracy and consistency of the messages coming from the organization

(Carney & Jorden, 1993; Seitel, 1983). Message management is not an easy task and usually involves more than one person. Every organization should have multiple spokespersons. While multiple spokespersons may seem to contradict the view that the organization "speaks with one voice," really it does not. First, one person cannot be relied upon to be available all of the time. That individual might be on vacation thousands of miles away during a crisis and unable to reach the crisis control center in time. What if the crisis drags on for days, requiring 24-hour-a-day efforts from the CMT? No one person can perform effectively for 24 to 48 hours straight. Eventually, lack of sleep will take its toll on job performance. Therefore, each organization should a have pool of spokespersons, all selected and trained in advance of a crisis.

Second, it is an overstatement to equate the idea of one voice with one person. The concept of an organization speaking with one voice merely implies that the organization presents a consistent message. Working together, multiple spokepersons can share one voice. However, the team work so vital to the CMT becomes a premium here. The media want to question authoritative sources during a crisis. No one person in an organization is an authority on every subject. As a result, an organization may have a number of people available during one press conference. Each question is then answered by the person most qualified to address it (Lerbinger, 1997). The key is preparation of all spokespersons, including the sharing of all relevant information and the coordination of the questions and spokespersons.

Clearly, the spokesperson must be able to work with the media by listening to and responding to questions. Listening is essential because spokespersons cannot give appropriate answers to questions if they do not hear the question correctly (Stewart & Cash, 1997). Answering questions demands the ability to think quickly. Press conferences are not slow-moving events. The spokesperson must be able to answer questions rapidly. Compounding all of this is the fact that the spokesperson is doing the job in a time of high stress—the organization is in crisis and the media want answers immediately. A spokesperson must be able to handle stress well and not let stress interfere with handling media inquiries. The spokesperson is a member of the crisis team, so all the knowledge, skills, and traits in Table 5.1 still apply. However, the big difference between spokespersons and other crisis team members stems from the need to work with the media.

Crisis experts continually recommend that the spokesperson have media training, which usually means practicing responding to media questions: the spokesperson goes through rehearsals (Nicholas, 1995; Sonnenfeld, 1994). Furthermore, there is a variety of laundry lists for what spokespersons should and should not do (e.g., Katz, 1987; Lukaszewski, 1987; Pines, 1985). A sample list of spokesperson "Do's and Don'ts" includes be truthful, never say "no comment," be concise and clear, don't lose your temper or argue with journalists, correct errors or misinformation in questions that are asked, look pleasant on camera, and appear in control and concerned. While such lists are helpful, they fail to provide a systematic means of either selecting or training spokespersons.

I have helped organizations train spokespersons and determine who should and should not speak to the media. Trust me; not everyone can be an effective spokesperson.

Media-Specific Tasks of the Spokesperson

From watching television, we all recognize that some people are well suited to media appearances while others were not. Some people look good on television, and others look like criminals (Nicholas, 1995). Oddly, one task of the spokesperson is to be appealing to the viewers. This does not mean that spokespersons must be physically attractive. Rather, they must present material in an attractive fashion. Media training is often vague in explaining how to do this. Similar to the section on CMTs, Table 5.2 summarizes the primary tasks of spokespersons along with the salient knowledge, skills, and traits necessary to perform the pertinent tasks.

A mix of content and delivery concerns confronts any spokespersons giving public presentations. Content concerns emphasize the information being presented. The spokespersons must disseminate accurate information about the crisis situation (Mitchell, 1986; Trahan, 1993). The spokespersons must also have command over the crisis-related information if they are to convey this information to the media and other stakeholders. However, poor delivery skills can prevent a message from being received accurately (Holladay & Coombs, 1994; McCroskey, 1997). A spokesperson must be skilled at presenting messages to the target stakeholders, in this case the media. Each of the four spokesperson tasks will be explained, along with an analysis of the task's connection to content and delivery.

Appearing Pleasant on Camera

Appearing pleasant on camera is not a superficial observation that the spokesperson should look good. Instead, being pleasant on camera reflects a set of delivery skills that helps spokespersons achieve a

Table 5.2 Spokesperson Media Task Analysis

Task Statement	Knowledge	Skills	Traits
Appear pleasant on camera	1. Understand the value of proper delivery.	1. Strong delivery	1. Low communication apprehension
Answer questions effectively	1. Understand danger of long pauses. 2. Understand the steps to effective listening. 3. Appreciate the danger of "no comment" statements. 4. Understand the danger of arguing with reporters	1. Able to think quickly 2. Able to use the steps to effective listening 3. Able to use phrases other then "No comment" when an answer is not currently known 4. Able to stay calm under pressure	1. High stress tolerance 2. Low verbal aggressiveness
Present crisis information clearly	1. Appreciate the problems with jargon. 2. Understand the need to structure responses.	1. Able to avoid the use of jargon 2. Able to organize responses	
Handle difficult questions	1. Understand the characteristics of tough questions	1. Able to identify tough questions 2. Able to ask for questions to be reworded 3. Able to preface tough questions in a tactful manner 4. Able to challenge incorrect information in a question 5. Able to explain why an answer cannot be answered 6. Able to evaluate the appropriateness of multiple-choice responses in a question 7. Able to respond to questions with multiple parts	1. Low argumentativeness

number of important crisis objectives. Previously it was noted that the crisis management team must show concern and control during a crisis. Part of the perception of concern and control is developed through the way a spokesperson presents the crisis-related information. One way to better understand delivery is to consider it as part of communicator style, which is the way in which a person communicates; it reflects the way in which something is communicated (Norton, 1983). Communicator style also influences how the content of the message is interpreted. Style provides a frame for how people should view the content of a message (Holladay & Coombs, 1994).

Spokespersons would want to maximize the style elements that cultivate the perceptions of control and compassion. Compassion is developed through the attentive and friendly style elements. Attentive styles reflect empathy and listening by the spokesperson. Being friendly suggests that a person is confirming and giving positive recognition to others (Norton, 1983). The attentive and friendly style elements help to cultivate the perception that the spokesperson is compassionate because compassionate people are empathetic and confirming. The dominant style elements means a person is behaving in a confident and businesslike manner (Norton, 1983). The dominant style facilitates the perception that the spokesperson is in control of the situation.

Maximizing these three style elements requires attention to specific delivery factors. Spokespersons must learn to maintain consistent eye contact with the audience (i.e., looking at the audience or camera at least 60% of the time), use hand gestures to emphasize points, vary their voices to avoid a monotone delivery, be sure to change facial expressions to avoid being blanked faced, and avoid too many verbal disfluencies, such as "uhs," "erhs," and "uhms." Spokespersons should be trained to maximize these five delivery variables when they present material to the media and other stakeholders. Past research indicates that the five delivery factors promote the perception of dominance, attentiveness, and friendliness as well as increasing credibility (Burgoon, Birk, & Pfau, 1990; Holladay & Coombs, 1994). It is logical to conclude that spokespersons will be perceived more positively by stakeholders when maximizing these five delivery factors.

There is a flip side to delivery as well. Poor delivery leads to negative perceptions of the spokesperson. Poor delivery skills are often interpreted as signs of deception (de Turck & Miller, 1985; Feeley & de Turck, 1995). People doubt the believability of a message when these delivery factors are present: (a) weak eye contact, looking at people infrequently; (b) frequent disfluencies (e.g., "uhs," "uhms"); (c) the use of abnormal hand or arm movements associated with fidgeting; and

(d) overuse of hand gestures (de Turck & Miller, 1985; Feeley & de Turck, 1995). There are clues people look for when trying to detect deception. Four of them are the delivery factors just reviewed.

Although delivery has always been an important part of the presentation of a public message (Heinberg, 1963; McCroskey, 1997), content can never be forgotten because good delivery does not make up for lack of content. Rather, good delivery enhances the reception of a message while poor delivery detracts from it. Spokespersons should be trained to maximize the delivery factors that promote control and compassion while minimizing those that contribute to perceptions of deception. All of the delivery factors mentioned thus far can be taught. However, it helps if people do not exhibit the communication apprehension trait when speaking in public. While communication apprehension can be overcome, spokespersons who are not communication apprehensive start out at a higher delivery proficiency level. Media training for spokespersons should include efforts to make them aware of their delivery habits and to polish their delivery skills. Having trainees watch videotapes of their press conferences is an excellent method for improving delivery skills.

Answering Questions Effectively

Answering questions effectively means providing responses to the questions that are asked. Preparation is essential to effective answers. The spokesperson must know or be able to quickly retrieve the crisis information that has been collected to that point. Another part is listening to hear the question. Spokespersons should not answer the questions they wanted to be asked; they must hear and respond to the very questions asked by the reporters. Remember, spokespersons can give introductory remarks or a short briefing before fielding questions. They can use that time to deliver the core crisis message from the organization.

Sometimes the spokesperson does not know the answer. The correct response is to admit what you do not know but promise to deliver the information as soon as you get it (Stewart & Cash, 1997). Remember the rule to never say "no comment." That phrase triggers two negative events. First, 65% of stakeholders who hear or see "no comment" equate it with an admission of guilt (In a crisis, 1993). As David Pendery, senior manager of public relations for Quiznos said, "Anytime you decline to comment on a known crisis you'll appear naïve at best, incompetent at worst" (Hall, 2006). Second, "no comment" is a form of silence, which is a very passive response. As Richard Levick of Levick Strategic Communications noted, "there are two sides to every story and, when you say 'no comment' the media gets the entire story and you don't get your side of the story" (Levick, 2005). In a crisis, being passive means that other actors in the crisis event get to speak and to interpret the crisis for your stakeholders (Hearit, 1994). The organization is allowing others who may be ill-informed, misinformed, or hold a grudge against the organization to define the crisis for stakeholders. An interpretation based on the wrong information or information supplied by an enemy can only hurt an organization's reputation.

A spokesperson also must be cordial and not argue with reporters (Mackinnon, 1996; Nicholas, 1995). Being cordial brings us back to the personality traits of a good crisis team member. A spokesperson should not be high in verbal aggressiveness or argumentativeness. Either trait can lead to a dispute with reporters. This does not mean that a spokesperson lets incorrect statements stand. Instead, the spokesperson corrects any errors or misinformation before answering a question but should not debate the error or misinformation (Mackinnon, 1996). Handling stress is a part of answering questions, too. An inability to handle stress reduces a spokesperson's ability to answer questions effectively because too much stress erodes task performance in general. Stress is high during media encounters due to the time pressure, the need to answer multiple questions from a variety of reporters (Balik, 1995), and the awareness of the huge number of possible hearers or readers. Participation in a mock crisis press conference is the best way to get a feel for the challenges a spokesperson faces.

Presenting Crisis Information Clearly

Presenting information clearly focuses on the content of the response. As such, it is related to answering questions effectively but has a narrower focus: ensuring that the stakeholders are able to understand what is said. The spokesperson's answers must be clear and concise. *Clear* means the answer is free of organizational jargon and overly technical terms and details (Mackinnon, 1996). Jargon is meaningless to those outside of the circle using it (Nicholas, 1995). As a result, jargon only clouds an answer. Overly technical information produces the same hazy reception of the message. In addition, technobabble makes people think the organization is using jargon to avoid telling the truth. It is best to use only the necessary technical information and explain it in such a way that nontechnical people can understand it. PepsiCo's handling of its 1993 syringe scare exemplifies how to translate technical information. In June of 1993, reports began to surface that syringes were being found in cans of Diet Pepsi. PepsiCo chose to focus on how it would be virtually impossible for a syringe to get into the can during bottling. PepsiCo reduced its bottling process to easily understandable terms for the news media and its consumers. PepsiCo believed and later proved the syringe scare was a hoax (Magiera, 1993; Mohr, 1994; Weinstein, 1993; Zinn & Regan, 1993). Clarity is aided by careful organization of a response (Stewart & Cash, 1997). An organized answer is easier to understand than a rambling one. Box 5.3 provides a short case of an organization that had difficultly presenting information clearly.

Box 5.3   **Merck's Technical Response**

VIOXX is an anti-inflammatory drug used to treat arthritis and acute pain. On September 30, 2004, Merck, the makers of VIOXX, recalled the product from the market. Merck made the voluntary recall when one of their clinical studies showed a connection between VIOXX and cardiovascular events, such as heart attacks and strokes. A clinical study uses careful control and treatment conditions to prove a cause and effect relationship between two things. This particular clinical study was designed to test the ability of VIOXX to help treat colorectal adenomas. In this case, VIOXX seemed to cause cardiovascular events.

Shortly after the recall, many in the medical community claimed Merck had known of the potential connection between VIOXX and cardiovascular events for years. A study published in August 2001 by the *Journal of the American Medical Association* (Mukherjee, Nissen, & Topol, 2001) indicated that there was a connection. Now consumers have to wonder, "Should Merck have recalled VIOXX sooner?" Merck's answer was "No." Merck explained that the published study was based on a meta-analysis. A meta-analysis looks at a variety of study for trends. Meta-analyses do not have the strict control and treatment conditions found in a clinical study. From a research methods perspective, other factors could have been responsible for the link between VIOXX and cardiovascular events found in the study published by the *Journal of the American Medical Associations*. Merck said it acted when it had clear cause–effect proof from a clinical study. Much of the research methods jargon and details have been trimmed from this description, but even this reduced version is highly technical. Probably few of Merck's consumers had the depth of knowledge needed to appreciate its argument.

Handling Difficult Questions

During a press conference, not all questions are of equal caliber. Watching any press conference on television makes apparent the frequent exceedingly long and complicated questions, questions that are multiple questions (asking for several pieces of information), tricky or tough questions, questions that are based on erroneous information, and multiple choice questions with unacceptable choice options. These five examples represent the difficult questions faced by a spokesperson. The spokesperson must learn to recognize difficult questions and to respond appropriately. Recognition involves practicing listening to questions delivered in the press conference format. Each of the five tough questions has identifiable features.

Recognition is easier than providing responses to tough questions. Still, there are response strategies for each of the five tough questions. For long, complicated questions, ask for the question to be repeated, rephrased, or explained. These strategies give the media representative a chance to improve the question's wording and clarity while providing the spokesperson with more time to construct a response. Multiple questions in one question can be handled in one of two ways. First, the spokesperson can choose which part of the question to respond to. The spokesperson should select the part of the question that fits best with providing the organization's desired message. Second, a spokesperson can address all parts of the question. When responding to all or multiple parts of a question, the spokesperson should number each part and the answer to each part. The additional structure helps to clarify the answer for other audience members.

Questions that are tricky or tough need a tactful preface to the answer. The spokesperson must convey to the audience that the question is tough or tricky and that a longer than usual answer is needed to address the question. It may also be the case that the tricky or tough question cannot be answered, and the spokesperson must explain why (Stewart & Cash, 1997). A question based upon erroneous information must be challenged and corrected (Nicholas, 1995). The spokesperson must make sure that misinformation is removed from the crisis information being presented at the press conference. For multiple choice questions, the spokesperson must determine if the response options are fair (Stewart & Cash, 1997). Why should a spokesperson choose a response when the two options might have the organization categorized as being heartless or stupid? The spokesperson should explain that the options are unreasonable or inappropriate and develop an option that fits with the appropriate answer to the question. Training helps a spokesperson identify and develop effective responses to the difficult questions.

University Application: Possible Crises

As a student, you are part of your university's organization. A crisis on campus could affect you. One way to begin applying many of the concepts in this book is to use them to examine your university from a crisis perspective. Either as a group or individually, list the possible crises that could hit your campus. Consider the wide range of personnel, geographic, and operations risks. Your list will probably be longer than you first thought it would be.

❖ CONCLUSION

The preparation phase of crisis management anticipates the occurrence of crises. The organization musters the resources necessary to effectively manage the crises that may befall it. Diagnosing vulnerabilities assesses the likelihood and impact of potential organizational crises, and crisis types are groupings of similar crises. An organization cannot prepare for all crises but can prepare for the major crisis types. The diagnosis of vulnerabilities and the information about crisis types are used to construct the crisis portfolio, the individual crisis plans for each of the major crisis types.

The crisis team is responsible for managing the actual crisis. Therefore, it is essential to carefully select and to fully train each crisis team member. The spokesperson is a specialized role within the crisis management process and provides a vital link to stakeholders. Spokespersons must also be carefully selected and thoroughly trained. Failure to select and train crisis team members and spokespersons methodically is a recipe for disastrous crisis management. A crisis team is lost without a crisis management plan. Chapter 6 concludes our discussion of crisis preparation by focusing on the CMP and crisis control center.

❖ DISCUSSION QUESTIONS

1. How do you think customers would react to Merck's technical reasons for not recalling VIOXX earlier?

2. In June of 2005, a four-year-old boy died after riding Mission Space at Epcot Center in Disney World. Who at Disney would

the news media want at a press conference? Would the CEO be a good choice? Why or why not?

3. What barriers are there to getting an accurate diagnosis of an organization's vulnerabilities? What can be done to overcome those barriers?

6

Crisis Preparation: Part II

I f an organization has done any crisis preparation, it is usually the drafting of the crisis management plan (CMP). While important, a CMP is not a magic insurance policy that protects an organization from a crisis. Nor is it a step-by-step set of instructions for what to do when a crisis hits. Laboring under either of these two assumptions will result in a rude awakening when a crisis does hit. An organization having only a CMP it has never tested is no better off than an organization with no CMP. Both will stumble and lose precious time as the crisis management clock starts to tick. This chapter examines functional CMPs and the related crisis communication system that are necessary to navigate the waves of a crisis.

❖ THE CRISIS MANAGEMENT PLAN

The core sermon preached by crisis converts is the need for a detailed, usable CMP. It must contain the information needed to manage a crisis but should not be overly long and cumbersome. Long CMPs look nice on shelves as they collect dust but are not practical when a crisis hits (Barton, 2001; Coombs, 2006a).

Value

As mentioned previously, crises are time-pressured events where quick responses are essential. During a crisis, time should not be wasted finding needed background information, deciding who will do what, and trying to determine the sequence of events (Barton, 2001). A CMP helps to reduce response time by gathering these elements together beforehand. In addition to speed, the CMP helps create an organized and efficient response. With some framework in place, the chaos surrounding a crisis is reduced and the event is less stressful (Corporate Leadership Council, 2003). A CMP creates a system that can save lives, reduce an organization's exposure to risks, and permit remedial actions without embarrassment and scrutiny (Barton, 1995).

Many large organizations have recognized the need for CMPs (Barton, 2001; Lerbinger, 1997). Still, in 2005 only 60% of major companies, up from 53% in 1984, have them (AMA, 2005). The numbers indicate that the message is still not being heard by all organizations. Sometimes it takes a crisis to reinforce the need for a CMP. The phrase "better late than never" comes to mind. In reality, all organizations should have CMPs because all organizations are at risk of a crisis, no matter how careful they are about their policies and operations.

Components

For CMPs, bigger is not always better. A CMP must be manageable, not filling a large binder and difficult to use. The most desirable CMP is a short document that is user friendly. CMPs can be placed in an easy to use flipchart format, bound at the top, and with each section having a different tab for easy identification. Additional format options are keeping copies of the CMP on CDs, data sticks, or on secure Intranet sites. Whatever the format, the CMP should be considered flexible and usable (Coombs, 2006a).

The CMP is, at its roots, a communication document and involves identifying who to contact and how. Contact information is provided for team members and additional experts that might be useful to the team. In fact, some crisis experts refer to the CMP as the *crisis communication plan* (e.g., Barry, 1984; Fearn-Banks, 2001). A crisis communication plan is a major part of the larger CMP. A CMP also includes methods and means for documenting what is said and done during a crisis. It can include reminders, in checklist form, of key actions that typically are taken during a crisis. However, it is important not to rely on a checklist for things that must be done. Each crisis is unique, and the CMP is a reference tool, not a step-by-step formula.

Following are the main components typically comprised in a CMP:

1. *Cover Page.* The cover page identifies the document as the CMP, notes that the document is confidential, provides the most recent revision date, and records the number of copies. The confidentiality statement reminds employees that the CMP should not be copied or shown to people outside the organization. Recording how many is used to control the number of copies in circulation. The revision date allows for a quick check to determine how up to date the CMP is.

2. *Introduction.* The introduction is a message typically written by the CEO. It is used to highlight the importance of the CMP and to persuade employees to take it seriously.

3. *Acknowledgment Forms.* The acknowledgment form is a removable page that employees sign and return to human resources, where it is placed in their personnel files. It is a signed affidavit saying the employee has read and understands the CMP. Having the signed documents in their personnel files encourages employees to take the CMP very seriously.

4. *Rehearsal Dates Page.* The rehearsal dates page records when the plan has been practiced and is another check on how up to date the plan and the crisis team are. Each person holding a copy of the CMP is responsible for keeping this page current.

5. *First-Action Page.* This section lists the incident commanders, how to reach them, how to activate the CMP (who should place the calls), and when it should be activated (when a situation is defined as a crisis). This section is the means of starting the crisis management process.

6. *Crisis Management Team Contact Sheet.* The contact sheet lists the names and contact information of all the members of the team, their areas of expertise, any outside consultants that may be needed, and any outside agents that may need to be contacted, such as insurance or emergency personnel. The CMT contact sheet section indicates who to contact, tells why they are relevant to a crisis, and provides a variety of means for contacting each person. This document is sometimes called the *crisis directory.* The CMT contact sheet provides an easy-to-use system for identifying and reaching members of the crisis team.

7. *Crisis Risk Assessment Section.* Every organization should anticipate what crises it may face. The crisis risk assessment identifies possible crises and evaluates the risk of each crisis in terms of likelihood

and impact. (Likelihood is the probability of the crisis occurring, while impact is the amount of damage [financial, structural, environmental, reputational, or human] the crisis could inflict on the organization.) The crisis risk assessment overviews the variety of crises an organization may most likely face and is not an exhaustive analysis of all possibilities. (Crisis assessment was detailed in Chapter 5.)

8. *Incident Report Section*. Crisis teams must keep accurate records of what has been done during a crisis. The incident report sheets are tools used to record this vital documentation. Crisis teams need this information when evaluating their crisis management efforts, and the organization needs this information when handling lawsuits or government investigations triggered by the crisis. The documentation centers on identifying when the incident was first apparent, where the crisis occurred, when various people and organizations were contacted about the crisis, and what actions were taken by whom and with what result.

9. *Proprietary Information Section*. While crisis managers often preach full disclosure of information, there are some policies and factual information organizations should not reveal. The proprietary information section reminds managers that certain information is confidential and cannot be released to stakeholders without CEO authorization or review by legal council (Tyler, 1997). For example, an organization should never give away trade secrets that provide its competitive edge in the marketplace without an extremely compelling reason (Barton, 2001). On a related note, an organization should never release the names of victims until family members have been notified.

10. *CMT Communication Strategy Worksheet*. Crisis managers must remember that communication is strategic—it serves a distinct purpose. The worksheet reminds CMT members of what it means to be strategic and to document crisis actions. Crisis managers are prompted to consider who they are talking to (the exact stakeholder), to record the specific audience to record the specific goal, to consider what they are trying to achieve with this communication goal, and to attach a copy of the actual message that was sent to the audience (Barton, 2001). Crisis managers can add other pertinent reminders that are specific to their organizations. For example, reminders about the use of specific technical terms can be added. A sample technical term reminder might describe the difference between "venting" and "releasing." Each organization should develop its own set of additional reminders.

11. *Secondary Contact Sheet.* Stakeholders others than those listed on the CMT Contact Sheet may need to be contacted during a crisis. These stakeholders may have information the organization needs or may need to be notified about the crisis. The secondary contact sheet identifies the stakeholders to be contacted and who in the organization is responsible for communicating with this stakeholder. Stakeholder type, contact name or names, organizational affiliation (if applicable), title, contact information, and documentation (when contact was made and by whom) should be included on the sheet.

12. *Stakeholder Contact Worksheets.* During a crisis, various stakeholders will be contacting the organization. Foremost among those are usually the media, but other stakeholders may request information and need a response during a crisis. The Stakeholder Contact Worksheet section should begin with the specific procedures that should be used when a call is received (Barton, 2001). The procedures should specify where all calls should be routed and who will answer the calls. The focus typically is on identifying a spokesperson to respond to the media, a topic discussed earlier in the chapter. However, the organization should not overlook other stakeholders who may be seeking information, such as community leaders, employees, employees' families, and investors. Although a lower priority than the media during a crisis, these other stakeholders have legitimate information needs. Neglecting these stakeholders injures the organization-stakeholder relationship. Organizations must develop procedures for all stakeholders that might contact the organization, not just the media. In addition to having clear procedures, careful documentation is essential. To record this information, multiple copies of a Stakeholder Contact Worksheet should be included in the CMP. The worksheet should include who contacted the organization, when the contact was made, the channel used to contact the organization, the specific inquiry, the response, and follow-up that was promised, and details of that follow-up.

13. *Business Continuity Plan (BC).* One organizational goal during a crisis is to resume business as usual as soon as possible. This section details what the organization will do if the crisis damages the facility or vital equipment needed to conduct business. While this plan may be a separate document, the CMP must acknowledge and recommend its use when necessary. This section should include conditions when the BC is to be used.

14. *Crisis Control Center Description.* When the CMP is activated, team members need to know where they should assemble. Some progressive organizations have developed special crisis control centers, sometimes called *crisis command centers.* Team members know to go directly to the crisis control center when they are contacted.

15. *Postcrisis Evaluation Forms.* Once a crisis is over, the CMT must assess its efforts. (As Chapter 9 will detail, an organization must learn from its crises.) Since the crisis management effort is primarily an exercise in communication—information collection and dissemination—the evaluation form focuses on communication (Barton, 2001; Egelhoff & Sen, 1992; Fearn-Banks, 2001). The evaluation form contains sections on the notification system used by the CMT and on its information collection efforts. The information collected through the form will help the CMT to correct weaknesses and maintain the strengths of the CMP.

Including all 15 points need not make for an excessively long CMP. However, it is a formal document as opposed to a functional one. Key points of the CMP, such as numbers 5, 6, 8, and 11, can be extracted to create a reduced version of the plan. This abbreviated version can be placed on pocket and wallet cards that all crisis team members are required to carry at all times. It is best to keep the CMP lean. If necessary, move some aspects of the CMP to a Crisis Appendix.

Crisis Appendix

Even the list of 15 elements just discussed can become lengthy. As a result, you may wish to create a Crisis Appendix to supplement the core CMP. The Crisis Appendix reflects a knowledge management aspect of crisis management. A Crisis Appendix is a crisis knowledge database that can contain precollected information, templates, and past crisis knowledge. For instance, a Crisis Appendix is an excellent place to store extended lists of potential experts and the documentation you will need for recording the team's actions.

The Crisis Appendix can contain the supplemental or background information you might need to know in a crisis, placed in an easily accessible format. An effective way to organize this information is to think of the questions you are likely to be asked in a crisis, such as, What is your organization's safety record? When was your last product recall? How often is maintenance performed on the equipment in question? You can store answers and information related to these and other questions. Your precollected information will reflect your organization's crisis risks. That means you should precollect information related to the crises most likely to affect your organization.

Templates are prewritten statements that require only a few blanks to be filled in before they are released. A number of different news releases can be drafted ahead of time and approved by the legal department. The team simply fills in the details from the current crisis, such as date, location, number of injuries, amount of damage, and so on. Time is saved, as the core message is written and approved before the crisis. Last, an organization should store what it has learned from past crises and exercises. Chapter 9 elaborates on organizational memory and learning. The idea is that the organization uses past experience to guide current actions by repeating previous successes and avoiding past mistakes. Knowledge from past crises or exercises may be useful to current crisis management efforts, so it should be available to the crisis management team.

University Application: Preparation

Do you know what to do if the building you are in right now caught on fire? Of course you get out of the building, but where should you assemble? Is there a procedure for checking in or out once you evacuate? If you do not know this information, see if you can find it. A good place to start would be your university's Internet site. What other emergency situations should you be prepared for on campus, and how has your university prepared you for them?

The CMP Is Not Enough

The danger of a CMP is that it can provide managers with a false sense of security. Some managers feel that if they have a CMP, they are protected when a crisis hits. Three flaws challenge this assumption. First, the CMP is a general guideline for action; it represents contingencies. Crisis teams must adapt the CMP to match a specific crisis. Mindlessly following a CMP in lock-step fashion is a recipe for disaster (Fink, 1986; Littlejohn, 1983). The CMT is invaluable in adapting the CMP to contingencies and handling those factors never addressed in the CMP (Barton, 2001; Regester, 1989).

Second, the CMP is a living document. Organizations change, their operating environments change, and their personnel changes; thus, the

CMP must be updated regularly. At least once or twice a year, the CMP should be examined for necessary changes. Moreover, a crisis manager should review the CMP weekly to see if updates are necessary.

Third, a CMP has little value if it is not tested and practiced in simulations or exercises. This point cannot be stressed too strongly. Practice reveals the holes or weaknesses that must be addressed before a real crisis occurs (Wilsenbilt, 1989). For example, at an airport in Texas, a serious flaw was discovered during the crisis drill for an airplane crash. Because airport personnel had the wrong radio frequency for contacting emergency personnel in the town, their radios were worthless during the drill. This is a common problem in disaster responses and was one of many problems during hurricane Katrina. Changing the frequencies was a simple procedure, but the problem would not have been discovered without the drill. Fortunately, the drill rather than an actual crisis revealed this serious problem in the CMP. Furthermore, practice is the only way for team members to gain experience enacting the plan. Practice also builds team confidence that they can handle a crisis. The dangers of an unrehearsed team have already been addressed. Managers must not let having a CMP lull them into a false sense of security. An ongoing approach to crisis management should prevent this complacency.

Other Related Plans

Organizations should create emergency preparedness and business continuity plans that will interface with the CMP. If a crisis requires an evacuation or providing shelter-in-place, the emergency preparedness plan is in effect as well. How do the two plans coordinate with one another? This is a question that exercises can answer and can help to enable smooth coordination. Of particular concern is overlapping memberships or resource demands of the two plans. The CMP and emergency preparedness plan should complement one another and not compete in any way.

As noted in the 15 elements of a CMP, the Business Continuity Plan (BC) outlines efforts that are to be taken to either keep the organization running during the incident or to return to normal operations as soon as possible after the incident. Again, the organization should determine if overlapping membership or resource demands exist between the BC and the CMP. Also the BC and crisis teams should coordinate messages. For instance, if an alternative location is used temporarily to maintain production, workers need to be told where and when to report for work. Suppliers and customers need to know if there will be a disruption in the supply chain, the extent of that disruption, and its estimated time span.

An excellent example of coordinating the CMP and BC is the West Pharmaceuticals plant explosion in Kinston, North Carolina. West Pharmaceuticals told customers the length of time it would take before production in their other facilities would offset the loss of the Kinston facility. Employees were told they would be working at other facilities until the Kinston facility was rebuilt. Employees were instructed where they would go and how they would be rotated home every so many weeks to have time with their families.

❖ PREPARATION OF THE CRISIS COMMUNICATION SYSTEM

With the personnel and CMP in place, crisis managers must make sure the physical setup of the communication system is prepared. Elements of the crisis communication system include the notification system, crisis communication center, and online applications. Preparation entails determining if the crisis communication system is sufficient to meet the needs of the CMT and to verify that the system is operational—that it works.

Mass Notification System

There are times when the crisis team must send a simple message to large a number of people. This is called *mass notification*. Although mass notification typically involves employees, it also can include community members who need to be given safety information covering evacuation or shelter-in-place. Mass notification is done through an automated messaging system, which sends a message by phone, text message, e-mail, or a combination of these to a preset list of people. The easiest way to engage in mass notification is to outsource it. A number of different vendors, such as MessageOne, provide an array of automated messaging options. The crisis team can use automated messaging systems to inform employees that a crisis has occurred and warn the community about safety risks. The messages need to be short. Employees and community members should be told where to go to find additional information, such as a phone number, an Internet site, or an internal Intranet site for employees only. Community members should be informed of any safety risks as soon as possible. Moreover, it is critical that employees learn about the crisis from the organization, not the news media. The mass notification system may be used whenever the crisis management process demands a short message be sent to multiple people.

Crisis Control Center

The review of the CMP noted that organizations should have a crisis control center. Such a center serves many functions: It is a place for the CMT to meet and discuss the crisis, it is an information collection center, and it is a place for briefing the media. Ideally the crisis control center is a separate area in the organization devoted solely to crisis management and equipped to meet the needs of the CMT. Large, geographically dispersed organizations should have crisis control centers at all major facilities. Multiple crisis control centers provide two benefits. First, a global company cannot expect to handle all crises effectively from one location. Extreme distances and time zone differences will hamper the crisis management effort. Second, multiple crisis control centers provide natural backups. If a crisis such as a fire or earthquake were to destroy an entire facility, the organization could use one of its other crisis control centers. Large-scale crises, such as hurricane Katrina, reinforced the need to have backups that are geographically distant from the site of the crisis. Some smaller organizations may use public relations agencies to house their crisis responses and use the agency's facilities for the crisis control center.

To fulfill its various functions, the ideal crisis control center will have a scenario-planning room in which the CMT members can meet, a communication center for monitoring information (TV monitors, phones, computers, and wire service), and a press room for briefings. The crisis control center should be fully equipped and operational at all times. Part of being prepared is having backups for all the necessary equipment. The specific equipment will vary according to the needs of the specific organization. There must be sufficient equipment and backups for the center. The equipment must be checked regularly to ensure that it is in working order.

The crisis control center should also be stocked with food and drinks to keep the crisis team going and have administrative support to help assist it with basics tasks, such as making copies or taking inquiries. The crisis control center must have dedicated phones lines, redundant Internet access, wireless connectivity, and the ability to track the news media. It follows that IT support is essential, too (Well-provisioned, 2005).

Some crisis experts have argued that a crisis control center should be mobile or even virtual. A mobile center can be deployed anywhere. You do not have to worry if your facility is shut down, unless the mobile center was at the site of the crisis. A mobile unit would have the same equipment needs as the stationary crisis control center. The main difference is that there would be no media briefing room due to space limitations at a mobile site. However, media briefings could be handled in a separate mobile facility; rented space, such as a meeting room in a hotel; or outdoor space, weather permitting. Virtual and partially distributed teams can stay linked through wireless communication and the Internet. Even team decisions can be made through conference calls or online meetings. As noted before, the problem with virtual and partially distributed teams is the potential for equipment to fail. This risk is greatest for virtual teams because all communication is mediated. Partially distributed teams are preferable to virtual teams because you have the option to base your response from the traditional crisis communication center and to use technology to allow some team members to stay involved when they are in the field or cannot get to the crisis control center.

University Application: Crisis Command Center

Identify a location on campus that would make an excellent crisis command center. What makes that location an excellent choice? Next, create a list of all the equipment you believe should be in the crisis command center. Be sure to consider the need for backup or alternative equipment.

The Intranet and Internet

Intranets are custom-made for crises. Intranets are like the Internet but are self-contained within an organization—only organization members have access to the information, and even then, access to sensitive information is limited to those with the proper clearance (Hibbard, 1997). The beauty of an Intranet is the speed of accessing information for the CMT and other employees. The CMT can access information directly through a computer instead of through telephone calls. If the crisis team needs financial information, it can retrieve the information on the computer—no need to place a call. Collecting and analyzing information is crucial during a crisis. Crisis teams gather raw data, transform the data into usable information (create knowledge), store the knowledge, and communicate it to others (Egelhoff & Sen, 1992). An Intranet is ideal for meeting these needs (National Research Council, 1996; Reeves, 1996). Motorola, for example, uses an Intranet as part of its crisis management efforts. It stores crisis-relevant information on its Intranet (e.g., financial and product information) and uses the system to facilitate the exchange of information during a crisis.

An Intranet allows immediate access to data about the organization; it is a place to store information, can provide a site where the crisis situation and relevant information is updated regularly, can be accessed by any employee, and allows communication to others in the organization via e-mail. Granted, not all crisis-relevant information can be collected via an Intranet. For instance, interviewing witnesses to an accident in a facility must be done in person. However, any precrisis background data needed about the organization, such as product ingredients or safety records, can be located there (for instance, in a Crisis Appendix). Moreover, e-mail and an Intranet are not always appropriate means of communicating crisis-related information to employees. Still, employee e-mail can be effective at times, and a regularly updated summary of crisis information allows employees to access what they want when they want it.

The Internet allows outside stakeholders to access your organizational information. Outside stakeholders can make e-mail inquiries or visit a Web page to access organizational information. In situations when it is an appropriate channel, e-mail can be used to reach government officials, media representatives, activist groups, stockholders, and many other stakeholders. The only limit is whether or not your target stakeholders have e-mail and you have the correct addresses. A Web page can post updated information about the crisis. Again, stakeholders have the option of deciding what information they examine and when they examine it. As mentioned, Odwalla developed a Web page when it needed to recall some of its fruit drinks in 1996. The voluntary recall and consumer communications were launched because of reports that people were becoming ill from E. coli in Odwalla fruit drinks (Nearly 200, 1996). The Web site identified the exact products under recall, how to return these products, and the reasons for the recall—the exact information customers needed to receive. Sample messages included Odwalla's completion of the recall (November 2), an update on the recall (November 1), confirmation that the FDA found E. coli (November 4), and condolences to the Denver family whose child died from E. coli poisoning (November 8).

An organization should also create a crisis dark site. A dark site is a section of a Web site or a completely separate Web site that has content but no active links. When a crisis hits, the CMT can activate the link, and the dark site becomes accessible. West Pharmaceuticals used a part of their Web site when the Kinston facility was destroyed. BP used a separate Web site to address the deadly 2005 explosion at its Texas City, Texas, facility. A significant amount of information can be placed on a crisis site before a crisis. Such information would include background information on the facility or product, photographs of the facility (for media use), maps of the facility, and links to relevant third-party experts (Corporate Leadership Council, 2003). Specific information about the crisis can be added as it becomes known. Again, templates or holding statements can speed the posting of information. The templates or holding statements are a series of fill-in-blank statements for the media. The focus is on basic information: what happened, where it happened, the cause if known, and next steps to be taken (Business Roundtable, 2002).

Stakeholders do turn to the Web to find information about a crisis. Oddly, researchers have found that only about 60% of organizations in crisis use the Internet (Perry, Taylor, & Doerfel, 2003). The failure to use the Internet in a crisis will increasingly be a liability for organizations because stakeholders increasingly use the Internet as a means to get information quickly. If an organization does not address the crisis online, stakeholders may wonder why. There is a need to tell the organization's side of the story, and the Internet provides an ideal place to tell that story. Unlike the news media, the Internet provides an organization unlimited space to talk about the crisis. We return to the need to tell "your side of the story" in Chapter 8.

Crisis management is moving toward using the Internet more fully. Major agencies, such as Hill & Knowlton, Ketchum, and Burson-Marsteller, feature the Internet in their discussions of crisis management client services. Their focus is on preparing dark sites for clients and monitoring the Internet for crisis-related information (e.g., Barritt, 2004). Integrating the Internet into the crisis management effort is becoming an expectation as the media and other stakeholders increasingly turn to the Internet when seeking crisis information (Lackluster online, 2002). Not having an Internet component to your crisis management effort may be viewed negatively by stakeholders.

The Internet also provides access to information outside of the organization. Some forms of external information required during a crisis can be drawn from it. In particular, government agencies provide information on regulations and reporting procedures. Other sources might be relevant, depending upon the type of crisis being experienced. For instance, industry accident data are useful during an organization's own accident crisis. The CMT can also monitor what is being said about the organization and the crisis in the online world, including the media and consumer-generated media. As with monitoring the traditional media, the CMT needs to know what is being said and what the stakeholders know in order to determine the accuracy of the crisis information being disseminated and if the organization's crisis message is getting through to stakeholders. The Intranet and Internet can be valuable information processing and delivery tools when used properly during a crisis. Remember, the Intranet and Internet do not make all other information-gathering and dissemination tools and channels obsolete. Always use the channel that is most effective for the communication situation (Clampitt, 1991; Rupp, 1996).

❖ CONCLUSION

The CMP and crisis control center complete the discussion of the six elements of crisis preparation. The CMP should be meticulously crafted before a crisis occurs. This chapter reviewed the various elements of a useful CMP. Also, the crisis communication system must be in working order. The CMP prescribes how and when to communicate during a crisis. An excellent CMP and CMT are useless if the physical structure of the communication system is not in proper working order. Calls cannot be made without working phones, and online data cannot be accessed without working computer stations. All six of the preparation elements should be reviewed and updated regularly to maintain a state of readiness for crises.

❖ DISCUSSION QUESTIONS

1. Would you choose to have a virtual crisis team? Why or why not?

2. What are the dangers of becoming overly dependent on the Internet or Intranet during a crisis?

7

Crisis Recognition

A n actual crisis puts an organization's crisis preparation to the test.
We deceive ourselves into believing that crises are easy to spot.
We think all crises are like giant icebergs in the North Atlantic on a clear
summer's day, relatively simple to see and to avoid. It is true that crises
are easy to locate when there is an obvious trigger event: a train derails,
a natural gas pipeline explodes, E. coli is found in a frozen lasagna,
an employee is wounded by a coworker, or some other identifiable
event. The obvious crises make it easy to realize the need to implement
the crisis management plan. However, not all crises are obvious.

As the definition of crisis in Chapter 1 noted, crises are symbolic as
well as objective. People can disagree on whether or not a situation is a
crisis. Some crises, particularly those involving conflicts with outside
groups, are hard to see. As strange as this may sound, an organization
may not even know it is in a crisis (Kamer, 1996). A situation becomes
a crisis when key stakeholders agree it is a crisis. Unfortunately, some
members of management may wish to deny that the organization is in
a crisis even when stakeholders are screaming that it exists (Fink, Beak,
& Taddeo, 1971; Pauchant & Mitroff, 1992). Similarly, management
may refuse to take preventative actions addressing warning signs. The
first part of this chapter details how crisis team members might "sell"
a crisis to top management in an organization. The recommendations
hold true for selling warning signs, too.

To review, the crisis team begins to understand a crisis once they have uncovered it. The team members need to collect data, convert the raw data into knowledge (usable information), store the knowledge, and relay the necessary knowledge to internal and, perhaps, to external organization stakeholders, such as expert and governmental organizations. The CMT is engaging in knowledge management. The CMT must collect accurate crisis data quickly (Darling, 1994; Mitchell, 1986). The crisis team analyzes the information to create the crisis-related knowledge that is used to (a) guide decision making and (b) create the messages sent to various stakeholders. Without crisis-related knowledge, the crisis team cannot make decisions or take actions to ameliorate the effects of the crisis. Actions include making statements to the media because this stakeholder is the most likely to be pressuring the organization for crisis information.

Crisis management team members must be aware of the problems associated with information collection, knowledge creation, and knowledge management. The second part of this chapter reviews research concerning the pitfalls associated with information collection, processing, and dissemination, along with ideas for combating these problems.

What Would You Do?

Glass in the Baby Food

You work for Gerber, the baby food company. In the same month, there are reports of pieces of glass appearing in Gerber products and in Beech-Nut baby food, your competitor. An internal investigation and an investigation by the Food and Drug Administration can find no glass contamination at your facilities. Management strongly suspects product tampering. Reports of glass in Beech-Nut products appeared a week before reports of glass in Gerber's. It could be people trying to cash in on the product scare—they put the glass in hoping to get money from Gerber. Beech-Nut has just announced a product recall related to the glass. What do you recommend Gerber do and why?

❖ SELLING THE CRISIS

While more the exception than the rule, some crises are not obvious or easily accepted. A problem can be ignored or not deemed worthy of the label *crisis* (Billings, Milburn, & Schaalman, 1980). Whether or not a problem is defined as a crisis is significant; framing a problem as a crisis changes how the organization responds to it. When a problem becomes defined as a crisis, the organization expends more resources on it and works harder to discover an explanation for it (Dutton, 1986). Part of expending resources includes activation of the CMP. While some crises may be hard to see, others are simply ignored.

As I've stressed, stakeholder perception matters during a crisis (Augustine, 1995; Frank, 1994; Higbee, 1992). If your customers define a situation as a crisis, it is a crisis, even if the dominant coalition (those managers in the organization who make decisions) chooses to initially define it as a noncrisis. We have to go no further than the Intel Pentium chip flaw fiasco to recognize the wisdom of these words. Intel knew in the summer of 1994 that the chip was flawed; it could make mistakes on certain advanced mathematical calculations. However, Intel ignored customer concerns about the flaw. Intel even failed to grasp the significance of having the flaw posted on the Internet. After generating greater customer animosity, Intel eventually agreed that the situation was a crisis, and in December of 1994, it replaced the defective chip (Gonzalez-Herrero & Pratt, 1996). It may fall to the crisis team to convince the dominant coalition to accept the stakeholder perception that a crisis exists. A crisis is taken more seriously and is given more attention than a noncrisis. The issue for crisis managers becomes how to sell a problem as a crisis to the dominant coalition.

Crisis Framing: A Symbolic Response to Crises

Organizational environments are filled with ambiguous events. Organization members must frequently decide if something is important or try to determine why something happened (Fairhurst & Sarr, 1996). Crises are part of the ambiguity encountered by organizations. All problems within organizations are framed in some way. A *frame* is the way a problem is presented, the meaning one attaches to the problem (Fairhurst & Sarr, 1996). A frame affects interpretations of the problem by highlighting certain of its features while masking other features (Dutton & Ashford, 1993). There can be competing frames. For example, abortion has been framed as both freedom of choice and murder. Crisis managers need to create a frame that will provoke the most desirable response from top management. Three factors play a role in developing an appealing crisis frame: (1) the crisis dimensions, (2) the expertise of the dominant coalition, and (3) the persuasiveness of the presentation.

Crisis Dimensions

Crises vary along three dimensions: (1) perceived importance, (2) immediacy, and (3) uncertainty. Like warning signs, actual crises differ in the amount of loss that can occur and the likelihood of the loss if the CMP is not enacted. Failure to act can allow damage to spread to other areas of an organization, into surrounding communities, and to additional stakeholders. For instance, fire or toxic gas can spread to other parts of a facility or into the community, and shareholders can suffer when financial damage from a product harm crisis is not contained.

Perceived importance is related to the crisis assessment dimensions of impact and likelihood; it varies with the value of the possible loss (impact) and the probability of the loss (likelihood). The greater the possible loss or probability of loss, the greater the perceived importance of a crisis (Billings et al., 1980; Dutton, 1986). For instance, a faulty product that affects a few customers has less perceived importance than a faulty product used by hundreds of thousands of customers, if the potential harms from the defects are equal. Perceived importance is the key to framing warning signs. As has been discussed, crisis managers use likelihood and impact to rate warning signs (refer back to Chapter 3). Similarly, crisis managers need to emphasize the danger of ignoring warnings when presenting them to the dominant coalition.

Immediacy refers to the time pressure involved with the crisis. Time pressure has two components: (1) how quickly the crisis will hit and (2) the degree of stakeholder pressure to take action. The sooner a crisis can produce harm, the greater its immediacy. A tampered product that endangers customers' lives has greater immediacy than an initial complaint about moral violations by an activist group. A tampered product places people in immediate danger while moral violations tend to involve philosophical debates.

Comparing two cases will clarify the idea of immediacy. Early in 1990, an antiabortion group had urged Dayton Hudson Corporation to end its grant to Planned Parenthood (Kelly, 1990). In September of 1990, Dayton withdrew its funding from Planned Parenthood. Dayton wanted to avoid being drawn into the abortion debate. Management felt that providing Planned Parenthood funding could tie them to abortion. Women's groups were angered by the decision. Dayton officials had time to consider their options and to study consumer attitudes. The grant was eventually restored. The moral debate did not require immediate action. In contrast, Burroughs Wellcome Company experienced extreme immediacy when two people in Washington state died from taking cyanide-laced Sudafed 12-hour capsules in March of 1991.

Burroughs had to remove the products from the shelves and warn customers fast (Dagnoli & Colford, 1991; Kiley, 1991). The product safety concern did require immediate action.

Intense pressure from key stakeholders is another form of time pressure. When primary stakeholders (e.g., employees, customers) want action now, the crisis has immediacy. For example, the 1997 UPS drivers' strike gave the crisis immediacy. UPS was delivering only 10% of its packages and losing millions of dollars (Sewell, 1997). A company cannot survive under such conditions. Pressure from employees gave the UPS crisis immediacy.

Uncertainty is the amount of ambiguity associated with a problem. The larger the amount of ambiguity surrounding a crisis, the greater its uncertainty. People are drawn to and have a need to reduce uncertainty. Organizations are no different (Dutton, 1986). Organizations need to know what is going on in their operations and why. How can a problem be corrected if it is not understood? Low uncertainty problems can be explained and corrected using common organizational rules and procedures. High uncertainty problems demand the type of extra attention crisis management can deliver. A comparison of similar crises helps to illustrate the power of ambiguity.

On December 10, 1995, American Airlines Flight 965 from Miami to Cali, Colombia, crashed into a mountain, killing 160 of the 164 people on board. On July 17, 1996, TWA Flight 800 from New York to Paris exploded 12 miles off the coast of Long Island, killing all 230 people on board. The Searchbank data base listed five articles dedicated to Flight 965 and 141 for Flight 800. One reason for the different levels of media interest was the variation in ambiguity.

For Flight 965, investigators quickly identified the automated guidance system as the cause of the crash. The final report, released seven months later, confirmed that the plane was following the wrong directional beacon, causing the automated guidance system to fly the plane into the side of a mountain (Dornheim, 1996, McGraw, 1996).

The cause of Flight 800's explosion was investigated and debated for over 17 months. Missiles, terrorist bombs, lightning strikes, meteorites, and mechanical failures all surfaced as possible causes (Duffy & Beddingfield, 1996; Gray, 1996). The National Transportation Safety Board's final report ruled out all but mechanical failure. The evidence suggested that a small electrical charge ignited the fumes in an empty fuel tank that then exploded and destroyed the plane. More than 10 years later, the cause of Flight 800's crash is still being debated online. Flight 800 remains a mystery because of the ambiguity surrounding the explosion. The mystery helped to hold media and public attention for over a year. Furthermore, a Herculean effort went into discovering the mysterious cause of the explosion and reducing the ambiguity.

Ambiguity demands to be resolved. Organizations must expend extra effort and resources when crisis ambiguity increases. The CMP can focus the attention required by an ambiguous crisis. The easiest crisis to sell is one that is perceived as very important, is very immediate, and has high uncertainty. Crisis managers must maximize as many of the crisis dimensions as possible when they frame the crisis for the dominant coalition.

Expertise of the Dominant Coalition

Organizational politics creeps into crisis management. Part of successful politicking is in knowing the people with whom you are dealing. The management personnel that make up the dominant coalition will possess varying types of expertise. Their expertise affects their comfort zone for dealing with problems. Managers like to successfully solve problems. Not surprisingly, they are more likely to be successful when dealing with problems within their expertise—their comfort zones. Comfort increases because they can identify more easily with the problem. Crisis managers must be sensitive to the expertise of the dominant coalition when framing a crisis. The crisis frame should be adapted to the coalition by reflecting some aspect of their expertise (Dutton & Ashford, 1993). If the dominant coalition has financial expertise, the CMT should make sure the crisis frame includes a financial component. One way to tap expertise is to use jargon, the language of a profession. A message using jargon from the dominant coalition's area of expertise cultivates a sense of familiarity with the situation (Fairhurst & Sarr, 1996). While not a completely rational reaction, the dominant coalition will want to manage crises they feel they can resolve successfully. A crisis leads stakeholders to question the dominant coalition's competence. Successful crisis management restores the perception of the dominant coalition's competence, while failure further erodes it (Dutton, 1986; Pearson & Clair, 1998). Hence, top management prefers crises it can feel comfortable with. The same holds true for prodromes. Any Dilbert cartoon reminds us that the organizational world does not run on pure logic.

Persuasiveness of the Presentation

Crisis managers will have an opportunity to convince the dominant coalition that a problem is a crisis. The crisis managers must use their persuasive skills when given the opportunity to argue for a crisis. People are persuaded by three basic factors: (1) credibility, (2) emotion, and (3) reason (Larson 1989; Tan, 1985).

Credibility is a concept that is used in persuasion and is defined as the receiver's attitude toward the communicator. For crisis management, the organization is the communicator and the stakeholders are the receivers. Credibility is a very important concept because it has a significant effect on the persuasiveness of a message (McCroskey, 1997). Research has proven that credibility can be divided into two components: expertise and trustworthiness. *Expertise* is the communicator's knowledge about the subject. An expert organization will appear to be competent, capable, and effective (Kouzes & Posner, 1993). *Trustworthiness* is the communicator's goodwill toward or concern for the receivers. A trustworthy organization is truthful land ethical and considers the impact of its actions on stakeholders when making decisions (Allen & Caillouet, 1994; Kouzes & Posner, 1993). To be credible, crisis managers need to have a record of successful task completion demonstrating their expertise. Having a reputation as being honest enhances their trustworthiness (McCroskey, 1997).

Emotion centers on how the message is presented (McCroskey, 1997). To heighten the emotionality, a crisis should be presented in a dramatic fashion. A crisis is dramatic when it is novel. Vivid examples and stories help to create a dramatic presentation. The drama and emotion make the message more interesting and easier to understand, and they catch the attention of management (Dutton & Ashford, 1993; Larson, 1989). Management and other targets of persuasion do not evaluate information on the basis of emotion alone; they also rely on logic.

Reason, a rational appeal, stirs our intellect (Larson, 1989). The use of facts (verifiable information) and logical evidence persuades people. However, facts do not speak for themselves. Crisis managers can spin the facts by emphasizing the dangers of a situation. Lotteries sell tickets by telling people they cannot win if they do not play, not by reporting the odds against winning. To convince management of a crisis situation, crisis managers would feature information that supports the strong likelihood and impact of a crisis while downplaying information that erodes either. Both sides of the issue must be presented because one-sided arguments are ineffective with educated audiences, such as managers (Tan, 1985). Crisis managers who use emotions to capture the dominant coalition's attention must then use compelling rational evidence (e.g., statistics or expert testimony) to support the acceptance of the crisis (Dutton & Ashford, 1993). The message designed to sell the crisis or warning sign should begin dramatically with vivid stories and examples, then move to reasoned arguments to reinforce its acceptance.

A hypothetical example demonstrates the use of emotion and reason. Imagine you work for Juice-Is-Us, a fresh vegetable juice maker. Evidence suggests that a recent shipment of tomato juice could be tainted with E. coli. You want to have the situation treated as a crisis. One option is to state the statistical probability of E. coli contamination and to note that the effects would be bad for the company. Another option is to describe in detail the effects of E. coli on the human body. Retell an actual case of a person who suffered from E. coli. Vivid examples and a story reinforce the dangers by bringing them to life. Next, present the information by noting the possibility of people contracting the disease, not the probability that they will not: spin the information. Add the possibility that regulatory agencies and law enforcement officials, such as the FBI, could investigate the situation. Last, reinforce your case with statistics about the likelihood of contamination, the potential number of consumers affected, and the potential financial and reputational impact of any E. coli poisonings or deaths. As you can see, the second option provides a much more persuasive argument for enacting the CMP.

Resistance to Crises

Not all problems rise to the level of crisis in an organization. As stated in the opening of the chapter, crises can be contested, symbolic issues. Natural disasters, malevolence, technical and human accidents, organizational misdeeds, and workplace violence tend to be obvious crises where most stakeholders would agree on the interpretation. Challenges and rumors are two crisis types where contrasting interpretations abound. At least one stakeholder group will see a crisis while the organization does not. The different interpretations can cause an organization to overlook a crisis. It is foolish arrogance to believe that only the organization can place the crisis label on a situation. Crisis interpretations are socially co-created by primary stakeholders, secondary stakeholders (especially the news media), and the organization. If primary stakeholders believe a crisis exists, it does. Remember the Audi 5000 case from earlier in the book? Audi never did agree with the customers over the sudden acceleration problems with the 5000. The contested crisis generated years of bad press and consumer ill will before Audi recalled the 5000 (Sullivan, 1990; Versical, 1987).

Karl Weick (1979, 1993) is a social psychologist who has studied crises and whose ideas have been applied to crisis management

(Seeger, Sellnow, & Ulmer, 2003). Weick's (1979) model of information processing provides a theoretical explanation for crises being missed. He uses the term *enactment* to explain how people in organizations make sense of events such as crisis. The process begins when there is some change in the organization's environment—an event occurs. Through enactment, managers isolate pieces of information about that event for closer inspection. The managers then try to make sense of and give meaning to this information through the process of *selection*. (In knowledge management, this is when information is converted into knowledge). Selection guides how the managers respond to the event. Last, *retention* explains what information the managers store for future use. Enactment is the key to the entire model. The information that is chosen for further attention shapes how managers see and react to their environment. If managers enact information that does not indicate a crisis, the organization will not respond to the event as a crisis. Weick's idea of enactment is that managers actively shape and create the environments to which they react by imposing their interpretations on the information. Managers may enact an event very differently from stakeholders and create a conflict over whether or not a crisis exists.

Crisis managers should evaluate all stakeholder claims that a crisis exists by examining or reexamining the information. First, they must determine if the facts are correct: Are the claims accurate? Inaccurate claims should be corrected immediately, thereby diffusing the crisis. Second, if true, determine if other stakeholders accept the interpretation of the situation as a crisis. Will more stakeholders in a particular group or other stakeholder groups support the crisis interpretation? In Audi's case, would more customers as well as government regulators see the sudden acceleration as a crisis? A crisis interpretation gains power and salience when it spreads among stakeholders. A crisis manager must decide if the values and interests embodied in the crisis interpretation will appeal to other stakeholders. Such decisions require a clear understanding of one's stakeholders.

Here's an example. In 1990, Philip Morris was challenged for having a high number of billboards selling cigarettes in inner-city areas. The crisis interpretation painted Philip Morris as a racist organization that exploited minorities in the inner city. About 40 different demonstrations were launched against the company by Rev. Calvin Butts, an inner-city, antitobacco advocate. Philip Morris was worried about being labeled a racist organization that exploits minorities. The company ended the advertising campaign due to fear of a spreading crisis interpretation. They agreed to reduce the number of cigarette billboards in inner-city areas and to join a council that would examine outdoor advertising practices in such areas (Fahey & Dagnoli, 1990). The lesson to be learned here is that if crisis managers believe a crisis interpretation will resonate with other stakeholders, they must work to convince the dominant coalition to accept it as a crisis.

Another scenario involving missed crises is when the dominant coalition purposefully refuses to see one. Embezzlement and successful computer hackings are common crises that are purposely not seen. Even when internal or external audits discover embezzlement, most organizations hide it. The FBI believes that only 10% of all embezzlements are reported. Embezzlement is embarrassing, and many organizations fear that reporting it will encourage more theft or anger shareholders, clients, or customers (Strauss, 1998). Similar reasons exist for not disclosing computer hackings; organizations do not want to appear weak or vulnerable. However, some states, such as California, require disclosure of computer hacking that places individuals' identity at risk (Hopper, 2002). I have had firsthand experience with laws requiring this kind of disclosure. My mortgage company (ABN-Amro) was forced to tell me and other customers when its data tape containing mortgage information was misplaced by a package delivery service (DHL).

Each organization and industry has its own type of crises that are purposely ignored. The organization may take actions to address the problem but choose to keep the situation quiet to avoid involving most stakeholders. The organization is engaging in a form of cover-up. Any cover-up is dangerous; it could be exposed later and trigger a different and more severe crisis (Barton, 2001).

As mentioned, crisis managers can affect the acceptance or rejection of a crisis by how they frame its presentation to the dominant coalition. Crisis managers must have information to support the frame and articulate it in a compelling fashion. Frame development begins with information. Crisis managers need information that indicates that a problem is (a) important—damage will occur or become more severe by spreading, (b) immediate—there are pressures to act now, or (c) uncertain—there is ambiguity surrounding the situation. Any of these three can signal a crisis; if all three are present, it is a compelling situation.

To underline the importance of these points, let me review: Crisis managers should consider the dominant coalition's expertise and basic elements of persuasion when selling the frame. The dominant coalition must be familiar and comfortable with the crisis—see it as within their realm of expertise. Jargon is one way to link a crisis to the dominant coalition's expertise. Vivid stories and examples serve to capture the dominant coalition's attention. The facts about the importance, immediacy, and uncertainty of the crisis are then offered to support the acceptance of the crisis label.

It falls to the crisis managers to cure organizational blindness by convincing management to openly acknowledge a situation as a crisis. Crisis managers should sell a situation as a crisis because they believe enacting the CMP will improve the situation and benefit the organization or its stakeholders or both. Selling crises is even more difficult when the dominant coalition is purposely ignoring the crisis.

Organizations can be blind to warning signs as well, and the recommendations for selling crises can also be applied to selling prodromes. For instance, a semiconductor manufacturer ignored evidence for eight years that its lax operating procedures were poisoning workers. A lawsuit by 30 workers alleging widespread ills and workplace abuses brought the problem to light. The case was settled out of court (Smith, 1998).

❖ CRISES AND INFORMATION NEEDS

Crises can be regarded as information-poor and knowledge-poor situations. A crisis begins as an unknown and must become a known. A typical crisis requires large amounts of information because initially little is known, it is a rapidly changing situation, and often the changes in the situation are more random than predictable. These factors indicate that the information demands of a crisis are complex (Barge, 1994). There is pressure on a crisis team to acquire information and to process it into knowledge quickly and accurately if the team is to operate effectively in a crisis. Understanding and coping with the information and knowledge demands of a crisis is part of crisis management.

Crises as Information Processing and Knowledge Management

Egelhoff and Sen (1992), Seeger et al. (2003), and Weick (1993) have all identified information processing as a major task during crisis management, while Wang and Belardo (2005) have emphasized knowledge management as central to crisis management. These are complementary perspectives because information processing is how knowledge is created. Situation awareness is a term used to describe this information-processing and knowledge-creating aspect of crisis management. In general, situation awareness describes the point at which the crisis team feels it has enough information and knowledge to make a decision (Kolfschoten & Appelman, 2006). More specially, situation awareness involves perceptions of the situation and environment, comprehension of them, and the ability to project future states (Endsley, 1995). For the crisis team, situation awareness indicates that it has a perception and understanding of the crisis situation and the ability to predict the effects of the crisis and to determine what actions are needed to address it.

A sample crisis illustrates the process of moving from the unknown to the known and creating situation awareness: There is an explosion in an aerosol can facility. The crisis team should know: the location of the explosion, the employees working in the area at the time, the chemicals involved in the process, and the exact tasks performed in the area of the explosion. What the crisis team does not know but needs to know includes who was injured, the nature and severity of the injuries, what emergency actions were taken after the explosion, the amount of damage to the facility, the need to suspend operations, and possible causes of the explosion. The crisis team collects information until they have the requisite knowledge and information about the crisis necessary to make decisions.

The Unknown

The crisis begins with a trigger event or someone convincing management that a crisis exists. Either way, the organization is faced with a problem that now commands the crisis team's attention and demands some resolution. The first task of the crisis management team is to determine what they need to know about the crisis, what they already know, and what they do not know. What they need to know is the information and knowledge required to enact the CMP and to make decisions. What is already known would be the previously collected crisis information and knowledge. What they do not know is the difference between what is needed and what exists in the crisis data bank (all the previously collected crisis information and knowledge, including the CMP and Crisis Appendix). Understanding the three informational concerns allows the crisis team to assess how much it knows and what it needs to gather in order to cope with the crisis and to reach situation awareness. The team then must try to reduce what they do not know by collecting crisis-relevant information.

❖ INFORMATION GATHERING

Information gathering should be an organized search, not a wild scavenger hunt. In fact, knowledge management strategies were created in large part to aid information collection and analysis. The crisis team must prioritize the information needs, know where to go, and who to ask in order to collect the information (Clampitt, 1991). The team must prioritize the information it needs because information needs are not equal. High priority information should receive immediate attention and greater effort (Geraghty & Desouza, 2005). For example, during an industrial accident that vents dangerous gas, the crisis team must know the direction and intensity of the gas cloud before it worries about the cause of the gas venting. Each crisis will determine its own information priorities.

Knowing that certain information is needed is pointless if the team does not know where to get it. Links to organization members and external stakeholders become valuable when a crisis team requires information, because the links are the sources for the requisite information (Pearson & Clair, 1998; Wang & Belardo, 2005). It behooves a crisis team to know the sources of potential crisis-relevant information and knowledge before a crisis hits. Identifying sources of knowledge is known as a knowledge map and fits with the CMT contact sheet in the CMP. The idea of developing a crisis knowledge map is discussed shortly.

❖ INFORMATION PROCESSING: THE KNOWN

Raw information is a starting point, not an end point, when trying to understand a crisis. The crisis team must determine what the pieces of information mean. What is typically called making sense out of information is information processing. Through processing the information, the team determines if it actually has assembled the knowledge it needed. Only by analyzing information can a team determine if enough knowledge of the requisite kind has been collected to convert the unknown into the known. The crisis managers must determine if they have enough knowledge to make effective decisions, if they have reached situation awareness. If there is a knowledge deficit, the information gathering continues. If there is enough knowledge, decisions are made about what the organization will do and what it will say about the crisis, the domain of Chapter 8.

❖ INFORMATION-PROCESSING PROBLEMS

The crisis management literature treats information processing as a rather simple task. Crisis managers are told to mobilize their resources and to gather all possible information (Mitchell, 1986). We are led to believe that information is easy to collect and to analyze. However, this is not the case. Research in organizational and small-group communication has found consistent flaws which plague information collecting and processing as well as knowledge sharing (Rollins & Halinen, 2005; Stohl & Redding, 1987). By understanding these flaws, we can construct better mechanisms for crisis team information collecting and processing. Crisis managers should be aware of five flaws: (1) serial reproduction errors, (2) the MUM effect, (3) message overload, (4) information acquisition biases, and (5) group decision-making errors.

Serial Reproduction Errors

Have you ever received a message that has traveled through three or four different people before reaching you? The odds are that the message made little sense or was far from accurate. This distortion is known as the *serial reproduction problem* or *serial transmission effect*. The more people a message passes through before reaching its final destination, the greater the likelihood of the message being distorted (Daniels et al., 1997). Obviously, inaccurate information is problematic during a crisis. It leads to public embarrassment through misstatements to the media and dangerous miscues by a crisis team that has based its decisions on inaccurate information. Remember the emotional pain caused by wrong information during the Sago mine disaster in West Virginia in early January of 2006?

The MUM Effect

One critical source of crisis-related information would be members of the organization. Not surprisingly, people in organizations have a tendency to withhold negative information completely (e.g., information that makes them look bad) or alter the information to make it less damaging (Stohl & Redding, 1987). This phenomenon is known as the MUM effect, acting to block the flow of negative or unpleasant information in an organization (Tesser & Rosen, 1975). Crises involve negative situations. Things have gone wrong and threaten the organization in some way (Barton, 2001). Organization members may be reluctant to provide negative information, especially if it could make them or their organization unit look bad.

Some people attribute the explosion of the space shuttle Challenger to the MUM effect (Goldhaber, 1990). The night before the Challenger launch, 15 engineers at Morton Thiokol argued against the launch. Morton Thiokol makes the solid rocket boosters (SRBs) which help to lift the space shuttle into orbit. The SRBs have O-rings (rubber circles) that seal gaps and prevent improper ignition of the solid fuels. The O-rings have no backup. If an O-ring fails, the solid rocket fuel can ignite improperly, explode, and destroy the vehicle. Everyone at NASA was aware of the potential consequences of an O-ring failure. The engineers felt the weather was too cold and would prevent the O-rings from functioning properly. (O-ring failure was determined later to be the cause of the explosion). Morton Thiokol originally refused to approve the launch. After another meeting, the decision was reversed, and Morton Thiokol green-lighted the launch. Middle managers at NASA never told either Arnold Aldrich, the manager of the entire space shuttle program, or Jesse Moore, NASA's associate administrator responsible for the final launch decision, about Morton Thiokol's launch concerns (Boffey, 1986; Mecham, 1986; Sanger, 1986). We can speculate whether either of these two men would have stopped the launch had they known about Morton Thiokol's concerns. However, NASA managers illustrated the MUM effect by not relaying negative information to their superiors. No crisis team can afford to have negative information withheld or modified just to keep a short-term peace or to protect team members.

Message Overload

A common problem experienced by people in organizations is message overload, when people are given more information than they can competently manage (Geraghty & Desouza, 2005; Stohl & Redding, 1987). The risk of information overload is great during a crisis. As noted earlier, crises are information poor, which demands the collecting and processing of large amounts of information to compensate for this information void. The demand for information can produce a vast flow of data into the crisis team. However, the danger is that the information flow becomes overwhelming and blocks the process instead of helping to close the gap between the unknown and the known in the crisis.

Information Acquisition Bias

Because the amount of available information exceeds the human ability to make sense of it, people naturally use selective perception, which means we each focus on certain aspects of the information; we encounter and disregard the rest (Barge, 1994). Weick's (1979) idea of enactment is related to selective perception. The risk in crisis management is as follows: Early on in the crisis, crisis team members form impressions about the nature of the crisis. All subsequent information and knowledge are tested against this initial perception or crisis frame. The crisis team tends to seek information that confirms the initial impression while discounting information that contradicts this impression. Unfortunately, the initial perception may blind the crisis team to critical information and knowledge needed for its decision-making efforts. Another risk arises when members define any new crisis in terms of past crises (Barge, 1994). Rather than treating a new crisis as a novel event, crisis teams can simply view it as a version of some previous crisis. If the past crisis is a poor match, the crisis team applies the wrong template when it addresses the new crisis. The crisis team manages the wrong crisis because it mistakes the new crisis for the old one. In either instance, important nuances about the current crisis are lost. The crisis team discounts potentially important information because of the blinders from initial impressions or baggage from past crises.

These two information acquisition biases can be demonstrated by returning to the case of TWA Flight 800 discussed earlier in this chapter. Initial reports indicated that a terrorist bomb was responsible for the incident. The pattern of the blast and discovery of microscopic PETN traces, a plastic explosive, on salvaged pieces of the plane were the best evidence. Investigators could have relied on their initial perceptions and examined only the circumstantial evidence supporting the bomb explanation. The remainder of the investigation could have ignored all other possible causes. Another reason to suspect terrorism was the similarity to the Pan Am Flight 103 bombing over Lockerbie, Scotland, in 1988. The radar tapes and the voice and flight data recordings of Flight 800 were very similar to Flight 103's. Investigators could have examined all the remaining evidence through the lens of a previous crisis. As it turned out, Pan Am Flight 103's template was the wrong one to apply to TWA Flight 800 (Gray, 1996; Watson, 1996). Had either of these information acquisition biases been used, the investigators would have ignored the clues to the real cause of the explosion: mechanical failure.

Group Decision-Making Errors

Groups are prone to decision-making errors when they fail to use critical-thinking skills. Critical thinking is a process of carefully evaluating information (Williams & Olaniran, 1994). Two tendencies contribute to poor group decision making. First, the group fails to see a problem or fails to identify the correct cause of the problem. The group is led to ignore problems or to solve the wrong problems. Second, the group improperly evaluates its alternatives for solving a problem (Hirokawa & Rost, 1992). Improper evaluation can lead the group to select an ineffective alternative for solving the problem. Both types of errors result in poor decision making. In each instance, the root cause of the error can be traced to the careless handling of information.

Summary

The purpose for reviewing information gathering and processing errors was twofold. First, the errors highlight how difficult information gathering and processing can be. Crisis team members should not underestimate these problems. Second, realization of the problems can help to develop more effective information-gathering and -processing mechanisms for crisis teams. The information gathering and processing should become more effective when the crisis team is trying to counter those errors.

❖ INFORMATION-PROCESSING MECHANISMS

Information-processing mechanisms are designed to aid crisis teams in both the collecting and processing of crisis-relevant information. The information-processing mechanisms involve both structural and procedural elements. The structural elements focus on how to collect information. The procedural elements center on how to prevent or reduce processing errors.

Structural Elements

Let me stress once again that crisis managers need to access sources that have information (potential knowledge) they might need during a crisis. Crisis managers must seek out needed information that is not a part of their already assembled crisis database. Communication consultants recognize the value of networks when collecting information. Networks are relationships with other people. Stronger networks lead to better information gathering and more accurate understanding of problems (Barge, 1994; Clampitt, 1991; Geraghty & Desouza, 2005). Crisis management teams must develop connections they can use to collect crisis-related information. I call the system the *crisis knowledge map*. The crisis knowledge map is composed of external and internal stakeholder networks.

Internal Stakeholder Network. The internal stakeholder network is composed of the people within the crisis team's organization. The foundation of the internal stakeholder network stems from the networks of the individual team members. Their contacts and information sources become the team's sources. The crisis team then looks to expand the list by asking each contact for others who may know about the subject (Barge, 1994). The crisis team should formalize the information by developing a list of contacts for various types of information that might be needed during a crisis, developing an Internal Stakeholder Section for a Crisis Knowledge Map Directory. The Crisis Knowledge Map Directory lists multiple contacts for various types of information the team may need. The Crisis Knowledge Map Directory can be an appendix to the CMP or a separate document. The Crisis Knowledge Map Directory starts with a listing of the expertise required, which is a way of categorizing people by the type of knowledge they possess. The expertise designation is followed by basic contact information: name, organization and title, phone numbers, pager number, fax number, and e-mail. Multiple contact points are important because if one fails, another can be tried until the person is contacted.

External Stakeholder Network. The external stakeholder network is composed of people outside of the crisis team's organization. Common members would include customers, government officials, suppliers, distributors, community members, competitors, and investors (Pearson & Mitroff, 1993). Any external stakeholder could be a part of this network. The Secondary Contact Sheet from the CMP is an essential resource. The Secondary Contact Sheet provides contact people for all stakeholder groups—and it indicates who in the organization handles each particular stakeholder. The crisis team converts the information from the Secondary Contact Sheet into an external stakeholder section for the Crisis Knowledge Map Directory. The structure of the external section parallels that of the internal section. The difference is that the external section would include the contact person or persons for the various stakeholder groups. The crisis team would have the option of direct contact with the external stakeholder or the use of the organization's contact person or persons. A contact person is helpful when a positive relationship has been established. The stakeholder should be more open with the contact person given the history of a positive relationship with that person versus having no relational history with a member of the crisis team. The open relationship should make it easier for the contact person to solicit higher quality information from the external stakeholder.

Crisis Information Logs. During a crisis, it is critical to track the amount and movement of crisis-related information and knowledge within the organization. Crisis information logs are a useful tool for monitoring information and knowledge flow. Logs record when a crisis team member makes an information request and the result of that request. By logging information requests and receipts, the crisis team knows what information it has and what information it still needs. The log starts with the standard concerns: the time and date of the request, what is requested, requested from whom, the channel used to make the request, and requested by whom. Once the information is received, the time, date, channel used to deliver the information, and sources are recorded along with the name of the person who received the information. Administrative support staff can help keep the crisis information logs. The CMT needs administrative support to help with this and other tasks during the crisis management process.

Once again, the next step is to evaluate and process the information into knowledge. Team members must decide if any follow-up information is needed or if the received information is sufficient. The log notes when the information was processed (knowledge created) and by whom. Accepted criteria for evaluating information are clarity, timeliness, and depth. *Clarity* means that the information has one interpretation, not multiple interpretations, and people can easily understand what the message means. *Timeliness* means that the information is current and received when needed. *Depth* means that the information seems complete—it answers the questions asked (Barge, 1994).

A hypothetical example demonstrates clarity, timeliness, and depth: Imagine that a hurricane hits the central manufacturing facility of your power tool company. The CMT wants to know when operations will resume. Does your CMT want to hear "in a reasonable amount of time" (lack of clarity) or "in 5 to 6 days" (clarity)? The CMT needs to know what alternatives are available for maintaining production. Does your CMT want a business resumption plan that has not been revised in three years (is not timely) or a current business resumption plan (timely)? Last, the CMT needs to know about injured workers, people who were on duty when the hurricane struck. Does your CMT want to learn there were 10 injuries (lack of depth) or the exact names of those injured and the extent of their injuries (depth)? The CMT works best when it receives quality information.

Precision should be stressed in the logs. The information is to be recorded as it is received and not summarized or modified. Precise written records help to eliminate some of the factors that promote serial reproduction errors. Also, having a written record reduces the number of sources used to transmit a message, which again serves to reduce the likelihood of serial reproduction errors.

The crisis information log records when information is requested, when it is received, and if it has been processed. Time and date help to assess the timeliness of information. Channels are useful in evaluation. The log can help to evaluate the extent to which specific channels were effective in requesting and sending information. Noting who the information was requested from helps to determine if better sources could be used in the future. The source of the information indicates the believability of the information, due in part to the credibility of the source. The log also tracks if, when, and by whom the information was processed. Overall, the log helps the crisis team to monitor its information collection and processing efforts. Crisis teams must collect and store accurate information about the progression of events in a crisis because such documentation is central to postcrisis evaluation, crisis-related lawsuits, and governmental investigations triggered by the crisis.

Procedural Efforts

The procedural efforts are all actions that can be taken to overcome various information-processing problems. A priority system is one way to combat information overload by using selective criteria to establish the perceived importance of information (Geraghty & Desouza, 2005; Stohl & Redding, 1987). Prioritization is a multistep process involving evaluation, storage, and retrieval. When incoming information is logged, it is also evaluated. A simple priority system might use three categories: (1) immediate, (2) routine, and (3) miscellaneous. *Immediate* refers to information the crisis team requires for pressing decisions or actions. *Routine* is the basic information a crisis team typically needs during the course of a crisis management effort. *Miscellaneous* is information that is received, has no apparent value, but does have some relationship to the crisis.

Routine and miscellaneous information is stored until the crisis team has time for or need of it. Information might be stored on paper or in computer files or both. Retrieval involves extracting the desired information from the information queue. Storage and retrieval require categorizing the information by topic. The information is assigned a general topic area and a list of key subjects it covers. The process is similar to cataloging books in a library. Chapter 9 provides additional recommendations for storage and retrieval.

Allowing the crisis team to focus on the high priority information reduces the message load, thereby decreasing information overload. The message priority system should reflect the crisis team's information needs. A contaminated food recall crisis will illustrate and clarify the priority process: Nine top priorities at the start of a food recall include (1) identifying affected consumers, (2) locating the source of the contamination, and (3) informing consumers about the recall. Information related to any of these three topics would be categorized as immediate during the initial phase of the crisis. Suppose the crisis team received the following information: (1) results of production facility inspections, (2) newspaper stories about the company's crisis management efforts, (3) projected costs of the recall, (4) confirmation that the recall information is being reported in the news media, (5) projections on lost market share, (6) estimated recovery time, (7) confirmed cases of consumer illnesses, (8) consumer reactions to the recall, and (9) Internet newsgroup discussion linking the recall to a government conspiracy.

Information chunks 1 (inspection results), 4 (confirmation of recall in the news media) and 7 (cases of illness) would be recognized as immediate priority. In each case, the information relates directly to the initial priorities of the crisis team. Information chunks 2, 3, 5, 6, and 8 would be routine priority. Eventually the crisis team will need to assess the financial damage (2 and 5), project recovery time (6), and evaluate their crisis management performance (2 and 8). Information chunk 9 is miscellaneous because there probably is no government conspiracy here, but the information does pertain to the crisis. When a lot of information is being received and the risk of information overload is high, crisis teams would benefit from an information priority system.

Data splitting is a technique used to combat information acquisition bias. Date splitting divides information into smaller units for more effective analysis. A big block of information is reduced to smaller units of information. The crisis team can examine these units of information more carefully because the smaller units are easier to examine in detail. In addition, smaller units act to break patterns that could feed into preexisting information processing biases (Barge, 1994). Let us return to the TWA Flight 800 case. Data splitting would include considering the flight data and radar records separately before placing each into the larger picture of the investigation.

Unfortunately, there is no simple technique for handling the MUM effect. The only proven means is an open communication system in which people engage in the candid disclosure and receipt of facts, even if it is bad news (Redding, 1972). Openness is developed through trust and past interactions with one another (Barge, 1994). The crisis team members must work to earn the trust of organization members and demonstrate that there will not be negative sanctions for passing along information that indicates member mistakes or errors. In a similar way, open and positive relationships with external stakeholders facilitate the flow of accurate information from outside sources (Grunig, 1992).

Group decision-making errors can be combated through vigilance and the devil's advocate technique. The discussion of crisis team selection touched on vigilance, a form of critical thinking. The four primary elements of vigilance are (1) problem analysis, (2) standards for evaluating alternative choices, (3) understanding the important positive aspects of an alternative choice, and (4) understanding the important negative aspects of an alternative choice. The four elements serve to counter the two group decision-making errors. Problem analysis counters the failure of the group to identify the correct cause of the problem, while standards for evaluating alternative choices and understanding the important positive and negative aspects of an alternative choice all serve to compensate for the group improperly evaluating alternatives for solving the problem (Hirokawa & Rost, 1992). The devil's advocate technique ensures that some group member always voices opposition to a group's plan. The opposition is supposed to lead the group to reevaluate their decisions and reminds the group to examine weaknesses it may have glossed over originally (Barge, 1994).

Training

Stress can be the enemy of the crisis team. While stress can enhance performance by making people more alert and react faster, it can also create problems such as freezing, misplaced aggression, and ignoring new tools and techniques. Training helps to reduce stress and to promote team dynamics that help to mitigate stress. Part of crisis team training can be on stress-proofing team members. People can learn techniques to help reduce stress in pressure situations. When a team has an open and supportive climate, stress is reduced. Part of training can reinforce the value of open communication and the value of cooperation and support for team members (Paton & Flin, 1999). Training is critical to team learning. In times of stress, people retreat to what is comfortable. New tools and techniques for crisis communication will not be used if team members do not feel comfortable using them before a crisis. The team will ignore the new tools and techniques and go back to what they know. New tools and techniques would include new software, hardware, or decision support techniques such as thinkLets

(Kolfschoten & Appelman, 2006). If it's important for a crisis team to integrate a new technology or technique into their work, then make sure the members are familiar and comfortable with using it (Hiltz, 2006).

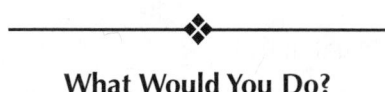

What Would You Do?

Sprint and the Baby

A local NBC station in Los Angeles, California, reports that Sprint refused to help parents whose 10-month-old child was in the backseat of a stolen car. The Cochrans were loading their car in their Riverside, California, driveway. They had placed the 10-month-old in the car and had returned to get their second child when the thieves struck. The parents claimed that Sprint would not provide global positioning information from the parents' cell phone unless proper channels were used. The story also said that Sprint needed a $25 fee to be paid before they would even help the authorities. The child and the car were recovered safely less than two hours after the theft. Bloggers were irate with Sprint and helped to spread the story. Why would this event be a reputational crisis?

Sprint's policy is that law enforcement personnel, not the regular consumer, must submit a faxed request to get access to global positioning data. The process takes only a few minutes. The policy is necessary because people could use the global positioning data for stalking or child abductions. There is no fee for law enforcement. Clearly the customer representative did not know or understand the policies. What can Sprint do to alleviate this crisis and prevent a repeat of this kind?

❖ CONCLUSION

A crisis cannot be managed effectively if the organization is blind to its details. At times, crisis team members will have to sell a crisis to the dominant coalition before action can be taken to resolve the crisis. This chapter began by offering suggestions for crisis selling. Once the existence of a crisis is recognized, information must be collected and processed into knowledge vital to its successful management. Crisis teams need accurate and timely information if they are to have the knowledge they need to make effective decisions quickly. While it sounds easy, numerous problems can hinder information gathering and processing. The main problems were reviewed and procedures and techniques suggested that crisis management teams can adopt to improve their information gathering and processing capabilities. Taken together, the material in this chapter prepares the crisis team for identifying the crisis and processing the information into the knowledge needed to resolve the crisis.

❖ DISCUSSION QUESTIONS

1. Bribery and computer hacking are two crises that are often unreported. What other crises are organizations likely to hide? What types of information does a university prefer potential students not have?

2. Organizations keep saying how much customer service means to them. Why are so many crises caused by not paying enough attention to consumers?

8

Crisis Response

❖ ❖ ❖

O nce a crisis hits, the crisis team must work to (a) prevent it from spreading to unaffected areas of the organization or the environment and (b) limit its duration (Mitroff, 1994). Communication presents unique challenges during the response phase. Internally, the crisis team must collect and process information in order to make decisions, which have been discussed in earlier chapters. Externally, stakeholders must be informed about the crisis and actions must be taken to address it, including reporting the organization's progress toward recovery.

❖

What Would You Do?

BP and Texas City: Act 2

You are the spokesperson for BP, and it is about an hour into the crisis. The crisis team is assembled in the designated crisis control center. Local fire crews and BP's own fire crews are dealing with the flames. Local emergency crews are on the scene attending to the injured. The crisis team has learned there are fatalities. A construction trailer near the explosion was hit hard. Many of the injured and killed were contractors working for BP; they were in the trailer. The local and national news media have sent crews to the site. The flames and smoke will make for dramatic visuals on the news. The crisis team will hold a briefing in a few minutes. What information are you likely to have that you can share with the news media? What questions do you anticipate being asked but cannot answer at this time? How will you handle those questions?

❖

Discussions of external crisis communication must include form and content. *Form* is how the response should be presented. *Content* is what is said.

❖ FORM AND THE CRISIS RESPONSE

The form of a crisis response is mentioned more frequently in the crisis management writings than any other topic. The crisis response includes the first public statements the spokesperson makes about the crisis. This first statement typically is delivered through the mass media, hence the concern in crisis management with media relations (e.g., Barton, 2001; Fearn-Banks, 2001; Lerbinger, 1997). The focus on the initial response stems from the fact that first impressions form quickly and color the remainder of stakeholders' reception of the crisis communication efforts (Sen & Egelhoff, 1991). In any crisis, stakeholder information needs occur simultaneously with the crisis team's information needs.

The form recommendations for crisis communications are to be quick, consistent, and open. It is important to keep in mind that crisis communication transpires in times of stress. Stakeholders will not be at their best for receiving information. Research suggests that people's ability to process information is reduced by up to 80% during emotionally charged situations, such as crises (Gilman, 2004). Crisis teams must take care to craft and to send crisis messages so that they can be clearly and easily understood.

Responding Quickly

The terms *quick* and *quickly* are synonymous with crisis response. The need for speed in crisis communication continues to escalate as technology accelerates the spread of information, thereby actually reducing the amount of time a crisis team has for responding (Barton, 2001). The media report crises very quickly, including posting the stories online. It some cases, the key stakeholders affected by the crisis learn about it from media reports before they have been officially notified, creating a bad situation for the organization. The quicker the stakeholders can hear about a crisis from the media, the quicker the crisis team must respond. Obviously, speed increases risks. As the crisis team must act quickly, it can make mistakes. The primary risk associated with speed is the potential for inaccuracies (Smith & Hayne, 1997).

Johnson & Johnson committed a quickness mistake when handling the original Tylenol product tampering crisis. In 1982, seven people in the Chicago area died from taking cyanide-laced Extra-Strength Tylenol capsules. A reporter asked if cyanide was used in the Tylenol manufacturing facility, and the Johnson & Johnson spokesperson responded that there was no cyanide in the plant that produced Tylenol. The statement was in error; the testing laboratories at the production facility did use cyanide. At the time of the press conference, the spokesperson did not have all the relevant information, and the error was corrected as soon as it was discovered (Berg & Robb, 1992; Leon, 1983; Snyder, 1983). However, speed does not have to mean mistakes, and the benefits of a rapid initial response far outweigh the risks.

It is accurate to say that a crisis creates an information void. Nature abhors a vacuum. Any information void will be filled somehow and by someone. The media have deadlines, so they are driven to fill the information void quickly. The media demands trigger a chain reaction effect. The media are going to report on a crisis. Stakeholders may find that the news media are their primary or initial source of crisis-related information (Fearn-Banks, 2001), with the Internet increasing in use as well (Lackluster, 2002). If the crisis team does not supply the initial crisis information to the media, some other groups will, and they may be ill informed, misinformed, or motivated to harm the organization. The information void can become filled with rumor and speculation, not facts (Caruba, 1994). Whatever the case, the initial crisis information may well be incorrect and may intensify the damage created by the crisis. A quick response helps to ensure that stakeholders receive accurate crisis-related information and hear the organization's side of the story.

Silence is a very passive response and reflects uncertainty and passivity, the exact opposite of what an organization should be attempting to create. A silence response suggests that an organization is not in control and is not trying to take control of how it or the crisis is perceived by stakeholders (Hearit, 1994). Silence allows others to take control of the situation (Brummett, 1980) and define the crisis for stakeholders. A quick response helps to create the impression of control and is necessary to get the organization's definition of the crisis—its side of the story—into the media and out to the stakeholders (Heath, 1994; Kempner, 1995; Mitchell, 1986). To explain in detail, from the stakeholders' viewpoint, a rapid response demonstrates that the organization is taking action and is capable of responding to a crisis (Darling, 1994; Maynard, 1993). Conversely, a slow response makes an organization appear to be incompetent (Donath, 1984). Control is important to credibility; it is part of the organization's expertise. A crisis indicates a lack of control in and by the organization (Heath, 1994). A quick response is a first step in reasserting organizational control and reestablishing organizational credibility (Augustine, 1995).

There are limits to being able to respond quickly. In some crises, it takes time to collect and to process the necessary information. Large-scale accidents produce great confusion. A January 1998 explosion at a Sierra Chemical dynamite manufacturing facility 10 miles east of Reno, Nevada, exemplifies the limits to quickness. Initial reports on January 7 listed eight injured, three known dead, and two missing. A report later that same day listed six injured, five missing, and no confirmed deaths. The next day, officials had the final count: six injured and four missing, presumed to be dead. It seems one of the five people originally listed as missing had not reported to work on January 7 (Ryan, 1998; Several missing, 1998). There was a repeat of the speed error problem during the 2006 Sago mine tragedy in West Virginia. Relatives were told that all the miners were alive, when in fact only one survived. This fateful error added to the suffering of the families and townspeople. It takes time to collect some types of information.

A crisis team might have to appear before the media with an incomplete story. That is OK. There is no sin in telling the media the crisis team does not know something but will provide the information as soon as possible. Consider a variation to the Sierra Chemical case: The Sierra Chemical crisis team decides to delay a press conference until it has all of the information about the explosion. In the mean time, the local news media are telling people about suspected causes. Perhaps a disgruntled, former employee claims the accident was due to mismanagement. Mismanagement is the explanatory theme reported as a likely cause of the blast because no other reasons are forthcoming. The initial news stories have Sierra Chemical responsible for the workers' deaths and injuries. This theme frames the thinking of reporters and other stakeholders. Speculation and rumor inadvertently become crisis fact, at least for awhile. Better to have the spokesperson saying the cause or extent of damages is still under investigation than stakeholders being fed inaccurate information.

Lack of information and knowledge coupled with the need for a fast response can beget two media communication "sins." The first is "no comment." The danger is that stakeholders hear "we're guilty" instead of "no comment" (refer back to Chapter 5's discussion of spokesperson training for more on no-comment statements and silence.) Better to say the information is not yet available but will be reported to the media as soon as it is received. This brings up the second sin: not delivering on the information promised to the media (Birch, 1994; Gonzalez-Herrero & Pratt, 1995). A good organization–media relationship is built on trust, and trust requires an organization to deliver on its promises. Failure to provide promised information damages the organization–media relationship, thereby eroding the organization's credibility with the media. If information is promised, it had better be delivered in some way.

Speaking With One Voice: Consistency

The organization must deliver consistent messages to stakeholders, and a unified response promotes consistency. As has been mentioned before, consistency does not mean having just one person speak for the organization every time there is a public statement, as some crisis experts recommend (Carney & Jorden, 1993). Rather, speaking with one voice means coordinating the efforts of the official spokespersons and discouraging other organizational members from becoming unofficial spokespersons (Seitel, 1983). Chapter 5 detailed this point in the spokesperson discussion. The crisis team must ensure that the team of spokespersons is well prepared to ensure consistency in their responses. Spokespersons sharing the same information base are more consistent than those who do not. Consistency is essential to building the credibility of the response. A consistent message is more believable than an inconsistent one (Clampitt, 1991; Garvin, 1996).

There is no way to ensure the consistency or accuracy of messages from unofficial spokespersons, and these can be any employee the media happen to persuade to answer questions. The CMP specifies the process for handling inquiries. The process should be reinforced to employees so that they fight the urge to speak for the company. It is hard for employees to resist the opportunity to be on the local news. A camera crew appears as an employee is leaving work. The employee has a chance to be on television. Why not comment on the crisis? Most employees are not aware of the perils of talking to reporters thirsty for a scoop. Again, speculation and rumor can enter the media through comments made by unofficial spokespersons. And of course, employees will talk to friends and family about the crisis. The best defense against inappropriate employee comments is to keep employees informed. They should receive timely updates through a mix of the Intranet, mass notifications, and briefings. If employees understand the crisis, they can better articulate it to the media, friends, and family. The CMP and crisis training can help to avoid inconsistency.

Openness

The openness of an organization is a multifaceted concept. Openness means (a) availability to the media, (b) willingness to disclose information, and (c) honesty. *Availability* means that a spokesperson will answer inquiries in a timely fashion, immediately if the information is available. In a crisis, the focus is on the media, but other stakeholders may ask or demand that their questions be answered. Neighbors of a facility may want to know how a chemical leak might affect them, or investors might want to know the financial impact of the crisis. The foundation for availability should have been developed prior to the crisis. The organization should have a history of being responsive to the needs of stakeholders. During a crisis, this responsiveness takes the form of spokespersons or other crisis team members making every reasonable attempt to respond to questions promptly. Reasonableness is an important qualifier.

As I've mentioned, sometimes the situation does not allow for an immediate response. When delays are necessary, tell stakeholders why the question cannot be answered and when they might be able to expect a response (Stewart & Cash, 1997). Never let a request go unacknowledged, or you risk damaging the stakeholder–organization relationship. Communication with stakeholders is a two-way process. You must honor their requests if you expect them to accept the organization's messages.

A typical struggle in crisis management is between the legal perspective for limited disclosure of crisis-related-information and the public relations perspective for full disclosure (Fitzpatrick & Rubin, 1995; Kaufmann, Kesner, & Hazen, 1994; Twardy, 1994; Tyler, 1997). The choice actually is on a continuum between saying as little as possible (limited disclosure) or revealing everything the organization knows about the crisis (full disclosure). Cautious full disclosure is preached heavily in crisis management circles (Kaufmann et al., 1994). However, full disclosure is rarely always possible or advisable. Some crisis-related information may be proprietary, covered by privacy laws, involve company policies, or be sensitive. This means some information cannot be disseminated publicly. At other times, full disclosure could exacerbate a crisis by escalating the direct and indirect costs of litigation. Direct costs involve the amount of money awarded to plaintiffs while indirect costs include trial costs, personnel matters, lost work time, deaths, serious injuries, and possible regulatory changes (Kaufmann et al., 1994). Organizations must consider their responsibility to stockholders, creditors, and employees as well as to victims

(Tyler, 1997). Simply put, there are times when an organization must protect its financial assets. Crisis managers choose what level of disclosure to employ during a crisis.

The disclosure debate raises the question of honesty. A common recommendation for crisis managers is to be honest and not lie to stakeholders. Stakeholders are angrier when an organization lies about a crisis than when an organization has a crisis (Caruba, 1994). Limited disclosure—not revealing critical information—is not meant to be a form of deception. In fact, an organization should fully disclose any and all information about a crisis if there are risks of further harm or even death resulting from the crisis. Limited disclosure should not be used as a form of stonewalling. It should be used to disclose only the information stakeholders need to know. Of course, what stakeholders need to know is difficult to define, and each crisis management team should establish guidelines for when it will utilize full or limited disclosure. (See Kaufmann et al. (1994) and Tyler (1997) for discussions about the ethics and procedures for using limited disclosure.) Remember, lack of honesty seriously damages organizational-stakeholder relationships— destroys the organization's reputation—and can lead to massive monetary awards against the organization in future lawsuits (Fitzpatrick, 1995).

❖ CONTENT AND THE CRISIS RESPONSE

What is actually said during a crisis has serious ramifications for the success of the crisis management effort. As mentioned, key goals in the crisis management process are to prevent or minimize damage, maintain the organization's operations, and repair reputational damage. Clear communication is essential to each of these three goals. Crisis response content can be divided into three sequential categories: (1) instructing information, (2) adjusting information, and (3) reputation management. The first messages must present instructing information followed by adjusting information then reputation repair (Sturges, 1994). Again, clarity is a concern as emotions will reduce stakeholders' ability to process information.

Instructing Information

Instructing information focuses on telling stakeholders what to do to protect themselves physically in the crisis. People are the first priority in any crisis, so instructing information must come first. When a crisis hits, stakeholders want to know what happened, and they need to know how the crisis will or might affect them. Stakeholders should be told if there is anything they themselves need to do in order to protect themselves. Stakeholders may need to know to evacuate an area, find adequate shelter in-place, to boil drinking water, to go somewhere for assistance, or to return a defective product (Sturges, 1994). Instructing information satisfies the needs of both the stakeholders and the crisis team. The stakeholders receive the information they require to protect themselves; the crisis team cultivates the perception that the organization is once more in control of the situation.

Product harm and accidents illustrate the need for instructing information. Products can be defective and place the users at risk. Here's an example: In June of 2006, HP recalled the Firmware update program for its Photosmart R707 digital cameras. A defect in the Firmware caused single-use, nonrechargeable batteries to overheat and become a fire hazard when the AC power adapter or HP R-series docking station was used. The Firmware was unable to properly control battery charging, so an update was created and made available to consumers (Important safety, 2006). Here's another: On average, 40,000 people each year either must be evacuated or sheltered in place because of a chemical release (Kleindorfer, Freeman, & Lowe, 2000). In May of 2004, residents within a one-mile radius of a BioLab warehouse in Conyers, Georgia, were asked to evacuate. The evacuation was necessary because a fire at the warehouse released toxic smoke from burning pool treatment chemicals (Intense chemical, 2004).

Business continuity creates a second type of instructing information—how the crisis affects business operations. As noted in the crisis management plan discussion, business continuity plans outline what the organization will do to maintain operations and to restore business as usual. Various stakeholders must receive information about the implementation of the business continuity plan. For example, maintaining operations may involve renting equipment, using different facilities, and even hiring other employees. In terms of business continuity, this is known as *interim processing* (Myers, 1993). All the people and vendors necessary to get the interim processing phase up and running must be contacted and given specific instructions. Moreover, employees, suppliers, and distributors must know how the interim processing affects them. When and where do employees report to work? When and where are deliveries to be made? Is the supply chain disrupted, and if so, how long is it expected to be? These are critical questions that the crisis team must answer through instructing information.

Once business is restored to normal, the relevant stakeholders must be informed of the change as well (Myers, 1993).

At this point, the crisis team must consider connecting with employee assistance programs. Employees need to know such instructing information as how they will be paid during the crisis and how benefits information will be processed. Human resources people are important crisis team members when it comes to handling employee assistance concerns.

What Would You Do?

Diamond Pet Foods and Toxic Dog Food: Act 1

In late 2005, reports began to surface of dogs suffering from aflatoxin in their food and at least 76 dying from it. Aflatoxin is a fungus on corn that can damage a dog's liver. The Food and Drug Administration found that all of the stricken dogs were eating Diamond pet food. The company tests all corn shipments for aflatoxin and rejects shipments that test too high. Diamond Pet Foods has decided to recall the related dog food products. What type of instructing information would consumers need? What other messages would you include in your crisis response and why? What would you do to help make sure pet owners hear of this recall? What other groups might be willing to help get your message to owners?

Adjusting Information

Adjusting information responses help stakeholders cope psychologically with the crisis. Stress is created by the uncertainty and potential harm of a crisis. On a basic level, stakeholders need to know what happened: the what, when, where, why, and how information about the crisis (Ammerman, 1995; Bergman, 1994). Stakeholders are reassured when they know what happened. Moreover, stakeholders want information about what is being done to prevent a repeat of the crisis and to protect them from future crises. Communicating action taken to prevent a similar crisis is known as *corrective action*. Corrective action reduces psychological stress by reassuring stakeholders that their safety is a priority (Sellnow, Ulmer, & Snider, 1998). Stakeholders are reassured when they know the crisis situation is being controlled. Instructing information furthers the perception that the organization has regained control of the situation. It is desirable to present corrective action as early as possible in the crisis response. The limitation to corrective action is that it may take time to develop. The cause of a crisis may take weeks or months to uncover (Ray, 1999). Corrective actions cannot be developed until the cause is known. If an attempt is made without solid knowledge, it is speculating, and that violates a basic "Don't" of crisis communication. If crisis managers speculate and are wrong, they appear to be deceptive or incompetent.

A variation of corrective action is the *renewal response strategy*, which takes a positive approach to crisis communication. The focus is on rebuilding confidence and restoring the organization, not on assigning or averting blame (Seeger & Ulmer, 2001; Sellnow, Seeger, & Ulmer, 2002; Ulmer & Sellnow, 2002; Ulmer, Sellnow, & Seeger, 2006). Ulmer's (2001) study of Malden Mills's recovery from a devastating fire illustrated renewal. The owner, Aaron Feurstein, pledged to rebuild the mill and to pay workers until the mill was rebuilt. For renewal to work, the organization needs a favorable reputation, or the promises of renewal will ring hollow. The renewal pledge must be consistent with the organization's core values (Ulmer & Sellnow, 2002). Though limited as to when it can be employed, renewal can be a very powerful and positive crisis response.

Employee assistance programs are critical for adjusting information. Crises are traumatic incidents that can produce debilitating levels of stress. Traumatic stress incidents overwhelm a person's ability to cope. Seeing people injured or killed in accidents, workplace violence, or natural disasters all qualify as traumatic stress incidents. Immediate and long-term interventions, such as defusing and debriefing, may be necessary to help employees and perhaps other stakeholders to adjust properly. Defusing sessions are conducted immediately after the crisis and provide a framework to help people cope. Debriefing sessions are therapeutic interventions at the group or individual level. Any type of traumatic stress response should be handled by qualified professionals.

Crises have the potential to create an entirely new class of stakeholders: the victims. Victims are those people who have suffered physically, mentally, or financially from the crisis. For instance, employees may be injured in an industrial accident, customers may be traumatized by the violence in an accident, or investors may lose dividends due to the costs of a recall or a drop in stock prices. Victims expect an organization to express concern for them (Patel & Reinsch, 2003; Sen & Egelhoff, 1991). Expressing compassion does not mean an organization necessarily admits responsibility. Rather, the spokesperson expresses sympathy and concern for the victims. Sympathy can be expressed without incurring the liability associated with taking responsibility for a crisis (Fitzpatrick, 1995; Tyler, 1997). The key is that the expression of concern cannot include an overt statement accepting responsibility. However, lawyers may still try to use expressions of concern against an organization in court. Texas, California, Florida, and Massachusetts all have laws that prohibit statements of concern as being used as evidence to prove fault in civil cases (Cohen, 2002; Fuchs-Burnett, 2002). Expressions of concern do make victims feel better about the crisis and hold less animosity toward the organization (Cohen, 2002; Kellerman, 2006).

What Would You Do?

Bausch & Lomb and ReNu with MoistureLoc: Act 2

It is April 10, 2006, and the FDA and CDC have posted warning about Fusarium keratitis on their Web sites. The messages note that ReNu with MoistureLoc was used by 26 of 30 people interviewed about having infections. The messages also note that Bausch & Lomb has stopped producing and shipping ReNu with MoistureLoc and that investigations so far have shown no proof that the product causes the infection. At this point, there has been no recall of the product. However, large retailers, such as Wal-Mart, Walgreens, CVS, and Rite Aid, are pulling the product from their shelves. Bausch & Lomb tells people about stopping shipments, gives people the warning signs of a Fusarium keratitis infection, and reminds people to properly clean their contact lens. Messages from the American Optometric Association reinforce the Bausch & Lomb message by saying improper cleaning can lead to Fusarium keratitis. Do you agree that this is the right response from Bausch & Lomb? From the retailers? What do you like or dislike about the response from Bausch & Lomb? From the retailers?

A slight complication appears. The government and news media report that similar outbreaks of Fusarium keratitis hit Singapore and Hong Kong in November of 2006. Bausch & Lomb voluntarily suspended sales of ReNu with MoistureLoc in those countries. Does that change your response at all if you are Bausch & Lomb?

Reputation Management

Reputations are threatened during any crisis. Research in marketing and public relations has begun to explore how crisis response strategies can be used to protect a reputation during a crisis (Coombs & Holladay, 2004, 2005; Dean, 2004). The belief is that communication (words and actions) affects how stakeholders perceive the organization in crisis (Allen & Caillouet, 1994; Benoit, 1995, 1997; Hearit, 1994, 1996, 2001). A variety of crisis responses strategies have been identified by researchers (e.g., Allen & Caillouet, 1994; Benoit, 1995). The crisis situation is recognized as an important influence in the selection of the crisis response strategy (Benson, 1988; Bradford & Garrett, 1995; Coombs, 1995; Hobbs, 1995). The key is in knowing when to use a particular response strategy. The problem has been in understanding when to use a particular strategy for a specific crisis situation. Attribution theory has been offered as a useful framework for fitting the crisis response to the crisis situation (e.g., Bradford & Garrett, 1995; Coombs, 1995, 2004a; Dean, 2004).

The Situational Crisis Communication Theory (SCCT) is part of a growing body of research that applies attribution theory to crisis management (Ahluwalia, Burnkrant, & Unnava, 2000; Dawar & Pillutla, 2000; Dean, 2004; Folkes, Koletsky, & Graham, 1987; Härtel, McColl-Kennedy, & McDonald, 1998). In public relations, the SCCT has used attribution theory to develop and test a set of recommendations for using crisis response strategies. Attribution theory is premised on the belief that people assign responsibility for negative, unexpected events (Weiner, 1986). Clearly, crises are unexpected and negative, so they provoke attributions of responsibility. In turn, these attributions shape how a stakeholder feels and behaves toward the organization. SCCT utilizes attribution theory to evaluate the reputational threat posed by the crisis situation and then recommends crisis response strategies based upon the reputational threat level.

To appreciate the SCCT recommendations, we need to define a set of crisis response strategies and explain how the reputational threat posed by a crisis is assessed.

❖ CRISIS RESPONSE STRATEGIES

Crisis response strategies represent the actual responses an organization uses to address a crisis. As has been mentioned, communication has both verbal and nonverbal aspects. Hence, crisis response strategies involve the words (verbal aspects) and actions (nonverbal aspects) the organization directs toward the crisis (Allen & Caillouet, 1994; Benoit, 1995).

Crisis response strategies were first examined as apologia or the use of communication to defend one's reputation from public attack (Ware & Linkugel, 1973). Since crises threaten reputations, it was believed that organizations would use apologia to defend their reputations (Dionisopolous & Vibbert, 1988). A number of crisis critics have applied the apologia strategies or stances to understand how organizations defend their reputations during a crisis (Hearit, 1994, 1996, 2001, 2006; Hobbs, 1995; Ice, 1991).

But apologia offered a rather limited number of crisis response strategies, and a belief grew that strategies other than those found in apologia were being used in crisis responses. The number of crisis response strategies was expanded by examining the concept of *accounts*. Accounts are statements people use to explain their behavior when that behavior is called into question. A crisis response can be a form of account. Similar to apologia, accounts involve protecting one's reputation from a threat (Benoit, 1995).

Benoit (1995, 1997) has developed a list of 14 "image restoration strategies" based on apologia and account research. Allen and Caillouet (1994) used impression management and accounts to develop a list of 20 "impression management strategies" an organization might use. Impression management is based on the idea that communication can be used to strategically shape the public reputation of an organization. Organizations use the "impression management strategies," what I term *crisis response strategies*, to repair reputational damage from a crisis.

Trying to specify the exact number of crisis response strategies is a losing proposition (Benoit, 1995). A more productive approach is to identify the most common strategies and to organize them in some useful fashion. A list of 10 common crisis communication strategies was derived by selecting those that appeared on two or more lists developed by crisis experts. These 10 strategies are defined in Table 8.1.

SCCT organizes crisis response strategies by determining if the intent of the strategy is to change perceptions of the crisis or of the organization in crisis. The strategies have been grouped into four postures, clusters of strategies that stakeholders perceive as similar to one another (Coombs, 2006b), as shown in Table 8.1. The denial strategies seek to remove any connection between the crisis and the organization. An organization will not be affected by a crisis if it is not involved in or responsible for the crisis. The denial posture includes attacking the accuser, denial, and scapegoating strategies. The diminishment strategies attempt to reduce attributions of organizational control over the crisis or the negative effects of the crisis. If the attributions for control of the crisis are viewed less negatively, the reputational threat to the organization is reduced. The diminishment posture includes the excusing and justification strategies. The rebuilding strategies try to improve the organization's reputation. Words are said and actions are taken designed to benefit stakeholders and to offset the negative effects of the

Table 8.1   Crisis Response Strategies, by Postures

Denial Posture

Attacking the Accuser:	The crisis manager confronts the person or group that claims that a crisis exists. The response may include a threat to use force (e.g., a lawsuit) against the accuser.
Denial:	The crisis manager states that no crisis exists. The response may include explaining why there is no crisis.
Scapegoating:	Some other person or group outside of the organization is blamed for the crisis.

Diminishment Posture

Excusing:	The crisis manager tries to minimize the organization's responsibility for the crisis. The response can include denying any intention to do harm or claiming that the organization had no control of the events which led to the crisis.
Justification:	The crisis manager tries to minimize the perceived damage associated with the crisis. The response can include stating that there were no serious damages or injuries or claiming that the victims deserved what they received.

Rebuilding Posture

Compensation:	The organization provides money or other gifts to the victims.
Apology:	The crisis manager publicly states that the organization takes full responsibility for the crisis and asks forgiveness.

Bolstering Posture

Reminding:	The organization tells stakeholders about its past good works.
Ingratiation:	The organization praises stakeholders.
Victimage:	The organization explains how it too is a victim of the crisis.

---

crisis. The rebuilding strategies include compensation and full apology. Apology is a complicated response, so Box 8.1 provides additional details. The denial, diminishment, and rebuilding postures also represent varying degrees of accommodation, the amount of concern the response shows for victims. It reflects the amount of responsibility an organization is perceived to have accepted for the crisis (Coombs, 2006b).

Box 8.1   The Apology

Apology is the most complex and perhaps controversial of the crisis response strategies. It is critical to differentiate between full and partial responses. A full apology must acknowledge the crisis, accept responsibility, include a promise not to repeat the crisis, and express concern and regret (Kellerman, 2006). A partial apology is typically just an expression of concern and regret. Why the split? The answer is legal liability. Accepting responsibility results in organizations losing lawsuits related to the crisis. If an organization says it is responsible, it must pay in court. As noted earlier, the expression of concern or regret does not carry the same liabilities (Cohen, 2002). A person must be careful when using the term *apology*. That is why full apology is specified and treated as separate from an expression of concern.

The bolstering strategies are supplemental to the other three postures. The bolstering strategies also seek to build a positive connection between the organization and the stakeholders. This posture includes the reminding, ingratiation, and victimage strategies. These three strategies focus on the organization, so they would seem rather egocentric if used alone, which is why they are considered supplemental.

Evaluating Reputational Threat

Three factors are used in SCCT to evaluate the reputational threat presented by a crisis: crisis type, crisis history, and prior reputation. These three factors are applied in a two-step process. The first step is to determine the crisis type, the frame that is used to interpret the crisis (see Chapter 5 to review the list of crisis types or frames used in SCCT). Research has found that each crisis type creates predictable attributions of crisis responsibility among stakeholders (Coombs & Holladay, 2002). Table 8.2 organizes the frames according to the levels of crisis responsibility they evoke. The Victim cluster produces very little crisis responsibility for the organization. Stakeholders see the organization as a victim of the crisis, not the cause of the crisis. The Accident cluster produces low attributions of organizational crisis responsibility. The crises are seen as largely uncontrollable by the organization and unintentional.

Table 8.2   Crisis Types, by Level of Responsibility

Victim Cluster: Very little attribution of crisis responsibility

    Natural disasters
    Rumors
    Workplace violence
    Malevolence

Accidental Crisis Cluster: Low attribution of crisis responsibility

    Challenges
    Technical-error accidents
    Technical-error product harm

Preventable Crisis Cluster: Strong attributions of crisis responsibility

    Human-error accidents
    Human-error product harm
    Organizational misdeeds

The Preventable cluster produces very strong attributions of organizational crisis responsibility. The organization willfully engaged in behaviors that led to the crisis (Coombs, 2005; Coombs & Holladay, 2001).

Crisis responsibility can be a threat to an organization's reputation because stronger attributions of crisis responsibility produce greater reputational damage (Coombs, 2004b; Coombs & Holladay, 1996; 2004). To determine the crisis type, look to see what cues are present and being used to describe the crisis. Most crises will fall easily into one of the crisis types. If the crisis type is ambiguous, the crisis team can attempt to shape which frame is selected. However, it is possible that the crisis team and stakeholders may disagree on the crisis type. If this is the case, the crisis team should seriously consider adopting the stakeholder's frame.

The second step in assessing the reputational threat is to modify the initial assessment, based upon crisis history and prior reputation. If an organization has had similar crises in the past, the current crisis will be a much greater reputational threat (Coombs, 2004a; Coombs & Holladay, 2004). The crisis history compounding the threat of the current crisis is known as the Velcro effect (Coombs & Holladay, 2002; Klein & Dawar, 2004). Similarly, an unfavorable prior reputation intensifies the reputational threat as well (Coombs & Holladay, 2006).

Table 8.3   SCCT Recommendations for Crisis Response Selection

1. Provide instructing information to all victims or potential victims in the form of warnings and directions for protecting themselves from harm.
2. Provide adjusting information to victims by expressing concern for them and providing corrective action when possible.

   Note: Providing instructing and adjusting information is enough of a response for victim crises with no crisis history or unfavorable prior reputation.
3. Use diminishment strategies for accident crises when there is no crisis history or unfavorable prior reputation.
4. Use diminishment strategies for victim crises when there is a crisis history or unfavorable prior reputation.
5. Use rebuilding strategies for accident crises when there is a crisis history or unfavorable prior reputation.
6. Use rebuilding strategies for any preventable crisis.
7. Use denial strategies in rumor crises.
8. Use denial strategies in challenges when the challenge is unwarranted.
9. Use corrective action (adjusting information) in challenges when other stakeholders are likely to support the challenge.
10. Use reinforcing strategies as supplements to the other response strategies.
11. Victimage response strategy should only be used with the victim cluster.
12. To be consistent, do not mix denial strategies with either the diminishment or rebuilding strategies.
13. Diminishment and rebuilding strategies can be used in combination with one another.

So what does this really mean? If an organization has a history of crises or a negative prior reputation, stakeholders will treat a victim crisis like an accidental crisis and an accidental crisis like an intentional one. In turn, crisis managers must adjust which crisis response strategies to use (Coombs, 2006a; Coombs & Holladay, 2002).

Once the reputational threat is assessed, the crisis team selects the recommended crisis response strategy. SCCT posits that as the reputational threat increases, crisis teams should use more accommodative strategies. Research using nonvictim stakeholders has found support for the SCCT-recommended strategies (Coombs & Holladay, 1996; 2004). Table 8.3 lists the crisis response recommendations from SCCT.

It is important to understand how stakeholders perceive crises and crisis response strategies. SCCT takes an audience-centered approach to crisis communication, considering how stakeholders react to the crisis situation and crisis response strategies. SCCT goes far beyond the typical case study approach to crisis communication that many feel has limited the field's development (Ahluwalia et al., 2000; Coombs & Schmidt, 2000).

With the threat to lives and property presented by a crisis, a focus on reputation may seem shallow. SCCT acknowledges that people are the first priority in a crisis. Only after instructing and adjusting information is provided should crisis managers turn their attention to reputation concerns. Reputation protection is a valuable aspect of crisis communication. Organizations invest a substantial amount of money and effort into building reputations.

Effects of Credibility and Prior Reputation on Crisis Response Strategies

Two additional points must be considered when discussing the crisis response strategies because they affect their use: credibility and prior reputation. As noted previously, credibility is composed of expertise and trustworthiness. Expertise is the organization's knowledge about the subject. An expert organization will appear to be competent, capable, and effective (Kouzes & Posner, 1993). Trustworthiness is the organization's goodwill toward or concern for its stakeholders. A trustworthy organization is truthful and ethical and considers how its actions will affect its stakeholders (Allen & Caillouet, 1994; Kouzes & Posner, 1993).

Although not referred to directly, credibility is an underlying theme in much of the crisis management literature. Two common refrains noted by crisis experts are that an organization must (1) establish control during a crisis and (2) show compassion during a crisis (e.g., Carney & Jorden, 1993; Frank, 1994; Sen & Egelhoff, 1991). When examining what is meant by control and compassion, a strong similarity is found to the expertise and trustworthiness dimensions of credibility. Control includes having accurate and complete information about the crisis (Bergman, 1994; Caruba, 1994; Kempner, 1995). Having information shows that the organization is an expert about the crisis. Compassion means showing concern and sensitivity for those affected by the crisis (Higbee, 1992; Mitchell, 1986). Compassion is consistent with trustworthiness. People trust those who seem to have their own best interests in mind. Thus, crisis experts have indirectly argued the importance of credibility during crisis management.

Believability is essential during any type of crisis event because there always can be competing interpretations. For this reason, crisis experts repeatedly emphasize that an organization must get its side of the story or version of the crisis out quickly (e.g., Heath, 1994;

Kempner, 1995). However, this advice has a hidden premise—it is assumed that stakeholders will believe what the organization says. The importance of believability is heightened when the crisis hinges on the stakeholders choosing between competing versions of the crisis story. In some crises, the accepted version will determine the success of the crisis management effort and affect the amount of damage inflicted by the crisis. Challenges and rumors are two types of crises which rest on the selection of competing crisis stories (Lerbinger, 1997). A closer look at challenges and rumors will clarify the importance of credibility to crisis management.

A challenge occurs when a stakeholder calls an organization's actions into question. The stakeholder claims that the organization is acting in ways that are inappropriate. Other stakeholders must decide whether to accept the claim of wrongdoing or to accept the organization's claim that its actions are appropriate (Lerbinger, 1997). Challenges are marked by ambiguity; there are some reasons why both sides may be correct. The ambiguity stems from the challenges being based either on morals or questions of product or service quality. A moral challenge is tied to some set of moral principles, such as a code of conduct. The U.N. Global Compact that recommends universal social and environment principles for companies is an example of such a code. A moral challenge does not involve the violation of any law or regulation. What is violated is a set of standards some stakeholders believe the organization should adhere to. Some examples include not buying furs because of the inhumane treatment of animals or not buying oil from Nigeria because of the Nigerian government's human rights abuses. The potential for a moral challenge is great since the world is composed of many diverse groups with conflicting views of appropriate conduct. During a moral challenge, stakeholders support the side that is the most believable or credible to them.

A quality of product or service challenge derives its ambiguity from how the data that measure quality are interpreted or from competing data sets that lead to different conclusions about the product or service quality. The Audi 5000 sudden-acceleration case exemplifies the ambiguity that can be associated with interpreting quality data. For a number of years, Audi 5000 drivers reported that the car would suddenly jump into gear and run. Sometimes there were deadly consequences, when people were unlucky enough to be in a vehicle's path at the time of the jump. Many customers defined the situation as a quality problem, a fault in the design of the Audi 5000's transmission system. Audi maintained that there was no reliable evidence that the transmission was faulty. Instead, Audi blamed the incidents on bad drivers. No definitive evidence supported either story; it all depended on how one interpreted the events. Eventually the 5000 was recalled and an antilocking device installed. Audi still maintained there was no problem, but stakeholders, including potential car buyers, found the Audi customers to have the more believable and credible story (Versical, 1987). Unless there is a government action, such as a recall or a jury decision in a lawsuit, challenges based upon quality are resolved by stakeholders selecting the story they feel comes from the most credible source and acting accordingly.

Rumors represent another form of crisis where believability is essential. A rumor occurs when an untruthful statement about an organization is circulated. The Snapple Beverage Company was hit by rumors that it supported the Ku Klux Klan and that the label on its popular ice tea drink depicted a slave ship. The rumor was centered in San Francisco, and Snapple launched a costly media campaign to combat the rumor. The trigger for the rumor seemed to be the kosher mark that Snapple, like hundreds of other companies, placed on its bottles (Gellene, 1993). The charges were false, and the organization spent thousands of dollars to correct the lies. Rumor experts recommend that organizations respond immediately to rumors by stating that the information is untrue and unjust (Gross, 1990). Once more, a premium is placed on the credibility and believability of the organization. Defusing a rumor requires that the organization be perceived as a credible channel of information—the stakeholders must believe that the organization is a source of accurate information. The organization must be more credible than the rumor.

The benefit of credibility is that it increases the believability of an organization's message. The more credible the organization, the more likely stakeholders are to believe and to accept the organization's definition of the crisis, to believe the organization's side of the story. A second characteristic of a favorable precrisis organization–stakeholder relationship would be stakeholders viewing the organization as credible.

An organization's reputation overlaps with credibility but is considered a separate construct. An organization's prior reputation can be likened to a bank account (an organizational bank that contains reputational capital). A favorable reputation builds up the account while a crisis subtracts from the account. Under certain limited circumstances (Coombs & Holladay, 2006), a favorable reputation can act as a shield to protect an organization from harm. In most cases, however, a crisis will inflict reputational damage, the loss of reputational capital.

An organization with a favorable reputation can experience stakeholders ignoring bad news about the organization because they are unlikely to believe that a good organization did anything bad. Crises can be one of the forms of bad news that is deflected by a strong reputation. The disbelief gives the organization the benefit of doubt during the initial phases of a crisis, which provides two advantages. First, it supplies a buffer against people assuming the worst. In a crisis, the worst is when stakeholders believe the organization is responsible for the crisis. A strong account suffers less from the withdrawals of a crisis. A favorable precrisis reputation means that an organization has reputational capital to spend, unlike those that are unknown or disliked.

While most people are quick to believe the worst about organizations, a favorable reputation can lead stakeholders to believe the best. In turn, this means the stakeholders would not jump to negative conclusions about the crisis. This position would be reevaluated once the facts about the crisis begin to emerge. A favorable reputation may also afford protection from the negative speculation that crises often produce. Negative speculation refers to the nonexpert opinions that often fill the information void created by a crisis. Organizations are wise to respond immediately to prevent this void. However, negative speculation may come more quickly than the facts during a crisis (Carney & Jorden, 1993). The negative speculation feeds into people's willingness to assume the worst about organizations, particularly corporations. A favorable reputation counters the negative speculation and the willingness to believe the worst. A favorable reputation should lead stakeholders to discount the negative speculation and to believe the best about an organization until that belief is proven to be unfounded. The stakeholders are predisposed to wait to hear the organization's side of the story before drawing conclusions about the crisis. A strong, favorable, precrisis organization–stakeholder relationship shields the organization from undue reputational harm and makes it easier for the organization to deliver its side of the story.

❖ FOLLOW-UP COMMUNICATION

With all the emphasis on initial response, it is easy to overlook follow-up communication with stakeholders. But crisis communication should continue throughout the life cycle of the crisis. Crisis teams must stay in touch with stakeholders. While the initial response has a mass media emphasis, follow-up communication can be better targeted to individual stakeholders. Better targeting means using the channels best suited to reaching particular stakeholder and tailoring the message to fit their unique needs (Carney & Jorden, 1993; Clampitt, 1991;

Fombrun & Shanley, 1990). For instance, major investors may learn about a crisis from the news media. Follow-up communication to investors would center on their primary concern, the financial implications of the crisis, , and use either calls or specially printed updates from the investor relations department. The external stakeholder network from the Crisis Knowledge Map Directory is valuable at this point. As noted in Chapter 7, the external stakeholder network will have the necessary contact information and preferred channels for reaching the stakeholders.

In addition to answering new inquiries, follow-up communication involves delivering any promised information and updating the stakeholders about new developments. As noted earlier, there are times when crisis managers do not have answers to stakeholder questions and do best to promise to pass the information along as soon as they receive it (Stewart & Cash, 1997). It is essential that the crisis team fulfill these promises. The crisis team must report to the stakeholders, even if it is only to say that the information was never found. Credibility and organizational reputation are built on matching words and deeds (Herbig, Milewicz, & Golden, 1994). The crisis managers' words include their promises, and their actions fulfill those promises. An organization loses credibility and damages the organization–stakeholder relationships when crisis managers fail to deliver on their information promises.

Updates inform stakeholders about the progress of the crisis management effort. Four pieces of information are crucial to updates. First, let stakeholders know how the recovery effort is progressing. Second, announce the cause of the crisis as soon as it is known, if the cause was not known at the time of the initial message. Third, inform stakeholders of any actions taken to prevent a repeat of the crisis, including when those changes have been implemented. Fourth, report to stakeholders any third-party support your organization is receiving. Third-party support means that outside groups are praising your crisis management efforts or agreeing with your assessment of the situation. Examples include noted crisis experts giving the crisis management effort a positive review in the news media or the government saying the organization's stated cause of the crisis is correct. Supplying these four kinds of information builds the credibility of the organization. Items 1, 2, and 3 reinforce a perception of control, while Item 4 provides added credibility with the endorsement of an outside expert.

Three final points about follow-up communication must be made. First, the spokespersons and crisis team should continue to field and to respond to inquiries throughout the crisis. The crisis team must track and answer all inquiries. Second, the spokesperson should continue to express compassion in the follow-up communications. Losing sight of the victims in later messages can call the initial concern into question. Was the organization simply posturing in the news media? The organizational compassion must be real and be reflected in the follow-up communication. Follow-up includes both words and actions (Bergman, 1994; Mitchell, 1986). If aid is promised to victims, make sure it appears. Third, employee assistance programs should continue monitoring and treating negative reactions to the traumatic event. Once more, tracking crisis information is critical. The crisis team should be recording what follow-up actions were promised on the Stakeholder Relations Worksheets. Again, credibility is based on the organization's words matching its actions.

University Application: Stakeholders

Fires are one of the primary risks faced by universities. When you have buildings, they can catch fire. Seton Hall was hit by a deadly dorm fire in the late 1990s, and my own campus had a classroom building fire during class time. In a crisis, such as a building fire, who are the likely key stakeholders for your university? Does it matter if the fire is in a dorm or a classroom building? Why or why not? What options does the university have for contacting these stakeholders? What challenges would the university face in trying to communicate with these stakeholders?

❖ CONCLUSION

The actions taken in the crisis response phase are informed by the crisis-related information and knowledge gathered during the crisis recognition phase. The crisis team seeks to contain the damage and to return to business as usual as soon as possible. Communication is essential to limiting the duration of the crisis because it is at the heart of the initial response, reputational management, informing stakeholders, and providing follow-up information. The initial response allows the crisis team to reestablish a sense of organizational control over events and to express compassion for victims. Taking early control of the crisis prevents rumors and speculation from needlessly intensifying the crisis damage. Moreover, the response must be quick and consistent while the organization remains open to communication with stakeholders.

Crisis communication is ideal for combating the reputational damage associated with a crisis. Crisis response strategies affect how stakeholders perceive the crisis and the organization in crisis. In addition, the crisis itself limits the type of crisis response strategies that can be used effectively. Crisis managers should select the crisis response strategies that fit best with their particular crisis situation. SCCT provides guidelines, not absolute rules, to help crisis managers select the most effective responses for protecting reputational assets in a given crisis situation. The Business Continuity Plan allows an organization to function during a crisis and to return to business as usual more quickly. Crisis managers must communicate to relevant stakeholders how the continuity plan affects their interaction with the organization. In addition to the initial response, crisis managers have a variety of follow-up information they must communicate to stakeholders, including delivery of previously promised information and updates regarding the progress of the crisis management efforts. The ongoing organization– stakeholder dialogue continues throughout the crisis management process.

Regular, two-way communication between the organization and the stakeholder is the life blood of a favorable organizational-stakeholder relationship. The dialogue must be maintained during good times and bad. Crises are part of the bad times. Remembering the importance of communicating with stakeholders aids the crisis management team in its efforts to contain and to recover from the crisis.

❖ DISCUSSION QUESTIONS

1. What are the advantages and disadvantages of using full apologies during a crisis? Do you think partial apologies have any real value? Why or why not?

2. As a crisis manager, how can you prepare for using instructing and adjusting information prior to a crisis?

3. Why does attribution theory seem so fitting for crisis communication?

4. What other crisis types would you add to Table 8.2?

9

Postcrisis Concerns

E ventually, all crises come to an end: The immediate effects of the crisis are passed and the organization returns to business as usual. However, crisis managers should not feel that their work is completed when the crisis ends. First, it is critical that crisis managers evaluate their efforts. Organizations learn to improve their crisis management through evaluation. Second, crises must still be monitored after they are resolved. Monitoring might involve cooperating in continuing investigations or supplying necessary updated information to stakeholders.

This chapter begins by examining the role of evaluation in crisis management learning. The evaluation efforts link back to earlier crisis management steps, thus reflecting the ongoing nature of crisis management. Evaluation is the key to improvement. One way to improve the crisis management process is by learning what the organization did right or wrong during a crisis. Evaluation yields insights into the crisis management effort and should be treated as crisis management lessons. Because lessons should be remembered, the idea of institutional or organizational memory is discussed after evaluation. The chapter ends by reviewing the follow-up activities a crisis manager may need to perform and how the postcrisis actions naturally lead back to crisis preparation.

❖ CRISIS EVALUATION

An actual crisis is a "tremendous opportunity for learning" (Pauchant & Mitroff, 1992, p. 158). Learning is accomplished through evaluation of the crisis management efforts in two distinct ways. First, how the organization dealt with the crisis, its crisis management performance, is evaluated, examining the efficacy of the CMP and its execution (Barton, 2001). The crisis team carefully examines all phases of its performance. Second, the crisis impact is evaluated, a review of the actual damage created by the crisis (Sen & Egelhoff, 1991). A natural link exists between the two forms of evaluation. The actual crisis damage should be less than the anticipated crisis damage if the crisis management efforts were effective. Thus, damage assessments provide a tangible indicator of crisis management success or failure.

Crisis Management Performance Evaluation

Crisis management performance is primarily a function of the quality of the CMP and the crisis team's ability to make it work. Failure could result from an ineffectual CMP, poor execution of the CMP, or both (Mitroff et al., 1996). An organization must understand the source of failure or success if it is to learn from either. What lessons are learned if the organization does not know what it did well or poorly? Moreover, there are certain structural features (i.e., technology and infrastructure) that can facilitate or inhibit crisis performance (Mitroff et al., 1996). All facets of the crisis management performance must be assessed to determine strengths and weaknesses.

Data Collection

Data collection is the first step in any evaluation process. Evaluation data comes from the crisis records, stakeholder feedback, organizational performance measures, Internet comments, and media coverage. The various crisis records document vital information, such as the notification process, the collection and processing of information, the reception and answering of stakeholder queries, the crisis-related messages sent by the organization, and significant decisions and actions taken by the CMT. The primary sources of crisis documentation are the Incident Report Sheets, the CMT Strategy Worksheets, the Stakeholder Contact Worksheets, and the Information Log Sheets. The crisis records should be reviewed to determine if there were any noticeable mistakes made by the CMT. For example, was important information not processed, were stakeholder queries ignored, or were inappropriate messages sent to stakeholders? Again, administrative help during the crisis is essential in completing the paperwork that is used in the postcrisis analysis.

All stakeholder groups involved in the crisis can be asked for feedback, including employees and external stakeholders. The feedback can be collected by structured surveys, interviews, or focus groups. Simple surveys seem to be the most effective method. They minimize the time demands placed on the stakeholders and ensure that the evaluators receive the information they want. Typical questions on such a survey include the person's role in the crisis, level of satisfaction with and ways to improve notification, comments on specific strengths or weaknesses in the crisis management performance, and suggestions for improving the CMP (Barton, 2001). Different evaluation forms are required for the crisis team members, employees, and external stakeholders because the three groups have different connections to the crisis management process. Obviously, it is more difficult to secure the cooperation of external stakeholders, but every effort must be made to gather data that will provide a holistic picture of the crisis management performance. Media coverage and Internet comments are two other types of stakeholder feedback. The CMT should collect the media reports and Internet comments about the crisis. The CMT may choose to hire an independent consulting firm to collect the crisis performance data.

Organizing and Analyzing the Crisis Management Performance Data

Once collected, the data must be organized for the analysis. A danger in evaluation is not performing a specific analysis. For crisis management, an overall "good" or "poor" performance evaluation would be too general. Specificity is the key to useful evaluation. Specify in detail what was done well and done poorly. The specifics tell organization evaluators what changes need to be made and what must be retained. Mitroff et al. (1996) provided a number of helpful suggestions for organizing and analyzing the crisis evaluation data. Mitroff suggested using four major crisis variables: crisis type, crisis phases, systems, and stakeholders. The four variables divide the evaluation data into small, discernible units. The crisis managers can target strengths and weaknesses more precisely when data are divided, a form of data splitting. The value of Mitroff's approach becomes clearer when the application of the specific crisis variables is considered.

Organizations face many different types of crises. Crisis teams may not handle all crises equally well. Crisis managers will want to compare evaluations from different crisis types to ascertain if there are patterns of strengths and weaknesses that are crisis specific (Mitroff et al., 1996; Pearson & Mitroff, 1993). Categorizing evaluations by crisis type permits cross-comparisons, which is one form of analysis.

As has been discussed earlier, crises move through distinct phases. Crisis management has been organized around three phases with each having subphases. Crisis teams may handle the phases and subphases with different degrees of success and failure. For instance, it may be adept at finding information but have problems articulating the organizational crisis response. Dividing the crisis evaluation data by crisis phases and subphases can help identify if the crisis team or CMP (or both) is weak in a particular part of the cycle. The crisis team could work on the skills associated with that segment, and the CMP could be revised to improve preparation for that target. Only by dividing evaluation data according to phases and subphases can the analysis reveal these types of specific strengths and weaknesses.

Systems include technology, human factors, infrastructure, culture, and emotions and beliefs. Technical systems organize the company's work and would include specific tasks along with the tools and materials necessary to complete them. Evaluators might ask, "Was the CMT hampered by lack of technical system support for crisis management?" The human factor system is the integration of people and machinery. It examines the fit between people and technology. Evaluators might ask, "Were the crisis management problems a function of a poor match between people and technology?"

Infrastructure refers to the connection of the crisis management team to the functioning of the organization. A permanent CMT should exist and be integrated into the operation of the organization. Some organizations may choose to use software programs designed to organize and facilitate the flow of crisis communication. One such program is Public Information & Emergency Response (PIER). A human factors evaluation would examine the fit between PIER and the crisis team. Evaluators might ask, "Did the CMT fail because it is not considered a functioning part of the organization?"

The cultural system refers to the extent to which the organization is oriented toward crisis preparation. Evaluators might ask, "Were the problems a function of cultural constraints, such as suppressing bad news?" Last, the emotional and belief system represents the dominant coalition's mindset about crisis management. Evaluators might ask, "Did the crisis management effort fail because the dominant coalition does not support crisis preparation or the crisis response?" The examination of system-specific concerns helps to determine if the crisis management performance might have been a function of structural factors rather than the CMP or the CMT (Mitroff et al., 1996).

The system variables reflect the ongoing nature of crisis management as well, since the evaluation of system variables is most appropriate during the preparation phase. An organization can and should identify system flaws before a crisis hits. However, sometimes the flaws are hidden and do not surface until an actual crisis occurs. For example, the dominant coalition may espouse support for crisis management until there is a crisis. Then their support may evaporate. Or the stress of the crisis management process may create unexpected problems in how people utilize technology.

Reactions from all stakeholders affected by the particular crisis are useful for a thorough evaluation. How did they feel about the crisis management performance? The only way to assess stakeholder reactions is to ask them. A cardinal rule in evaluation is to not assume you know how people feel about a message or action. By considering each stakeholder separately, an organization can determine specific strengths and weaknesses. The evaluators can determine which actions were effective or ineffective for specific stakeholder groups. For example, investors might be happy with the information given and how they received it, while the community may be disappointed with how they received their crisis-related information. Specific stakeholder reactions also will indicate which parts of the stakeholder network are effective or ineffective during crisis management.

Regardless of how the data are divided, the key is to identify the specific strengths and weaknesses of the crisis management plan, the performance of crisis management team, and structural features of the organization. Evaluations that are too general serve little purpose if the goal is to improve crisis management performance. The crisis management plan should be revised by building on the strengths and developing ways to correct the weaknesses.

Crisis team members must be evaluated for both individual-level and group-level factors. As noted in Chapter 5, certain knowledge, skills, and traits are helpful in a crisis team member. In addition, the crisis team must perform as a group. Thus, the group-level factors, such as group decision making, are relevant during evaluation. The crisis management evaluation data should yield assessments of how individual team members performed as well as how the team as a whole performed.

Impact Evaluation

The crisis management performance should help the organization by protecting it from damage in some way. Crisis management is designed to protect important organizational assets such as people, reputation, and financial concerns (Barton, 2001; Marcus & Goodman, 1991). The crisis management performance evaluation should include measures of damage factors that reflect success or failure in protecting these assets. The damage factors include financial, reputational, human, secondary financial, Internet frames, media frames, and media coverage duration. The financial factors are fairly standard: earnings per share, stock prices, sales, and market share (Baucus & Baucus, 1997; Baucus & Near, 1991; Sen & Egelhoff, 1991).

The reputational factors involve perceptions of the organization. Three related elements are relevant to assessing crisis effects on reputation: (1) the pre- and postcrisis reputation scores, (2) media and Internet coverage of the crisis, and (3) stakeholder feedback. Any organization that expends resources on managing its reputation should make the effort to track its reputation over time. The organization should assess its reputation on a regular basis by soliciting evaluations from stakeholders. Comparing pre- and postcrisis organizational reputations is the strongest indicator of the reputational impact of a crisis.

To reiterate, reputations are built from direct and indirect stakeholder experiences with the organization. During a crisis, stakeholders experience an organization through the media, the Internet, and its crisis management actions. The media portrayals of the organization and the crisis can be critical in shaping the perceptions of other stakeholders involved in the crisis (Fearn-Banks, 2001; Pearson & Clair, 1998). Stories of an uncaring organization in disarray erode a reputation and injure the stakeholder–organization relationship. The media's power intensifies when it is the primary channel for reaching stakeholders. The media stories become the central crisis experiences when stakeholders have no other contact with the organization and are dependent on the media for information. Experts believe stakeholder crisis evaluations will reflect the media depictions. Thus, if the media are critical of the organization, its reputation with stakeholders could suffer. Conversely, the reputation would be protected by favorable media portrayals (Nelkin, 1988). With the growing use of the Internet for crisis information, the Internet coverage of a crisis is important for the same reasons. Most stakeholders, especially those who are not victims, are most likely to experience the crisis through some combination of the news media and the Internet.

Organizations should use standard publicity analysis techniques to evaluate crisis coverage in the news and the Internet. Analysts can examine the media and Internet reports for positive and negative statements about the organization. To preserve important details, the positive and negative statements should be grouped by subphase to indicate precisely where the crisis managers were perceived as doing something good or bad.

Media and Internet coverage is an imprecise substitute for actual measures of reputation. Stakeholders do not always absorb and parrot impressions from the news media or Internet. The news media and Internet are not all-powerful. Stakeholders may disagree with the media reports, especially if the reports run counter to their perceptions of the organization.

Skilled crisis managers communicate to stakeholders through channels other than the news media and Internet, such as telephone, direct mail, or e-mail. A well-developed stakeholder network provides the foundation for more direct contact with stakeholders. Thus, assessing stakeholder satisfaction with the crisis management performance is critical. As noted previously, external feedback from stakeholders should be part of any crisis management performance evaluation. Negative feedback suggests there will be reputational damage because stakeholders perceive the crisis as mishandled. Conversely, positive feedback indicates that the CMT's good work might help to protect the reputation. Stakeholder evaluations have limitations when used to evaluate reputations; they are an imprecise substitute for actual reputation measures. As with the media and Internet coverage, other factors are at work. Media analysis, Internet analysis, and stakeholder feedback provide crude reputational indices but are useful when direct measures of reputation are lacking.

Human factors focus on victims, including deaths, injuries, disruptions (e.g., evacuations or changes in daily routines caused by the crisis), and environmental damage. Injuries, death, and disruptions can be recorded for quantity and severity for injuries and disruptions. Environmental damage is included with human factors because injuries and deaths are often associated with it, even though the victims are animals and plants in this case. Perhaps crisis management has no higher priority than to protect the human factors. Secondary financial factors are a reminder of the crisis because they continue to drain financial resources. These include lawsuits (number and total value) and new regulations. A large number of lawsuits or an expensive few drain an organization's financial resources. Court costs are a burden on top of any financial settlements. The litigation costs help to explain why some organizations settle lawsuits out of court while professing innocence and stating that the settlement was necessary to end the costly litigation process. MetPath Inc., a leading medical testing laboratory, paid $35 million to settle fraud charges while maintaining it did nothing wrong. The new regulations are actions the government takes in response to a crisis. For example, the government may enact regulations to prevent a repeat of a crisis. The U.S. government considered banning the use of capsules for over-the-counter medications after the Sudafed and second Tylenol tamperings. Compliance with new regulations can create a financial impact that lasts for years (Sen & Egelhoff, 1991).

Media frames refer to the success of placing the organization's side of the story in the media. The organization's side of the story involves accurate information about what happened in the crisis, the organization's response, and the organization's interpretation of the crisis. Analysts search for evidence markers of the organization's side of the story in the media reports. These include quotations from organizational spokespersons, media use of organizational sound bites, and accurate descriptions of the crisis event. Media frame success is measured two ways. First is a comparison of the amount of organizational frame material versus counter-frame materials in the media coverage. For instance, who was quoted more by the media, the organization or its critics? Second is the accuracy of the crisis-related information appearing in the media. The higher the percentage of information the organization considers accurate, the more successful its media frame efforts. The same holds true for the frames that appear in Internet reports of the crisis.

The duration of the crisis' media coverage is the final evaluative point. Effective crisis management tries to move a crisis out of the media (Higbee, 1992). A crisis moves out of the media by becoming uninteresting and losing its newsworthiness. Effective crisis management seeks to inform stakeholders and to bring closure to a crisis. Both actions reduce newsworthiness. The information vacuum created by a crisis makes it newsworthy. Once stakeholders have the facts, particularly the cause of the crisis, audience curiosity and interest fades. When actions indicate that a crisis is over, such as repaired damage or a return to normal operations, the situation loses the news value of being unusual. Conversely, crisis management errors, such as instigating conflict, prolong media coverage by sustaining the newsworthiness of a crisis. Two cases illustrate the relationship between newsworthiness and media coverage.

In May of 1985, E. F. Hutton officials pleaded guilty to 2,000 counts of wire and mail fraud and paid a $2 million fine. The story attracted mild media attention as people wondered what had happened at this high profile investment firm. In September of 1985, E. F. Hutton officials announced the results of former Attorney General Griffin Bell's investigation of the case. Bell had been hired by E. F. Hutton to find the cause of the crisis and to provide corrective measures. E. F. Hutton fired 14 executives criticized in the report and pledged to institute other reforms designed to prevent a repeat of the crisis (Koepp, 1985). The media quickly lost interest after the report was issued. Penalties had been paid, guilt admitted, the "why" question answered, and E. F. Hutton was working to prevent a repeat of the crisis. The crisis appeared resolved, stripping it of any newsworthiness.

In April of 1996, the Equal Employment Opportunity Commission (EEOC) filed a major sexual harassment lawsuit against Mitsubishi Motor Manufacturing of America Inc. Mitsubishi denied the charges and began a series of attacks against the EEOC. The response was deemed hostile by many observers and was highlighted by a media event when about 2,900 Mitsubishi workers demonstrated at EEOC offices in Chicago. Technically, the protest was organized by workers. However, Mitsubishi played a major role in facilitating the demonstration by allowing time off and helping to arrange bus transportation to Chicago (Annen & McCormick, 1997). The verbal barbs aimed at the EEOC and the litigation continued through 1997, as did the negative media coverage. When Mitsubishi's consultant, former Labor Secretary Lynn Martin, released a report on improving the workplace, the media greeted the announcement with skepticism and the crisis remained alive. The Mitsubishi–EEOC conflict kept the story alive by making it newsworthy. Crisis managers should try to reduce, not increase, the newsworthiness of a crisis. A CMT has erred when its actions prolong media coverage of the crisis.

An assessment of the financial, reputational, human, secondary financial, media and Internet frame, and media duration factors enable you to measure the final impact of the crisis. But how does this help with the evaluation of crisis management performance? Alone, these factors do not evaluate crisis performance. They simply describe the impact of the crisis. What crisis managers must do is compare the outcome to (a) the projections made about what the impact would have been if no actions were taken to manage the crisis and (b) the desired objectives of the crisis management team. While speculation is involved in both cases, careful projections can be made. Similar procedures are used in evaluating issues management efforts (Jones & Chase, 1979). Honesty is important. The CMT must not inflate the potential damage or low-ball their objectives if the exercise is to be meaningful. What the damage assessment provides is some "objective" verification that the effect of the crisis performance was positive, negative, or of no consequence to the organization.

Evaluation Summary

All of the various crisis performance data and analysis should be condensed into a final report, complete with an executive summary and recommendations. Remember, the purposes are learning and improving crisis performance, not placing blame. Once completed, the evaluation indicates (a) if the CMT did what it should have done and did so effectively, (b) if the CMP proved useful in anticipating and resolving situations created by the crisis, (c) if structural features facilitated or hindered the crisis management effort, and (d) the crisis damage. Combined, this evaluation identifies specific strengths and weaknesses of the CMT, the CMP, and the organization. Furthermore, the inclusion of damage analyses indicates if a crisis management performance is deemed successful. Sometimes a crisis team can execute a CMP well but still face massive damage, or a team can perform a suspect plan poorly yet the organization suffers little damage. For example, Johnson & Johnson had no CMP when it successfully managed the 1982 Tylenol tampering. There are exceptions to all rules, but crisis managers should not count on luck. It is much wiser to prepare.

❖ INSTITUTIONAL OR ORGANIZATIONAL MEMORY

As mentioned, analysis creates crisis lessons. But what use are crisis lessons if they cannot be recalled to help prevent a repeat of a mistake or to recreate a success? Remembering and recall are the domains of institutional or organizational memory (Pearson & Mitroff, 1993).

Knowledge management favors the term *organizational memory* as the repository of organizational knowledge (Li, YeZhuang, & Ying, 2004). Like people, organizations can store information and knowledge for later use (Weick, 1979). A crisis should not be wasted. "Direct experience with a crisis, although painful, teaches more than even the best scenario ever could" (Newsom, VanSlyke Turk, & Kruckeberg, 1996, p. 544). Evaluation reveals the lessons that hard experience teaches to the organization. And the crisis lessons must be remembered by becoming a part of institutional memory.

Effectively using institutional or organizational memory involves storage and retrieval (Li et al., 2004; Weick, 1979). First, there must be some means of recording and storing the crisis knowledge: the crisis documentation and the evaluation report, the crisis lessons. Storage options include hard copies and computer files. Either means requires redundancy and storage at multiple locations (Pauchant & Mitroff, 1992). Not all crisis information and knowledge are of the same quality. Some knowledge is more accurate—more fact than speculation—and more comprehensive—more complete and containing fewer potential errors (Garvin, 1996). Storage is more than recording knowledge; it also involves rating key crisis information for accuracy and comprehensiveness. The Intranet is a logical place to store crisis knowledge for easy retrieval.

The crisis knowledge must be easy to retrieve for later use. Retrieval involves being able to search and to locate specific details (Weick, 1979). Intranet systems can use their own search mechanisms. Careful organization and input of the crisis knowledge will permit easy searches and retrieval during later crisis management efforts. Again, recording is not a simple process. The crisis knowledge must be carefully and accurately stored if it is to be useful. Each organization must develop its own system for organizing crisis knowledge into a format that is searchable and retrievable.

Organizational memory requires one word of warning—do not become a slave to memory (Weick, 1979). Crisis managers must be willing to disregard past actions and knowledge if they do not fit well with a current crisis. Blindly following past successes can lead to blunders when the past crisis is not wholly consistent with the current crisis. Organizational memory of crises can help to create an information acquisition bias. The memory of past crises is both a blessing and a curse. However, the skilled crisis management team should be able to overcome the blind spot of information acquisition bias.

What Would You Do?

BP and Texas City: Act 3

It is now three days since the initial blast at Texas City. The news media has been running stories about other accidents at the Texas City plant. One story announces that BP has the worst safety record in the petrochemical industry. A total of 15 people have been killed and over 100 injured. Twelve of the injured are still hospitalized. The U.S. Chemical Safety and Hazard Investigation Board (CSB) investigation team is on site. The CSB is there to determine the cause of the blast. The CSB notes that key alarms were not working and that the startup was done even though important parts of the system were not working properly. Also, BP had not connected the damaged tower to a safety flare system. A recommendation to change the safety system had been made well before the accident, and BP management's own documents show that they were aware of the recommendation. What can you do to help craft an effective response to this crisis? What should BP be saying and doing now?

❖ POSTCRISIS ACTIONS

The responsibility of the crisis team continues until all crisis-related obligations are fulfilled. The postcrisis tasks can be divided into three groups: follow-up communication, cooperation with investigations, and crisis tracking. Even though the organization has returned to normal operations and the immediate effects have dissipated, the cause of the crisis may still be under investigation by government officials. The crisis team must be sure it cooperates with any investigation. Cooperation builds goodwill with the government agencies involved and indicates to other stakeholders that the organization is open and honest. Openness leads to the topic of follow-up communication.

Follow-up communication is an extension of the crisis recovery phase. Crisis managers maintain positive organizational–stakeholder relationships by keeping stakeholders informed about the crisis even when it is over and by continuing to answer new inquiries. Employee assistance efforts must continue as well, to help those overwhelmed by the trauma of the crisis. Crisis managers should update the stakeholders on the progress and results of ongoing investigations and the actions being taken to prevent a repeat of the crisis. In regards to preventing future crises, crisis managers might tell stakeholders when the changes have been completed and how well the changes are working. The changes actually become a part of the crisis prevention subphase, since the actions are designed to prevent future crises.

Any crisis must be monitored when it is over, even if no changes are initiated. Crisis tracking monitors the factors that produced the crisis to see if another threat may arise. Crisis tracking feeds back into signal detection and crisis preparation. Simply put, the postcrisis phase ends with crisis managers moving back to the actions involved in the precrisis phase of crisis management; the process is ongoing.

What Would You Do?

Diamond Pet Foods and Toxic Dog Food: Act 2

You are still actively recalling your product when a second problem arises. Some smaller news outlets are reporting that Diamond Pet Foods knew there was aflatoxin in the corn but used it anyway. The stories imply that your company knowingly put dogs at risk. There is no evidence to support this story, though it could be a result of Diamond Pet Foods management saying they did see high levels of aflatoxin being found in 2005 corn shipments. However, all shipments were tested as per company regulations, and problematic shipments were rejected. Does your company need to address this new concern? Why? If you decide that action is necessary, how will you address this new concern?

❖ CONCLUSION

Even when a crisis is perceived to be over, the efforts of the crisis management process remain in motion. The crisis management performance must be evaluated. Careful evaluation is essential to improved crisis management performance. The downside is that a thorough evaluation is time consuming and somewhat painful. Still, the rewards more than justify the expenditure of resources. Evaluation and crisis documentation should become a part of the functional institutional or organizational memory. A well-organized recording of crisis knowledge will allow the knowledge to be used effectively during future crisis management efforts. Last, the crisis team must help any continuing investigations, maintain the flow of follow-up information to stakeholders, and continue to track the crisis. In so doing, the crisis team has a natural segue back to the precrisis phase of crisis management, showing that crisis management can be an ongoing process.

❖ DISCUSSION QUESTIONS

1. How often do you feel key stakeholders should be updated with postcrisis information?

2. How can crisis logs help to make the postcrisis updates more effective?

3. What is the danger of having an organizational crisis memory?

4. What are some of the barriers you would face when conducting a postcrisis evaluation? How might you overcome those barriers?

10

Final Observations and Lessons

Here at the end of the book, I would like to highlight four very valuable lessons. One, crisis management is not a simple collection of various actions relevant only during a training drill or actual crisis. Rather, crisis management is an ongoing process of intricate, interwoven steps. Two, specific knowledge, skills, and traits are associated with effective crisis managers. Selection and training of crisis personnel should seek to maximize those knowledge, skills, and traits. Three, crisis management involves the development and maintenance of procedures designed to improve the flow of information and knowledge before, during, and after a crisis. Four, new technologies should be integrated into the crisis management process. Reviewing each of the four lessons reinforces the utility of the continuous crisis management approach to practitioners, researchers, and educators.

❖ CRISIS MANAGEMENT IS ONGOING

The call for crisis preparedness is the initial and continuing message delivered by crisis management advocates. As of 2005, just 60% of all major organizations had crisis management plans. It has been found that those that have plans do little in terms of exercises and crisis team training (AMA, 2005). There is a danger in mistaking crisis preparation for crisis management. Some organizations develop an unwarranted sense of security when they have completed their crisis preparation. Having a CMP, crisis team, crisis portfolio, and crisis communication system in place is but one stage in a larger process. Failure to appreciate the larger process prevents an organization from deriving the complete benefits from a crisis management program. Crisis management must become part of an organization's DNA (Coombs, 2006a).

Furthermore, crisis management must be viewed as a daily effort, not just as an as-needed concern. Crisis prevention best illustrates the daily nature of crisis management. New information from the crisis-sensing network must be processed and evaluated each day. In addition, current efforts to prevent crises, such as risk reduction, must be implemented and their effects monitored regularly. Even crisis preparation should not be stagnant. Organizations should routinely test and revise the various elements of crisis preparation. Revisions would include updating the CMP, upgrading or teaching new skills to the crisis management team, reassessing the crisis portfolio, and improving the crisis communication system. Because organizations, their personnel, the environment, and technology constantly change, the elements of crisis preparation also must change. Practice and going through actual crises provide the data for evaluating crisis management performance. The evaluation guides the revisions to crisis preparation and prevention. Furthermore, the follow-up from an actual crisis segues back to crisis prevention. Crisis management is not a limited resource that is drawn upon only during real or simulated crises. Instead, crisis management should be a daily activity performed by a distinct crisis management unit within the organization.

An organization should dedicate some personnel to crisis management on a full-time basis. While the crisis management team can be valuable operating as an ad hoc unit during a crisis, at least one person needs to monitor the everyday demands of the crisis management process.

Researchers can locate their work within the larger framework of the crisis management process. The contextualization helps researchers to develop links between their specific areas of crisis management study and the entire crisis management process. For instance, those studying crisis communication strategies focus on actions taken during the crisis event stage. Those researchers can explore more fully how their results might inform either the crisis preparation or crisis evaluation phases. Lessons about crisis communication can enhance preparation by establishing precrisis communication guidelines and aid in the follow-up communication required during the postcrisis phase.

Educators can structure their crisis management teaching around the three stages of the ongoing approach. Students would be taught the value of each stage, the tools necessary to develop each stage, and the importance of integrating the stages.

❖ KNOWLEDGE, SKILLS, AND TRAITS

The selection and training of crisis team members are generally rather primitive. In most organizations, crisis team selection is based almost exclusively on a person's functional position within an organization. As discussed in Chapter 5, the crisis team membership should indeed reflect key areas in the organization, such as operations, public relations, legal, and security (Littlejohn, 1983; Regester, 1989), and members should also be selected according to particular personal qualities. Team members need to be trained to execute the crisis management plan, a group-level skill. The spokespersons need to be selected for their knowledge base and media skills. Spokesperson training should emphasize practice media sessions—being asked questions in a mock press conference. Chapter 5 relates the merits and limitations of these practices. The value of improving the current selection and training of crisis teams warrants further attention.

Crisis Teams

An effective crisis team is critical to the success of the crisis management process. The best CMP and communication systems are of little value when used improperly. A fitting analogy is a state-of-the-art manufacturing facility being operated by poorly trained workers. No matter how good the equipment might be, the actual process and end product quality is poor because the workers do not know how to maximize the value of the equipment. The selection and training of crisis team members must seek to maximize the knowledge, skills, and traits that facilitate group performance. Decision-making effectiveness should be at the heart of the selection and training process. Crisis teams should be equipped for success through training on essential knowledge and skills, such as group decision making, conflict resolution, structuring arguments, listening skills, and managing stress.

Selection is another means for improving crisis team performance. Certain personality traits can help or hinder the team's functioning. The relevant traits identified in Chapter 5 include low group communication apprehension, a cooperative orientation, high tolerance for ambiguity, at least moderate argumentativeness, and low verbal aggressiveness. The value of these traits becomes apparent in the stress, communication demands, and conflicts that are natural in the work of a crisis team.

In an ideal world, crisis team members would be selected through a combination of trait evaluation and functional area. Each functional area would identify a pool of potential candidates for the crisis team. A trait assessment instrument would be given to all potential team members. The people with the most favorable profiles would be selected to represent their functional area on the crisis management team. Not all selection can be done in this fashion. However, trait assessment is beneficial, even when it is not used as grounds for selection.

One benefit of trait assessment is that it provides crisis team leaders with a more complete picture of their team members. Leaders can benefit from knowing about the strengths and weaknesses of each team member. For instance, what if the team member from operations has high group communication anxiety? The team leader must work to solicit input from the operations representative. Or say the team member from the legal department is high in verbal aggression. The team leader must monitor the legal representative to prevent personal attacks and the destructive use of conflict in the crisis team. A second benefit is that team members have a better understanding of their own strengths and weaknesses. Programs can be developed to help team members cope with limiting traits. The best examples are the programs developed to reduce communication apprehension. There are limits to these program—they cannot be expected to produce huge changes in all traits. Still, self-awareness is a powerful tool for people trying to work through their own limitations.

Spokespersons

The spokesperson is a special member of the CTM. The selection and training of spokespersons is more developed than is the case for general team selection and training. Spokespersons are frequently chosen in part because they have proven to be effective in dealing with the media. The proof might come from practice or from past actual experiences with the media. However, functional knowledge can also be a driving force for spokesperson selection. The media may want to question someone with direct knowledge of a particular subject. An environmental crisis demands an expert from the environmental unit while a production accident may require an operations expert from the manufacturing unit. As noted in Chapter 5, an organization must train a number of potential spokespersons to meet with the media.

It would be unfair to expect training to transform all spokespersons into dynamic, charismatic speakers. Not everyone will reach high levels of delivery proficiency. The goal should be to develop a set of core delivery competencies consisting of making eye contact with the audience at least 60% of the time, minimal fidgeting, minimal verbal disfluencies, varied vocal qualities, using hand gestures, and having an expressive face. The emphasis is placed on eliminating the negative delivery elements that foster perceptions of deception. Reducing the negative delivery factors will naturally expand the positive delivery factors that build credibility. Not everyone can become a dynamic speaker but all should be trainable to not look like they are lying.

The discussion of the knowledge, skills, and traits of crisis team members should help practitioners to develop more effective crisis teams. Specific ideas are provided for improving both the selection and training of crisis team members. These suggestions include screening tests for traits, developing crisis team training procedures, and assessing crisis team performance on a variety of individual-level skills, as well as group-level skills. Combined, the ideas should help to produce crisis teams that are well equipped and trained for the task. The same holds true for spokesperson training. A suggestion offered for expanding the media training is to include more delivery skills.

Researchers can find new avenues of inquiry embedded in the discussion of knowledge, skills, and traits. People have just begun to explore the actual functioning of crisis teams and the effectiveness of crisis spokespersons (e.g., William & Olaniran, 1994). The ideas for improving crisis teams and spokespersons are based on the small-group and public speaking research. While the ideas should be applicable, most have yet to be tested.

The knowledge, skills, and trait discussions offer educators specific topics and skills that should be taught to students. For instance, a crisis management course benefits from the inclusion of topics concerning small-group decision making and public speaking. The knowledge base for decision making and public speaking would be provided along with opportunities to practice skills and be evaluated on the performance of small-group decision making and delivery.

❖ CRISIS MANAGEMENT PROCEDURES

In presenting an ongoing approach, a number of procedures were developed to facilitate the crisis management process. The crisis-sensing network deserves special attention along with the value of public relations.

Crisis-Sensing Mechanism

The bulk of the crisis management writings focus on either the CMP (e.g., Katz, 1987) or how to respond to a crisis (e.g., Siomkos & Shrivastava, 1993). Both are critical subjects that any crisis manager should master. A danger develops as crisis mangers focus on the later stages of the crisis management process and devote insufficient attention to looking for potential crises. A well-rounded crisis management program divides attention equally between the precrisis, crisis event, and postcrisis stages.

The crisis-sensing mechanism operates every day as organizational units scan the environment and internal operations for potential crises. Whether the information is related to developing issues, risk, or relationship problems with stakeholders, crisis managers seek to locate and defuse potential crisis situations. The ongoing need to scan for crises reinforces the belief that crisis management is a full-time function. Furthermore, the way postcrisis monitoring of a crisis flows back into the crisis-sensing mechanism emphasizes the continuity between the various crisis management stages and substages. The continuous nature of crisis management is revealed in both its daily operation and the connection between its stages.

The crisis-sensing mechanism underscores the need to integrate organizational units. No one organizational unit monitors all the various sources that might reveal a crisis. Diverse information about external political and social issues, production, product safety, transportation, regulatory compliance, insurance risks, and customer complaints are just a part of the crisis-sensing mechanism. To operate effectively, the crisis management unit must receive timely information from all of the other organizational units collecting data relevant to crises. Without the integration of the various scanning mechanisms into the crisis-sensing mechanism, the crisis managers cannot be as effective in crisis detection and prevention as they should be. Integration demands that other organization units respect and cooperate with those assigned the task of crisis management.

Value to and of Public Relations Personnel

When we think about public relations and crises, the term *media relations* immediately comes to mind. Crisis management affords people in public relations an opportunity to move beyond media relations and into the dominant coalition—the group in the organization that makes decisions. To be in the dominant coalition, public relations people must demonstrate that they possess certain information that is critical to the operation of the organization (Grunig, Grunig, & Ehling, 1992). Being vital members of the CMT indicates the value of public relations to the dominant coalition. Public relations personnel can be vital because of their roles in the crisis-sensing network and the stakeholder communication network. Part of the public relations person's job is communication with stakeholders. Public relations helps to collect information about any problems with stakeholders—part of the crisis-sensing network. In addition, public relations people are trained to resolve these problems; this helps to build favorable organization—stakeholder relationships—part of maintaining the stakeholder communication network (Grunig & Repper, 1992).

Public relations personnel bring more to the crisis management team than media relations skills. The public relations person brings important information about stakeholders needed for decision making and is a vital link to stakeholders for monitoring and building relationships. By performing these critical tasks in crisis management, public relations personnel help to establish their value as members of the dominant coalition. Movement into the dominant coalition is highly valued by the field of public relations. The move to the dominant coalition helps to protect the integrity of public relations by preventing encroachment (people from other departments controlling public relations). In turn, the job of the public relations practitioner is more secure and receives higher pay (Kelly, 1994). Crisis management provides an opportunity for public relations personnel to demonstrate their full range of skills and value to the dominant coalition.

❖ NEW COMMUNICATION TECHNOLOGIES

I am not one to believe that new communication technologies, the Intranet and Internet to be more specific, replace all old technologies. The Intranet and Internet can be valuable additions to the crisis management process but do not revolutionize it. The Intranet provides an excellent location for storing crisis knowledge and databases as well as being an effective mechanism for informing employees. A variety of stakeholders know how to use the Internet to find information about a crisis. It follows that an organization should address crisis concerns on the Internet and have dark sites ready to go. Moreover, the Internet is an excellent source of information about warning signs and can provide information useful in evaluating crisis management efforts. Communication technologies also allow crisis teams to function as partially distributed teams. A crisis team is no longer constrained by the need for everyone to be in the same place. Such freedom allows a crisis team greater flexibility in operation and membership.

Always keep this motto in mind when engaged in crisis management: "Always have a backup plan." Technologies can fail. That means you cannot base your crisis management effort solely or in large part on the Intranet and Internet. Consider the need to notify employees of critical information. What if the Intranet site is down or many employees do not have access to computers? There is still the telephone, and if phones are down, you can try to reach them in person with messengers. Technology can be a great help in a crisis, but be prepared to manage the crisis with primitive technologies. Remember, if the computer and printer do not work, you can always use a manual pencil sharper, pencil, and paper. Also remember usability and comfort. People will not use technologies during a crisis if they are hard to use or they are unfamiliar. Make sure the human–technology interface is functional before a crisis. Training and exercises will help you to assess the human–technology fit for your crisis management efforts.

What Would You Do?

Tommy Hilfiger Insults Customers?

It comes to your attention that a negative story about your employer, Tommy Hilfiger, has appeared in a small newspaper and is now circulating on the Internet. The story claims that Hilfiger was on Oprah Winfrey's show and said he wished African Americans, Hispanics, and Asians would not wear his clothes because he did not make his clothes for them and that Oprah promptly threw him off the show. The Internet story includes a call to boycott Tommy Hilfiger's products. You try to verify this information and learn that Mr. Hilfiger has never appeared on Oprah's show, and you know that his advertising features diverse models. This is a rumor that could hurt the company. It is not a new rumor. A similar rumor was attached to Liz Claiborne in 1991. How would you fight the rumor? Consider what channels you would use, the content of your messages, and what people you could rally to your defense.

❖ FINAL THOUGHTS

Throughout this book, I have been synthesizing existing crisis management ideas with some new ideas to produce a framework for approaching crisis management. The framework is intended to be a tool for integrating the diverse writings and ideas about crisis management into a manageable guide. The crisis management process has been divided into three stages as a way to organize and synthesize the various crisis management insights. The three-stage model emphasizes the ongoing nature of the crisis management process. Crisis management never ends. At any given time, the crisis manager is simply working on different parts of the crisis management process. I believe the integrative power of the book offers unique insights into crisis management. I hope it has informed your views on the crisis management process.

❖ DISCUSSION QUESTIONS

1. What types of crises do you feel would be the most difficult to manage? What makes them so difficult to manage?

2. Do you feel not using new communication technologies in crisis communication will actually hurt a crisis response or simply look like an organization is behind the times? What is the true value of new communication technology to crisis communication?

3. If you could make five recommendations to an organization about crisis communication, what would they be? What is the value of each of your recommendations?

Appendix

Possible Case Studies

Disney	1997–2005	Boycott by American Family Association	
Union Carbide Corporation	1998	Nitrogen leak and asphyxiation	Hahnville, LA
Morton International Inc.	1998	Explosion and fire	Paterson, NJ
Sonat Exploration Co.	1998	Vessel failure	Pitkin, LA
Tosco Corporation	1999	Oil refinery fire	Martinez, CA
Concept Sciences Inc.	1999	Hydroxylamine explosion	
eBay	2000	Computer hacking	
Amazon.com	2000	Computer hacking	
Buy.com	2000	Computer hacking	
NuWood	2001	Workplace violence	Goshen, IN
Wendy's	2001	Challenged by PETA for not meeting animal welfare guidelines	
Bethlehem Steel Corporation	2001	Fire	Chesterton, IN
BP Amoco	2001	Hot plastic accident	Augusta, GA
Motiva Enterprises	2001	Refinery explosion and fire	Delaware City, DE
Georgia-Pacific	2002	Hydrogen sulfide gas leak	Pennington, AL
Third Coast Industries	2002	Fire	Brazoria County, TX
DPC Enterprises	2002	Chlorine transfer hose rupture and release	Festus, MO
Kaltech Industries	2002	Explosion	

Tyco International	2002	Executives stealing money	
Enron	2002	Illegally hiding debt from investors	
Adelphia Communications Corp.	2002	Illegally hiding debt from investors	
WorldCom Inc.	2002	Illegally hiding debt from investors	
HealthSouth	2002	Illegally hiding debt from investors	
Air Midwest	2003	Flight 5481 crash in Charlotte, NC, from improper maintenance	
Lockheed Martin	2003	Workplace violence	Meridian, MS
Chi-Chi's	2003	Hepatitis outbreak	Pittsburgh, PA
First Chemical Corporation	2003	Explosion of distillation tower	
BLSR Operating Ltd.	2003	Vapor cloud fire	Rosharon, TX
D.D. Williamson	2003	Vessel failure	Louisville, KY
Technic Inc.	2003	Explosion	Cranston, RI
Isotec	2003	Explosion of distillation tower	Miami Township, OH
West Pharmaceutical Services	2003	Explosion and fire	Kinston, NC
CTA Acoustics	2003	Explosion and fire	Corbin, KY
Honeywell	2003	Chlorine gas release	Baton Rouge, LA
Hayes Lemmerz	2003	Series of explosions	Huntington, IN
DPC Enterprises	2003	Chlorine gas leak	Glendale, AZ
Merck	2004	Heart attacks and strokes from VIOXX	
McDonald's	2004	CEO Jim Cantalupo dies of heart attack	
Giant Industries	2004	Gasoline component released and exploded	Gallup, NM
MFG Chemical	2004	Toxic allyl alcohol vapor release	
Formosa Plastics	2004	Polyvinyl chloride explosion	

Qwest Communications International	2005	Illegally hiding debt from investors	
San Francisco 49ers	2005	Improper team media training video	
Acetylene Service Company	2005	Gas explosion	Perth Amboy, NJ
Marcus Oil	2005	Storage tank failure	Houston, TX
BP Texas City	2005	Series of explosions	Texas City, TX
Ford Motor company	2005 & 2006	Boycott by American Family Association	
Synthron Inc.	2006	Explosion	
Cadbury	2006	Food poisoning from chocolate	
Dell, Apple, and Toshiba	2006	Defective laptop batteries	
HP	2006	Unethical means to obtain phone records	
Reebok	2006	Lead in child's bracelet	
Earthbound Farms and Dole	2006	E. coli in spinach	
Princess Cruises	2006	Fire on board a ship	
Princess Cruises	2006	Steering malfunction	

References

Abrams, A. L. (n.d.). Legal strategies: Crisis management and accident investigation. Retrieved September 12, 2006, from https://www.asse .org/Abrams%20Paper.pdf#search='abrams%20abrams%20crisis%20 management

Agle, B. R., Mitchell, R. K., & Sonnenfeld, J. A. (1999). Who matters to CEOs? An investigation of stakeholder attributes and salience, corporate performance, and CEO values. *Academy of Management Journal, 42,* 507–525.

Ahluwalia, R., Burnkrant, R. E., & Unnava, H. R. (2000). Consumer response to negative publicity: The moderating role of commitment. *Journal of Marketing Research, 27,* 203–214.

Allen, M. W., & Caillouet, R. H. (1994). Legitimation endeavors: Impression management strategies used by an organization in crisis. *Communication Monographs, 61,* 44–62.

Alsop, R. J. (2004). *The 18 immutable laws of corporate reputation: Creating, protecting, and repairing your most valuable asset.* New York: Free Press.

American Management Association. (2005). *AMA survey: Crisis management and security issues.* Retrieved September 21, 2006, from http://www.amanet .org/research/index.htm

Ammerman, D. (1995). What's a nice company like yours doing in a story like this? In L. Barton (Ed.), *New avenues in risk and crisis management* (Vol. 3, pp. 3–8). Las Vegas, NV: UNLV Small Business Development Center.

Annen, P., & McCormick, J. (1997, November 24). More than a tune-up: Tough going in a fight against sexual harassment. *Newsweek, 130*(21), 50–52.

Augustine, N. R. (1995, November/December). Managing the crisis you tried to prevent. *Harvard Business Review, 73*(6), 147–158.

Baker, M. (n.d.). Odwalla and the E. coli outbreak. Retrieved May 12, 2006, from http://www.mallenbaker.net/csr/CSRfiles/crisis05.html.

Balik, S. (1995, August). Media training: Boot camp for communicators. *Communication World, 12,* 22–25.

Barge, J. K. (1994). *Leadership: Communication skills for organizations and groups.* New York: St. Martin's.

Baron, R. A. (1983). *Behavior in organizations: Understanding and managing the human side of work.* Boston: Allyn & Bacon.

Barritt, T. (2004). *Risky business*. Retrieved Jan 3, 2006, from http://resources
.Ketchum.com/web/IC_Barritt.pdf

Barry, R. A. (1984, March). Crisis communications: What to do when the roof
falls in. *Business Marketing, 69,* 96–100.

Barton, L. (1995, August). *Your crisis management plan*. Paper presented at the
meeting of New Avenues in Crisis Management, Las Vegas, NV.

Barton, L. (2001). *Crisis in organizations II* (2nd ed.). Cincinnati, OH: College
Divisions South-Western.

Baskin, O., & Aronoff, C. (1988). *Public relations: The profession and the practice*
(2nd ed.). Dubuque, IA: William C. Brown.

Baucus, M. S., & Baucus, D. A. (1997). Paying the piper: An empirical examination of longer-term financial consequences of illegal corporate behavior.
Academy of Management Journal, 40(1), 129–151.

Baucus, M. S., & Near, J. P. (1991). Can illegal corporate behavior be predicted?
An event history analysis. *Academy of Management Journal, 34*(1), 9–36.

Bausch & Lomb: Crisis management 101. (2006, April 17). *BusinessWeek* online.
Retrieved April 20, 2006, from http://web.lexis-nexis.com/universe

Benoit, W. L. (1995). *Accounts, excuses, and apologies: A theory of image restoration*.
Albany: State University of New York Press.

Benoit, W. L. (1997). Image repair discourse and crisis communication. *Public
Relations Review, 23*(2), 177–180.

Benson, J. A. (1988). Crisis revisited: An analysis of strategies used by Tylenol
in the second tampering episode. *Central States Speech Journal, 39,* 49-66.

Beren, G., & van Riel, C. B. M. (2004). Corporate associations in the academic
literature: Three main streams of thought in the reputation measurement
literature. *Corporate Reputation Review, 7,* 161-178.

Berg, D. M., & Robb, S. (1992). Crisis management and the "paradigm case." In
E. L. Toth & R. L. Heath (Eds.), *Rhetorical and critical approaches to public relations* (pp. 93–110). Hillsdale, NJ: Lawrence Erlbaum.

Bergman, E. (1994, April). Crisis? What crisis? *Communication World, 11*(4), 9–13.

Billings, R. S., Milburn, T. W., & Schaalman, M. L. (1980). A model of crisis
perception: A theoretical and empirical analysis. *Administrative Science
Quarterly, 25,* 300–316.

Birch, J. (1994, Spring). New factors in crisis planning and response. *Public
Relations Quarterly, 39,* 31–34.

Birsch, D., & Fielder, J. H. (1994). *The Ford Pinto case: A study in applied ethics,
business, and technology*. Albany: State University of New York Press.

Blackshaw, P., & Nazzaro, M. (2004). Consumer-generated media (CGM) 101.
Retrieved September 21, 2005, from http://www.brandchannel.com/
images/Papers/222_CGM.pdf#search='intelliseek%20consumer%20
generated%20media%20101'

Blythe, B. T., & Stivariou, T. B. (2003). *Negligent failure to plan: The next liability
frontier*. Retrieved April 24, 2006, from http://www.occupationalhazards
.com.safety_zones/33/article.php?id=7316

Boffey, P. M. (1986, Feb. 19). Shuttle head says he was not told of cold readings. *New York Times*, A1.

Botan. C., & Taylor, M. (2004). Public relations: The state of the field. *Journal of Communications, 54* (4), 645–661.

Bradford, J. L., & Garrett, D. E. (1995). The effectiveness of corporate communicative responses to accusations of unethical behavior. *Journal of Business Ethics, 14,* 875–892.

Brewer, L., Chandler, R. C., & Ferrell, O. C. (2006). *Managing risks for corporate integrity: How to survive an ethical misconduct disaster.* Mason, OH: Thomson.

Brummett, B. (1980). Towards a theory of silence as a political strategy. *Quarterly Journal of Speech, 66,* 289–303.

Bryson, J. M. (2004). What to do when stakeholders matter: Stakeholder identification analysis techniques. *Public Management Review, 6,* 21–53.

Buchholz, R. A. (1990). *Essentials of public policy for management* (2nd ed.). Englewood Cliffs, NJ: Prentice Hall.

Burgoon, J. K., Birk, T., & Pfau, M. (1990). Nonverbal behaviors, persuasion and credibility. *Human Communication Research, 17,* 140–169.

Business Roundtable's post-9/11 crisis communication toolkit. (2002). Retrieved April 24, 2006, from http://www.brtable.org/pdf/722.pdf

Carney, A., & Jorden, A. (1993, August). Prepare for business-related crises. *Public Relations Journal 49,* 34–35.

Carroll, C. E., & McCombs, M. E. (2003). Agenda-setting effects of business news on the public's images and opinions about major corporations. *Corporate Reputation Review, 6,* 36–46.

Caruba, A. (1994). Crisis PR: Most are unprepared. *Occupational Hazards, 56* (9), 85.

Center, A. H., & Jackson, P. (1995). *Public relations practices: Managerial case studies and problems* (5th ed.). Englewood Cliffs, NJ: Prentice Hall.

Changing landscape of liability: A director's guide to trends in corporate environmental, social, and economic liability. (2002). Retrieved September 12, 2006, from http://www.sustainability.com/insight/liability-article.asp?id=180

Clampitt, P. G. (1991). *Communicating for managerial effectiveness.* Newbury Park, CA: Sage.

Clarkson, M. B. E. (1991). Defining, evaluating, and managing corporate social performance: A stakeholder management model. In J. E. Post (Ed.), *Research in corporate social performance and policy* (pp. 331–358). Greenwich, CT: JAI.

Clarkson, M. B. E. (1995). A stakeholder framework for analyzing and evaluating corporate social performance. *Academy of Management Review, 20,* 92-117.

Coalition of Immokalee workers, Taco Bell reach groundbreaking agreement. (2005). Retrieved September 12, 2006, from http://www.ciw-online.org/we%20won.html

Coates, J. F., Coates, V. T., Jarratt, J., & Heinz, L. (1986). *Issues management: How you can plan, organize, and manage for the future.* Mt. Airy, MD: Lomond.

Cohen, J. R. (2002). Legislating apology: The pros and cons. *University of Cincinnati Law Review, 70,* 819–895.

Coombs, W. T. (1992). The failure of the task force on food assistance: A case study of the role of legitimacy in issue management. *Journal of Public Relations Research, 4*(2), 101–122.

Coombs, W. T. (1995). Choosing the right words: The development of guidelines for the selection of the "appropriate" crisis response strategies. *Management Communication Quarterly, 8,* 447–476.

Coombs, W. T. (1998). The Internet as potential equalizer: New leverage for confronting social irresponsibility. *Public Relations Review, 24,* 289-304.

Coombs, W. T. (2002). Assessing online issue threats: Issue contagions and their effect on issue prioritization. *Journal of Public Affairs, 2*(4), 215-229.

Coombs, W. T. (2004a). A theoretical frame for post-crisis communication: Situational crisis communication theory. In M. J. Martinko (Ed.), *Attribution theory in the organizational sciences: Theoretical and empirical contributions* (pp. 275–296). Greenwich, CT: Information Age Publishing.

Coombs, W. T. (2004b). Impact of past crises on current crisis communications: Insights from situational crisis communication theory. *Journal of Business Communication, 41,* 265–289.

Coombs, W. T. (2005). The terrorist threat: Shifts in crisis management thinking and planning post-9/11. In D. O'Hair, R. Heath, & G. Ledlow (Eds.), *Communication, communities, and terrorism, Vol. III: Communication and the media* (pp. 211–225). Mahwah, NJ: Lawrence Erlbaum.

Coombs, W. T. (2006a). *Code red in the boardroom: Crisis management as organizational DNA.* Westport, CT: Praeger.

Coombs, W. T. (2006b). The protective powers of crisis response strategies: Managing reputational assets during a crisis. *Journal of Promotion Management, 12,* 241–259.

Coombs, W. T., & Chandler, R. C. (1996). Crisis teams: Revisiting their selection and training. In L. Barton (Ed.), *New avenues in risk and crisis management* (Vol. 5, pp. 7–15). Las Vegas: UNLV Small Business Development Center.

Coombs, W. T., & Holladay, S. J. (1996). Communication and attributions in a crisis: An experimental study of crisis communication. *Journal of Public Relations Research, 8*(4), 279–295.

Coombs, W. T., & Holladay, S. J. (2001). An extended examination of the crisis situation: A fusion of the relational management and symbolic approaches. *Journal of Public Relations Research, 13,* 321–340.

Coombs, W. T., & Holladay, S. J. (2002). Helping crisis managers protect reputational assets: Initial tests of the situational crisis communication theory. *Management Communication Quarterly, 16,* 165–186.

Coombs, W. T., & Holladay, S. J. (2004). Reasoned action in crisis communication: An attribution Theory-Based approach to crisis management. In D. P. Millar & R. L. Heath (Eds.), *Responding to crisis: A rhetorical approach to crisis communication* (pp. 95–115). Mahwah, NJ: Lawrence Erlbaum.

Coombs, W. T., & Holladay, S. J. (2005). Exploratory study of stakeholder emotions: Affect and crisis. In N. M. Ashkanasy, W. J. Zerbe, & C. E. J. Hartel (Eds.), *Research on emotion in organizations: Vol. 1: The effect of affect in organizational settings* (pp. 271–288). New York: Elsevier.

Coombs, W. T. & Holladay, S. J. (2006). Halo or reputational capital: Reputation and crisis management. *Journal of Communication Management, 10*(2), 123–137.

Coombs, W. T., & Schmidt, L. (2000). An empirical analysis of image restoration: Texaco's racism crisis. *Journal of Public Relations Research, 12*(2), 163–178.

Cooper, R. (1997, Summer). A historical look at the PepsiCo/Burma boycott. *The Boycott Quarterly*, 12-15.

Couretas, J. (1985, November). Preparing for the worst. *Business Marketing, 70*, 96–100.

Crable, R. E., & Vibbert. S. L. (1985). Managing issues and influencing public policy. *Public Relations Review, 11*, 3–16.

Creating the best crisis communications teams: One crisis at a time. (2003, January 27). *PR News*. Retrieved September 12, 2006, from http://web.lexis-nexis. com/universe

Corporate conscience award. (2003, October 8). Retrieved March 6, 2006, from http://www.chiquita.com/chiquita/announcements/releases/pr031008a.asp.

Corporate Leadership Council. (2003). *Crisis management strategies*. Retrieved September 12, 2006, from http://www.executiveboard.com/EXBD/Images/PDF/Crisis%20Management%20Strategies.pdf#search='corporate%20leadership%20council%20crisis%20management

Dagnoli, J., & Colford, S. W. (1991, March 18). Brief slump expected for Sudafed. *Advertising Age*, 53.

Daniels, T. D., Spiker, B. K., & Papa, M. J. (1997). *Perspectives on organizational communication* (4th ed.). Dubuque, IA: William C. Brown & Benchmark.

Darling, J. R. (1994). Crisis management in international business: Keys to effective decision making. *Leadership & Organizational Development Journal Annual, 15*(8), 3–8.

Davies, G., Chun, R., da Silva, R. V., & Roper, S. (2003). *Corporate reputation and competitiveness*. New York: Routledge.

Dawar, N., & Pillutla, M. M. (2000). Impact of product-harm crises on brand equity: The moderating role of consumer expectations. *Journal of Marketing Research, 27*, 215–226.

Dean, D. H. (2004). Consumer reaction to negative publicity: Effects of corporate reputation, response, and responsibility for a crisis event. *Journal of Business Communication, 41*, 192–211.

Denbow, C. J., & Culbertson, H. M. (1985). Linking beliefs and diagnosing image. *Public Relations Review, 11*, 29–37.

de Turck, M. A., & Miller, G. R. (1985). Deception and arousal: Isolating the behavioral correlates of deception. *Human Communication Research, 12*, 181–201.

Dilenschneider, R. L. (2000). *The corporate communications bible: Everything you need to know to become a public relations expert*. Beverly Hills, CA: New Millennium.

Dilenschneider, R. L., & Hyde, R. C. (1985, Jan./Feb.). Crisis communications: Planning for the unplanned. *Business Horizons, 28*, 35–38.

Dionisopolous, G. N., & Vibbert, S. L. (1988). CBS vs Mobil Oil: Charges of creative bookkeeping. In H. R. Ryan (Ed.), *Oratorical encounters: Selected studies and sources of 20th century political accusation and apologies* (pp. 214–252). Westport, CT: Greenwood.

Dobbin, B. (2006, April 12). Bausch & Lomb: Source of infection unknown. Retrieved September 21, 2006, from http://www.boston.com/business/articles/2006/04/12/bausch__lomb_source_of_infection_unknown/

Does Airborne really stave off colds? (2006). Retrieved September 13, 2006, from http://abcnews.go.com/GMA/Health/story?id=1664514&page=1

Donaldson, T., & Preston, L.E. (1995). The stakeholder theory of the corporation: Concepts, evidence, and implications. *Academy of Management Review, 20*, 65–91.

Donath, B. (1984, September). Why you need a crisis PR plan. *Business Marketing, 69*, 4.

Dornheim, M. A. (1996, Sept. 9). Recovered FMC memory puts new spin on Cali accident. *Aviation Week & Space Technology, 145*(11), 58–62.

Dowling, G. (2002). *Creating corporate reputations: Identity, image, and performance*. New York: Oxford University Press.

Dozier, D. M. (1992). The organizational roles of communications and public relations practitioners. In J. E. Grunig (Ed.), *Excellence in public relations and communication management* (pp. 327–356). Hillsdale, NJ: Lawrence Erlbaum.

Duffy, B., & Beddingfield, K. T. (1996, August 5). The sound of silence: More evidence from TWA Flight 800 suggests there was a bomb aboard. *U.S. News & World Report, 121*(5), 28–31.

Dutton, J. E. (1986). The processing of crisis and non-crisis strategic issues. *Journal of Management Studies, 23*(5), 501–517.

Dutton, J. E., & Ashford, S. J. (1993). Selling issues to top management. *Academy of Management Review, 18*(3) 397–428.

Dutton, J. E., & Duncan, R. B. (1987). The creation of momentum for change through the process of strategic issue diagnosis. *Strategic Management Journal, 8*, 279–295.

Dutton, J. E., & Jackson, S. E. (1987). Categorizing strategic issues: Links to organizational action. *Academy of Management Review, 12*, 76–90.

Dutton, J. E., & Ottensmeyer, E. (1987). Strategic issue management systems: Forms, functions, and context. *Academy of Management Review, 12*, 355–365.

Egelhoff, W. G., & Sen, F. (1992). An information-processing model of crisis management. *Management Communication Quarterly, 5*, 443–484.

Endsley, M. R. (1995). Toward a theory of situation awareness in dynamic systems. *Human Factors, 37*, 32–64.

Entine, J. (1998). Intoxicated by success: How to protect your company from inevitable corporate screw-ups. Retrieved September 13, 2006, from http://www.jonentine.com/ethical_edge/corp_screwups.htm

Entine, J. (1999). The Odwalla affair: Reassessing corporate social responsibility. Retrieved September 13, 2006, from http://www.jonentine.com/articles/odwalla.htm

Ewing, R. P. (1979, Winter). The uses of futurist techniques in issues management. *Public Relations Quarterly, 24*(4), 15–18.

Fahey, A., & Dagnoli, J. (1990, June 18). PM ready to deal with outdoor ad foes. *Advertising Age, 1,* 31.

Fairhurst, G. T., & Sarr, R. A. (1996). *The art of framing: Managing the language of leadership.* San Francisco: Jossey-Bass.

Fearn-Banks, K. (2001). *Crisis communications: A casebook approach* (2nd ed.). Mahwah, NJ: Lawrence Erlbaum.

Febreze warning. (1999). Retrieved September 13, 2006, from http://urbanlegends.about.com/library/blfebrez.htm

Feeley, T. H., & de Turck, M. A. (1995). *Global cue usage in behavioral lie detection. Communication Quarterly, 43*(4), 420–430.

Finet, D. (1994). Sociopolitical consequences of organizational expression. *Journal of Communication, 44*(4), 114–131.

Fink, S. (1986). *Crisis management: Planning for the inevitable.* New York: AMACOM.

Fink, S., Beak, J., & Taddeo, K. (1971). Organizational crisis and change. *Journal of Applied Behavioral Science, 7,* 15–37.

Fitzpatrick, K. R. (1995, Summer). Ten guidelines for reducing legal risks in crisis management. *Public Relations Quarterly, 40*(2), 33–38.

Fitzpatrick, K. R., & Rubin, M. S. (1995). Public relations vs. legal strategies in organizational crisis decisions. *Public Relations Review, 21*(1), 21–33.

Flin, R. (2006, June). *Naturalistic decision making and crisis management.* Paper presented at ISCRAM-TIEMS 2006, Summer School, Tilburg, the Netherlands.

Folkes, V. S., Koletsky, S., & Graham, J. L. 1987. A field study of causal inferences and consumer reaction: The view from the airport. *Journal of Consumer Research, 13,* 534–539.

Fombrun, C. J. (2005). Building corporate reputation through CSR initiatives: Evolving standards. *Corporate Reputation Review, 8,* 7–11.

Fombrun, C., & Shanley, M. (1990). What's in a name? Reputation building and corporate strategy. *Academy of Management Journal, 33*(2), 233–258.

Fombrun, C. J., & van Riel, C. B. M. (2004). *Fame & fortune: How successful companies build winning reputations.* New York: Prentice Hall.

Ford supports homosexual polygamy. (2006). Retrieved June 13, 2006, from http://media.afa.net/newdesign/ReleaseDetail.asp?id=3464

Frank, J. N. (1994, April). Plan ahead for effective crisis management, expert advises. *Beverage Industry, 85*(4), 22.

Fuchs-Burnett, T. (2002, May/July). Mass public corporate apology. *Dispute Resolution Journal, 57,* 26–32.

Garvin, A. P. (1996). *The art of being well informed.* Garden City Park, NY: Avery.

Gellene, D. (1993, October 22). New dispute brewing for Snapple. *New York Times,* D3.

Geraghty, K., & Desouza, K. C. (2005). Optimizing knowledge networks. Retrieved September 13, 2006, from http://www.eknowtion.com/show_articles.php?id=12

Gilman, A. (2004, September 27). Creating a message map for risk communication. *PR News.* Retrieved April 20, 2006, from http://web.lexis-nexis.com/universe

Goldhaber, G. M. (1990). *Organizational communication* (5th ed.). Dubuque, IA: William C. Brown.

Goldstein, I. L. (1993). *Training in organizations: Needs assessment, development and evaluation* (3rd ed.). Monterey, CA: Brooks/Cole.

Gonzalez-Herrero, A., & Pratt, C. B. (1995, Spring). How to manage a crisis before—or whenever—it hits. *Public Relations Quarterly, 40*(1), 25–29.

Gonzalez-Herrero, A., & Pratt, C. B. (1996). An integrated symmetrical model of crisis communications management. *Journal of Public Relations Research, 8*(2), 79–106.

Grant, T. (2006, June). *Network-centric crisis management: The 9/11 case.* Paper presented at ISCRAM-TIEMS 2006 Summer School, Tilburg, the Netherlands.

Gray, P. (1996, August 5). The search for sabotage. *Time, 148*(7), 28–32.

Gross, A. E. (1990, October 11). How Popeye's and Reebok confronted product rumors. *Adweek's Marketing Week, 31,* 27, 30.

Grunig, J. E. (1992). Communication, public relations, and effective organizations: An overview of the book. In J. E. Grunig (Ed.), *Excellence in public relations and communication management* (pp. 1–30). Hillsdale, NJ: Lawrence Erlbaum.

Grunig, J. E., & Repper, F. C. (1992). Strategic management, publics, and issues. In J. E. Grunig (Ed.), *Excellence in public relations and communication management* (pp. 117–158). Hillsdale, NJ: Lawrence Erlbaum.

Grunig, L. A., Grunig, J. E., & Ehling, W. P. (1992). What is an effective organization. In J. E. Grunig (Ed.), *Excellence in public relations and communication management* (pp. 65–90). Hillsdale, NJ: Lawrence Erlbaum.

Guth, D. W. (1995, Summer). Organizational crisis experience and public relations roles. *Public Relations Review, 21*(2) 123–136.

Hainsworth, B. E. (1990). Issues management: An overview. *Public Relations Review, 16*(1), 3–5.

Hall, P. (2006, Jan. 16). The PR sherp: PR experts address no comment and net mischief. *PR News.* Retrieved April 20, 2006, from http://web.lexis-nexis.com/universe

Halonen-Rollins, M., & Halinen-Kaila, A. (2005). *Customer knowledge management competence: Towards a theoretical framework.* Retrieved May 30, 2006, from http://csdl2.computer.org/comp/proceedings/hicss/2005/2268/08/22680240a.pdf#search='customer%20knowledge%20management%20competence'

Hanging in the Febreze. (1999). Retrieved May 5, 2004, from http://www.snopes.com/critters/crusader/febreze.asp

Härtel, C., McColl-Kennedy, J. R., & McDonald, L. (1998). Incorporating attribution theory and the theory of reasoned action within an affective events theory framework to produce a contingency predictive model of consumer reactions to organizational mishaps. *Advances in Consumer Research, 25,* 428–432.

Hays, C. L. (2003). *Wal-Mart opens wallet in effort to fix its image.* Retrieved September 21, 2004, from http://sfgate.com/cgi-bin/article.cgi?f=/c/a/2003/08/14/BU185832.DTL

Headley, L. O. (2005). *Failure to protect employees from terrorism may lead to liability.* Retrieved September 13, 2006, from http://www.law.com/jsp/tx/PubArticleFriendlyTX.jsp?id=1136455510408

Hearit, K. M. (1994, Summer). Apologies and public relations crises at Chrysler, Toshiba, and Volvo. *Public Relations Review, 20*(2), 113–125.

Hearit, K. M. (1996, Fall). The use of counter-attack in apologetic public relations crises: The case of General Motors vs. Dateline NBC. *Public Relations Review, 22*(3), 233–248.

Hearit, K. M. (2001). Corporate apologia: When an organization speaks in defense of itself. In R. L. Heath (Ed.), *Handbook of public relations* (pp. 501–511). Thousand Oaks, CA: Sage.

Hearit, K. M. (2006). *Crisis management by apology: Corporate response to allegations of wrongdoing.* Mahwah, NJ: Lawrence Erlbaum.

Heath, R. L. (1988). Organizational tactics for effective issues management. In R. L. Heath (Ed.), *Strategic issues management* (pp. 99-121). San Francisco: Jossey-Bass.

Heath, R. L. (1990). Corporate issues management: Theoretical underpinnings and research foundations. In J. E. Grunig & L. A. Grunig (Eds.), *Public relations research annual* (Vol. 2, pp. 29–66). Hillsdale, NJ: Lawrence Erlbaum.

Heath, R. L. (1994). *Management of corporate communication: From interpersonal contacts to external affairs.* Hillsdale, NJ: Lawrence Erlbaum.

Heath, R. L. (1997). *Strategic issues management: Organizations and public policy challenges.* Thousand Oaks, CA: Sage.

Heath, R. L. (1998). New communication technologies: An issues management point of view. *Public Relations Review, 24,* 273-288.

Heath, R. L., & Cousino, K. R. (1990, Spring). Issues management: End of first decade progress report. *Public Relations Review, 16*(1), 6–18.

Heath, R. L., & Nelson, R. A. (1986). *Issues management: Corporate public policy making in an information society.* Beverly Hills, CA: Sage.

Heinberg, P. (1963). Relationships of content and delivery to general effectiveness. *Speech Monographs, 30,* 105–107.

Herbig, P., Milewicz, J., & Golden, J. (1994). A model of reputation building and destruction. *Journal of Business Research, 31,* 23–31.

Hibbard, J. (1997, May 26). Shell oil shifts safety data to intranet. *Computerworld, 31*(21), 20–21.

Higbee, A. G. (1992, October). Shortening the crisis lifecycle: Seven rules to live by. *Occupational Hazards, 54,* 137–138.

Hiltz, S. R. (2006, June). *Partially distributed virtual teams: A tutorial, hands-on experience, and discussion of their use in emergency response.* Paper presented at ISCRAM-TIEMS 2006 Summer School, Tilburg, the Netherlands.

Hirokawa, R. Y. (1985). Discussion procedures and decision-making performance: A test of a functional perspective. *Human Communication Research, 12*, 203–224.

Hirokawa, R. Y. (1988). Group communication and decision making performance: A continued test of the functional perspective. *Human Communication Research, 14*, 487–515.

Hirokawa, R. Y., & Keyton, J. (1995). Perceived facilitators and inhibitors of effectiveness in organizational work teams. *Management Communication Quarterly, 8*(4), 424–446.

Hirokawa, R.Y., & Rost, K. (1992). Effective group decision making in organizations. *Management Communication Quarterly, 5*, 267–288.

Hobbs, J. D. (1995). Treachery by any other name: A case study of the Toshiba public relations crisis. *Management Communication Quarterly, 8*, 323–346.

Holladay, S. J., & Coombs, W. T. (1994). Speaking of visions and visions being spoken: An exploration of the effects of content and delivery on perceptions of leader charisma. *Management Communication Quarterly, 8*(2), 165–189.

Holtz, S. (1999). *Public relations on the net: Winning strategies to inform and influence the media, the investment community, the government, the public, and more!* New York: AMACOM.

Hon, L. C., & Grunig, J. E. (1999). Guidelines for measuring relationships in public relations. Retrieved September 25, 2005, from http://ipr.wieck.com/files/uploads/1999_MeasuringRelations.pdf

Hopper, D. I. (2002, April). *Technology: Hacking up, disclosure down, FBI survey 7.* Retrieved September 21, 2006, from http://seclists.org/isn/2002/Apr/0042.html

Husted, B. W., & Salazar, J. D. J. (2006). Taking Friedman seriously: Maximizing profits and social performance. *Journal of Management Studies, 43*, 75–91.

Ice, R. (1991). Corporate publics and rhetorical strategies: The case of Union Carbide's Bhopal crisis. *Management Communication Quarterly, 4*, 341–362.

Important message from Bausch & Lomb. (2006). Retrieved September 21, 2006, from http://www.bausch.com/en_US/corporate/corpcomm/news/2006_5_15_recall.aspx

Important safety information. (2006). Retrieved September 7, 2006, from http://h71036.www7.hp.com/hho/cache/323517-0-0-225-121.html?jumpid=ex_R602_go/r707safetyupdate

In a crisis. (1993, September). *Public Relations Journal, 49* (9), 10–11.

Intense chemical blaze 'very difficult to fight.' (2004). Retrieved September 13, 2006, from http://edition.cnn.com/2004/US/South/05/25/fire

Irvine, R. B., & Millar, D. P. (1996). Debunking the stereotypes of crisis management: The nature of business crises in the 1990's. In L. Barton (Ed.), *New avenues in risk and crisis management* (Vol. 5, pp. 51–63). Las Vegas, NV: UNLV Small Business Development Center.

Jones, B. L., & Chase, W. H. (1979, Summer). Managing public policy issues. *Public Relations Review, 5*(2), 3–23.

Kaiser, E. (2004). Wal-mart goes on PR offensive to repair image. Retrieved September 13, 2006, from http://www.forbes.com/newswire/2004/02/01/rtr1237512.html

Kamer, L. (1996). When the crisis is orchestrated: Corporate campaigns and their origins. In L. Barton (Ed.), *New avenues in risk and crisis management* (Vol. 5, pp. 64–72). Las Vegas: UNLV Small Business Development Center.

Katz, A. R. (1987, November). 10 steps to complete crisis planning. *Public Relations Journal, 43*, 46–7.

Kaufmann, J. B., Kesner, I. F., & Hazen, T. L. (1994, July/August). The myth of full disclosure: A look at organizational communications during crises. *Business Horizons, 37*, 29–39.

Kellerman, B. (2006, April). When should a leader apologize and when not? *Harvard Business Review*, 73–81.

Kelly, K. (1990, Sept. 24). Dayton Hudson finds there's no graceful way to flip-flop. *Business Week,* 50.

Kelly, K. S. (1994). Fund-raising encroachment and the potential of public relations departments in the nonprofit sector. *Journal of Public Relations Research, 6*(1), 1–22.

Kempner, M. W. (1995, March). Reputation management: How to handle the media during a crisis. *Risk Management, 42*(3), 43–47.

Kiley, D. (1991, March 11). Sudafed deaths spark a backlash against capsules. *Adweek's Marketing Week,* 6.

"Killer Coke" or innocent abroad? (2006, Jan. 23). *BusinessWeek, 3978,* 46–48.

Kilmann, R. H., & Thomas, K. W. (1975). Interpersonal conflict-handling behaviors as reflection of Jungian personality dimensions. *Psychological Reports, 37,* 971–980.

Klein, J., & Dawar, N. (2004). Corporate social responsibility and consumers' attributions and brand evaluations in a product-harm crisis. *International Journal of Marketing, 21,* 203–217.

Kleindorfer, P., Freeman, H., Lowe, R. (2000). *Accident epidemiology and the U.S. chemical industry: Preliminary results from RMP*Info.* Retrieved September 13, 2006, from http://opim.wharton.upenn.edu/risk/downloads/00–1-15.pdf

Koepp, S. (1985, September 16). Placing the blame at E. F. Hutton. *Time,* 54.

Kolfschoten, G. L., & Appelman, J. H. (2006, June). *Collaborative engineering in crisis situations.* Paper presented at ISCRAM-TIEMS 2006 Summer School, Tilburg, the Netherlands.

Kolfschoten, G. L., Briggs, R. O., de Vreede, G.J., Jacobs, P. H. M., & Appelman, J. H. (2006). A conceptual foundation of the thinkLet concept for collaboration engineering. *International Journal of Human-Computer Studies, 64,* 611–621.

Komaki, J., Heinzmann, A. T., & Lawson, L. (1980). Effects of training and feedback: Component analysis of a behavioral safety program. *Journal of Applied Psychology, 65,* 261–270.

Kouzes, J. M., & Posner, B. Z. (1993). *Credibility: How leaders gain and lose it, why people demand it.* San Francisco: Jossey-Bass.

Kreps, G. L. (1990). *Organizational communication: Theory and practice* (2nd ed.). New York: Longman.

Lackluster online PR no aid in crisis response. (2002). *PR News.* Retrieved April 20, 2006, from http://web.lexis-nexis.com/universe

Laczniak, R. N., DeCarlo, T. E., & Ramaswami, S. H. (2001). Consumers' responses to negative word-of-mouth communication: An attribution theory perspective. *Journal of Consumer Psychology, 11,* 57–73.

Larson, C. U. (1989). *Persuasion: Reception and responsibility* (5th ed.). Belmont, CA: Wadsworth.

Lauzen, M. M. (1995). Toward a model of environmental scanning. *Journal of Public Relations Research, 7*(3), 187–204.

Lawmakers blast Enron's "culture of corporate corruption." (2002). Retrieved September 13, 2006, from http://archives.cnn.com/2002/LAW/02/03/enron/

Ledingham, J. A. (2005). Relationship management theory. In R. L. Heath (Ed.), *Encyclopedia of public relations* (Vol. 2, pp. 740–745). Thousand Oaks, CA: Sage.

Leon, M. (1983). Tylenol fights back. *Public Relations Journal,* 10–14.

Lerbinger, O. (1997). *The crisis manager: Facing risk and responsibility.* Mahwah, NJ: Lawrence Erlbaum.

Levick, R. (2005, August 17). In staging responses to crises, complacency plays a big role. *PR News.* Retrieved April 20, 2006, from http://web.lexis-nexis.com/universe

Levitt, A. M. (1997). *Disaster planning and recovery: A guide for facility professionals.* New York: John Wiley.

Li, A., YeZhuang, T., & Ying, Q. Z. (2004). *An empirical study on the impact of organizational memory on organizational performance in manufacturing companies.* Retrieved May 30, 2006, from IEEE Computer Society web site: http://csdl2 .computer.org/persagen/DLPublication.jsp?pubtype=p&acronym =hicss

Littlejohn, R. F. (1983). *Crisis management: A team approach.* New York: American Management Association.

Loewendick, B. A. (1993, November). Laying your crisis on the table. *Training & Development,* 15–17.

Look behind the label (n.d.) Retrieved May 12, 2006, from http://www2 .marksandspencer.com/thecompany/trustyour_mands/index.shtml.

Lukaszewski, J. E. (1987, November). Anatomy of a crisis response. *Public Relations Journal, 43,* 45–7.

Mackinnon, P. (1996, July/August). When silence isn't golden. *Financial Executive, 12*(4), 45–48.

Magiera, M. (1993, June 21). Pepsi weathers tampering hoaxes: It's textbook case of how to come through a PR crisis. *Advertising Age,* 1.

Marcus, A. A., & Goodman, R. S. (1991). Victims and shareholders: The dilemmas of presenting corporate policy during a crisis. *Academy of Management Journal, 34,* 281–305.

Maynard, R. (1993, December). Handling a crisis effectively. *Nation's Business,* 54–55.

McCroskey, J. C. (1997). *An introduction to rhetorical communication* (7th ed.). Boston: Allyn & Bacon.

McGinley, L. (1997). Of mice and men: How Ex-Lax, trusted for nearly a century became a cancer risk. Retrieved September 13, 2006, from http://www.junkscience.com/news/exlax.html

McGraw, D. (1996, Jan. 8). Human error and a human tragedy: The aftermath of the American Airlines crash. *U.S. News & World Report, 120*(1), 38.

McKeen, J. D., Zack, M. H., & Singh, S. (2006). *Knowledge management and organizational performance: An exploratory study.* Retrieved May 30, 2006, from http://csdl2.computer.org/persagen/DLPublication.jsp?pubtype=p&acronym=hicss

Mecham, M. (1986, Feb. 19). Shuttle probe gets testy: Who knew about the cold and when? *USA Today,* 1A.

Meserve, J. (1999). *One company still dealing with Melissa.* Retrieved September 13, 2006, from http://www.networkworld.com/news/1999/0401melissa.html

Milas, G. H. (1996, February). Guidelines for organizing TQM teams. *IIE Solutions, 28*(2), 36–39.

Mitchell, R. K., Agle, R. A., & Wood, D. J. (1997). Toward a theory of stakeholder identification and salience: Defining the principle of who and what really counts. *Academy of Management Review, 22*(4), 853–886.

Mitchell, T. H. (1986, Autumn). Coping with a corporate crisis. *Canadian Business Review, 13,* 17–20.

Mitroff, I. I. (1994, Winter). Crisis management and environmentalism: A natural fit. *California Management Review, 36*(2), 101–113.

Mitroff, I. I., Harrington, K., & Gai, E. (1996, September). Thinking about the unthinkable. *Across the Board, 33*(8), 44–48.

Mitroff, I. I., & McWinney, W. (1987, August). Disaster by design and how to avoid it. *Training, 24,* 33–34, 37–8.

Mohr, B. (1994, March). The Pepsi challenge: Managing a crisis. *Prepared Foods,* 13–14.

Moore, R. H. (1979, November). Research by the conference board sheds light on problems of semantics, issue identification and classification—and some likely issues for the '80s. *Public Relations Journal, 35,* 43–46.

Mukherjee, D., Nissen, S. E., & Topol, E. J. (2001, August), Risk of cardiovascular events associated with selective cox-2 inhibitors. *Journal of the American Medical Association, 286*(8), 954–959.

Myers, K. N. (1993). *Total contingency planning for disasters: Managing risk, minimizing loss, ensuring business continuity.* New York: John Wiley.

National Research Council. (1996). *Computing and communications in the extreme: Research for crisis management and application.* Washington, DC: National Academy Press.

Nearly 200, *Odwalla Press Release,* October 31, 1996.

Nelkin, D. (1988). Risk reporting and the management of industrial crises. *Journal of Management Studies, 25,* 341–351.

New survey finds crisis training is primarily learned on the job. (2006, March 20). *PR News*. Retrieved April 20, 2006, from http://web.lexis-nexis.com/universe

Newsom, D., VanSlyke Turk, J., & Kruckeberg, D. (1996). *This is PR: The realities of public relations* (6th ed.). Belmont, CA: Wadsworth.

Nicholas, R. (1995, November, 23). Know comment. *Marketing*, 41–43.

Normand, M., McKittrick, M., Roberts, S., & Kline, S. (n.d.). *Enron: A cultural bankruptcy*. Retrieved September 13, 2006, from http://www.pages.drexel.edu/~mtm34/pdf/EnronStudy.pdf#search='normandenron'

Norton, R. W. (1983). *Communicator style: Theory, applications, and measures*. Beverly Hills, CA: Sage.

O'Connor, M. F. (1985). Methodology for corporate crisis decision-making. In S. J. Andriole (Ed.), *Corporate crisis management* (pp. 239–258). Princeton, NJ: Petrocelli.

O'Hair, D., Friedrich, G. W., Wiemann, J. M., & Wiemann, M. O. (1995). *Competent communication*. New York: St. Martin's.

Olaniran, B. A., & Williams, D. E. (2001). Anticipatory model of crisis management: A vigilant response to technological crises. In R. L. Heath (Ed.), *Handbook of public relations* (pp. 487–500). Thousand Oaks, CA: Sage.

Patel, A., & Reinsch, L. (2003). Companies can apologize: Corporate apologies and legal liability. *Business Communication Quarterly, 66*, 17–26.

Paton, D., & Flin, R. (1999). Disaster stress: An emergency management perspective. *Disaster Prevention and Management, 8*, 261–267.

Pauchant, T. C., & Mitroff, I. I. (1992). *Transforming the crisis-prone organization: Preventing individual, organizational, and environmental tragedies*. San Francisco: Jossey-Bass.

Paul, R., & Elder, L. (1995). *An educator's guide to critical thinking terms and concepts*. Retrieved March 24, 2006, from http://www.criticalthinking.org

Pearson, C. M., & Clair, J. A. (1998). Reframing crisis management. *Academy of Management Review, 23*(1), 59–76.

Pearson, C. M., & Mitroff, I. I. (1993). From crisis prone to crisis prepared: A framework for crisis management. *The Executive, 7*(1), 48–59.

Perry, D. C., Taylor, M., Doerfel, M. L. (2003). Internet-based communication in crisis management. *Management Communication Quarterly, 17*, 206–232.

PhRMA. (2005, August). *PhRMA guiding principles: Direct to consumer advertisements about prescription medicines*. Retrieved September 15, 2006, from http://www.phrma.org/files/DTCGuidingprinciples.pdf#search='phrma%20guiding%20principles%20direct'

Power shift: How the Internet gives consumers the upper hand—and what proactive automakers can do about it. (2006). *Nielsen BuzzMetrics*. Retrieved May 11, 2006, from http://www.nielsenbuzzmetrics.com/downloads/whitepapers/nbzm_wp_Automotive.pdf

Pines, W. L. (1985, Summer). How to handle a PR crisis: Five dos and five don'ts. *Public Relations Quarterly, 30*(2), 16–19.

Procter & Gamble files lawsuit against Vi-Jon Laboratories. (2006, February 15). [Press release]. Retrieved October 2, 2006, from http://news.thomasnet .com/companystory/477793

Procter & Gamble reaches settlement agreement with Vi-Jon Laboratories. (2006, April 18). *PR News Today.* Retrieved September, 13, 2006, from http://www.prnewstoday.com/release.htm?cat=household-consumer-cosmetics&dat=20060418&rl=CLTU02218042006–1

Pussycat dolls: Your voice = victory. Retrieved September 13, 2006, from http://www.dadsanddaughters.org/action/PussycatDollsPulled.html

Putnam, L. L., & Poole, M. S. (1987). Conflict and negotiation. In F. M. Jablin, L. L. Putnam, K. H. Roberts, & L. W. Porter (Eds.), *Handbook of organizational communication: An interdisciplinary perspective* (pp. 549–599). Newbury Park, CA: Sage.

Putnam, T. (1993, Spring). Boycotts are busting out all over. *Business and Society Review,* (85), 47–51.

Rancer, A. S., Baukus, R. A., & Infante, D. A. (1985). Relations between argumentativeness and belief structures about arguing. *Communication Education, 34,* 37–47.

Ray, S. J. (1999). *Strategic communication in crisis management: Lessons from the airline industry.* Westport, CT: Quorum.

Redding, W. C. (1972). *Communication within the organization.* Lafayette, IN: Purdue Research Foundation.

Reeves, M. (1996, November). Weaving a web at the office: Intranets are all the rage in networking technology. *Black Enterprise, 27*(4), 39–41.

Regester, M. (1989). *Crisis management: How to turn a crisis into an opportunity.* London: Hutchinson.

Richardson, B. (1994). Socio-technical disasters: Profile and prevalence. *Disaster Prevention and Management, 3*(4), 41–69.

Richmond, V. P., & McCroskey, J. C. (1997). *Communication: Apprehension, avoidance, and effectiveness* (5th ed.). Boston: Allyn & Bacon.

Rojas, B. (2006, March/April). Wal-Mart: Beyond business. *Continuity Insights,* 10–13.

Rollins, M., & Halinen, A. (2005 January). Customer knowledge management competence: Towards a theoretical framework. *Proceedings of the 38th Annual Hawaii International Conference on Systems Sciences.* Retrieved October 2, 2006, from http://csdl2.computer.org/persagen/DLPublication .jsp?pubtype=p&acronym=hicss

Rowley, T. J. (1997). Moving beyond dyadic ties: A network theory of stakeholder influence. *Academy of Management Review, 22*(4), 887–910.

Rupp, D. (1996, November). Tech versus touch. *HR Focus, 73*(11), 16–18.

Ryan, C. (1991). *Prime time activism: Media strategies for grassroots organizing.* Boston: South End Press.

Ryan, C. (1998). *Three killed in explosion at chemical plant outside Reno.* Retrieved September 13, 2006, from www.lasvegassun.com/sunbin/stories/ nevada/1998/jan/07/506675238.html

Sanger, D. E. (1986, Feb. 28). Communications channels at NASA: Warnings that faded along the way. *New York Times*, A13.

Savage, G. T., Nix, T. W., Whitehead, C. J., & Blair, J. D. (1991, May). Strategies for assessing and managing organizational stakeholders. *The Executive*, 5(2), 61–75.

Schuler, A. J. (2002). *Does corporate culture matter? The case of Enron*. Retrieved September 13, 2006, from http://www.schulersolutions.com/enron_s_corporate_culture.html

Scriven, M., & Paul, R. (1996). *Defining critical thinking*. Retrieved March 24, 2006, from http://www.criticalthinking.org

Seeger, M. W., Sellnow, T. L., & Ulmer, R. R. (2003). *Communication and organizational crisis*. Westport, CT: Praeger.

Seeger, M. & Ulmer, R. R. (2001). Virtuous responses to organizational crisis: Aaron Feuerstein and Milt Cole. *Journal of Business Ethics, 31*, 369–376.

Seitel, F. P. (1983, May). 10 myths of handling bad news. *Bank Marketing, 15*, 12–14.

Sellnow, T. L., Seeger, M. W., & Ulmer, R. R. (2002). Chaos theory, informational needs, and natural disasters. *Journal of Applied Communication Research, 30*, 269–292.

Sellnow, T. L., Ulmer, R. R., & Snider, M. (1998). The compatibility of corrective action in organizational crisis communication. *Communication Quarterly, 46*, 60–74.

Sen, F., & Egelhoff, W. G. (1991, Spring). Six years and counting: Leaning from crisis management at Bhopal. *Public Relations Review, 17*(1), 69–83.

Several missing in Nevada explosion. (1998). *CNN Interactive*. Retrieved October 2, 2006, from http://www.cnn.com/US/9801/07/reno.explosion.pm/

Sewell, D. (1997, August 12). Small businesses feeling the pain. *Houston Chronicle*. Retrieved October 2, 2006, from http://www.chron.com/content/chronicle/business/97/08/13/ups-impact.2-0.html

Shrivastava, P. (1993). Crisis theory/practice: Towards a sustainable future. *Industrial and Environmental Crisis Quarterly, 7*, 23–42.

Shrivastava, P., & Mitroff, I. I. (1987, Spring). Strategic management of corporate crises. *Columbia Journal of World Business, 22*, 5–11.

Siomkos, G., & Shrivastava, P. (1993). Responding to product liability crises. *Long Range Planning, 26*(5), 72–79.

Skinner, C., & Mersham, G. (n.d.). *Expect the unexpected*. September 20, 2006, from http://www.oup.com/word/za/expect_the_unexpected.doc

Smallwood, C. (1995). Risk and organizational behavior: Toward a theoretical framework. In L. Barton (Ed.), *New avenues in risk and crisis management* (Vol. 4, pp. 139–148). Las Vegas: UNLV Small Business Development Center.

Smith, E. B. (1998, January 13). The Zilog mystery: What made so many workers so sick? *USA Today*, B1, B3.

Smith, C. A. P., & Hayne, S. C. (1997). Decision making under time pressure: An investigation of decision speed and decision quality of computer-supported groups. *Management Communication Quarterly, 11*(1), 97–126.

Snyder, A. (1991, April 8). Do boycotts work? *Adweek's Marketing Week,* 16–18.

Snyder, L. (1983, Fall). An anniversary review and critique: The Tylenol crisis. *Public Relations Review, 9,* 24–34.

Sonnenfeld, S. (1994, July/August). Media policy—What media policy? *Harvard Business Review, 72*(4), 18-19.

Soper, R. H. (1995, August). *Crisis management strategy plan formulation and implementation.* Paper presented at the meeting of New Avenues in Crisis Management, Las Vegas, NV.

Stacks, D. W. (2002). *Primer of public relations research.* New York: Guilford.

Stewart, C. J., & Cash, W. B., Jr. (1997). *Interviewing: Principles and practices* (8th ed.). Dubuque, IA: William C. Brown.

Stewart, T. D. (2002). *Principles of research in communication.* Boston: Allyn & Bacon.

Stohl, C., & Coombs, W. T. (1988). Cooperation or cooptation: An analysis of quality circle training manuals. *Management Communication Quarterly, 2,* 63–89.

Stohl, C., & Redding, W. C. (1987). Messages and message exchange processes. In F. M. Jabling, L. L. Putnam, K. H. Roberts, & L. W. Porter (Eds.), *Handbook of organizational communication: An interdisciplinary perspective* (pp. 451–502). Newbury Park, CA: Sage.

Strauss, G. (1998, Jan. 13). Embezzlement growth is "dramatic." *USA Today,* 1A, 2A.

Study finds companies snooping on employee e-mail. Retrieved September 20, 2006, from http://www.redorbit.com/news/technology/524932/study_finds_companies_snooping_on_employee_email/index.html

Sturges, D. L. (1994). Communicating through crisis: A strategy for organizational survival. *Management Communication Quarterly, 7*(3), 297–316.

Sullivan, M. (1990). Measuring image spillover in umbrella-branded products. *Journal of Business, 63*(3), 309–329.

Tan, A. S. (1985). *Mass communication theories and research.* New York: John Wiley.

Tesser, A., & Rosen, S. (1975). The reluctance to transmit bad news. In L. Berkowitz (Ed.), *Advances in experimental social psychology* (Vol. 8, pp. 193–232). New York: Academic Press.

Trahan, J. V., III. (1993, Summer). Media relations in the eye of the storm. *Public Relations Quarterly, 38*(2), 31–33.

Tsui, J. (1993). Tolerance for ambiguity, uncertainty audit qualification and bankers' perceptions. *Psychological Reports, 72,* 915–919.

Twardy, S. A. (1994, Summer). Attorneys and public relations professionals must work hand-in-hand when responding to an environmental investigation. *Public Relations Quarterly, 39*(2), 15–6.

Tyler, L. (1997). Liability means never being able to say you're sorry: Corporate guilt, legal constraints, and defensiveness in corporate communication. *Management Communication Quarterly, 11*(1), 51–73.

Ulmer, R. R. (2001). Effective crisis management through established stakeholder relationships. *Management Communication Quarterly, 14,* 590–615.

Ulmer, R. R., & Sellnow, T. L. (2002). Crisis management and discourse of renewal: Understanding the potential for positive outcomes in crisis. *Public Relations Review, 28*, 361–365.

Ulmer, R. R., Sellnow, T. L., & Seeger, M. W. (2006). *Effective crisis communication: Moving from crisis to opportunity.* Thousand Oaks: Sage.

Versical, D. (1987, May). An anatomy: Dealers, critics review Audi's crises management. *Automotive News*, 1.

Wagstaff, J. (2006). Kryptonite' task and the real cluetrain lesson. Retrieved September 22, 2006, from http://loosewire.typepad.com/blog/2004/11/kryptonites_tas.html

Walsh, B. (1995, June 5). Beware of the crisis lovers. *Forbes, 155*(12), A17–18.

Wang, W. T., & Belardo, S. (2005). *Strategic integration: A knowledge management approach to crisis management.* Retrieved May 30, 2006, from http://csdl2 .computer.org/persagen/DLPublication.jsp?pubtype=p&acronym=hicss

Ware, B. L., & Linkugel, W. A. (1973). They spoke in defense of themselves: On the generic criticism of apologia. *Quarterly Journal of Speech, 59*, 273–283.

Watson, R. (1996, Sept. 2). Next, a 'Eureka' piece.' *Newsweek, 128*(10), 48–50.

Weddle, P. D. (2001.). Use the Internet to gain a crisis-management edge. Retrieved September 20, 2006, from http://www.careerjournal.com/hrcenter/weddlesguide/20011026-weddle124.html

Weick, K. E. (1979). *The social psychology of organizing* (2nd ed.). Reading, MA: Addison-Wesley.

Weick, K. E. (1988). Enacted sensemaking in crisis situations. *Journal of Management Studies, 25*, 305–317.

Weick, K. E. (1993). The collapse of sensemaking in organizations: The Mann Gulch disaster. *Administrative Science Quarterly, 38*, 628–652.

Weiner, B. 1986. *An attributional theory of motivation and emotion.* New York: Springer Verlag.

Weinstein, S. (1993, August). The hoax that failed. *Progressive Grocer, 72*(8), 17.

Well-provisioned war room and why you need one. (2005, October 26). *PR News.* Retrieved April 20, 2006, from http://web.lexis-nexis.com/universe

Werther, W. B., Jr., & Chandler, D. (2006). *Strategic corporate social responsibility: Stakeholders in a global environment.* Thousand Oaks, CA: Sage.

Williams, D. E., & Olaniran, B. A. (1994). Exxon's decision-making flaws: The hypervigilant response to the Valdez grounding. *Public Relations Review, 20*(1), 5–18.

Wilsenbilt, J. Z. (1989, Spring). Crisis management planning among U.S. corporations: Empirical evidence and a proposed framework. *SAM Advanced Management Journal*, 31–41.

Wilson, S., & Patterson, B. (1987, November). When the news hits the fan. *Business Marketing, 72*, 92–94.

Wood, D. J. (1991). Corporate social performance revisited. *Academy of Management Review, 16*, 691–718.

Zinn, L., & Regan, M. B. (1993, July 5). The right moves baby. *Business Week*, 31.

Index

About the Author

W. Timothy Coombs, PhD, Purdue University, is an associate professor in the Department of Communication Studies at Eastern Illinois University. He is the 2002 recipient of Jackson, Jackson & Wagner Behavioral Science Prize from the Public Relations Society of America for his crisis research, which led to the development and testing of the Situational Crisis Communication Theory (SCCT). SCCT provides recommendations about how crisis managers should respond to crises by evaluating key elements of the crisis situation. He has published widely in the areas of crisis management and preparedness. His research includes the award-winning book, *Ongoing Crisis Communication*, and his new book, *Code Red in the Boardroom: Crisis Management as Organizational DNA*. He was part of the Darden School of Management's Batten Institute's forum, "Defining Leadership: A Forum to Discuss Crisis Leadership Competency," and has a chapter in the related publication, *Executive Briefing on Crisis Leadership*. Dr. Coombs has lectured at various venues in the United States, Europe, and Australia on the subject of crisis management. He has also consulted with companies in the petrochemical and health care industries on crisis-related topics.